The Truth about Travel Nursing

Know More than Your Recruiter as a Travel Healthcare Professional

by
Kyle Schmidt

Contents

Introduction 1

Section 1: The Basics 5

   Chapter 1: The Basics 5

   Chapter 2: How the Business Works: The Short Story 12

Section 2: Agencies in Depth 19

   Chapter 3: Agencies: Differentiating by Size 19

   Chapter 4: Hospital-Agency Relationships: Direct Relationship and Vendor Management Services 26

Section 3: Working with the Agencies 39

   Chapter 5: Finding Agencies Finding You 39

   Chapter 6: Recruiters: The X Factor 53

   Chapter 7: Working with Multiple Agencies 60

Section 4: Compensation 64

   Chapter 8: Compensation: The Agency's Perspective 64

   Chapter 9: Understanding the Travel Compensation Package 69

Section 5: TAX FREE MONEY 84

   Chapter 10: Tax Free Money: Overview 84

   Chapter 11: Qualifying for Tax Free Stipends and Tax Deductions. 90

   Chapter 12: Tax Free Myths and Special Circumstances 103

   Chapter 13: Record Keeping for Tax Purposes 111

Section 6: Compensation: Determining What You Want 119

   Chapter 14: Lodging: Financial Considerations 119

   Chapter 15: Company Provided Housing 127

Chapter 16: Securing Your Own Lodging 132

Chapter 17: Medical Benefits...136

Chapter 18: 401K and Retirement Planning 142

Chapter 19: Travel Stipends 145

Chapter 20: Rental Cars...148

Chapter 21: License and Certification Reimbursements.............150

Chapter 22: Bonuses 152

Chapter 23: Extra Hours Pay 154

Chapter 24: Guaranteed Hours 157

Chapter 25: Shift Differential...159

Section 7: Additional Considerations...............................161

Chapter 26: Deciding Where to Travel 161

Chapter 27: Hospital Preferences....................................163

Chapter 28: Shift and Contract Length 165

Chapter 29: "Hybrid" Travel Contracts 167

Section 8: Securing and Completing Assignments 170

Chapter 30: Your Submission Profile 170

Chapter 31: The Green Light for Submission....................178

Chapter 32: What Happens When Your Profile is Submitted? 184

Chapter 33: The Interview...186

Chapter 34: The Offer and Confirmation 190

Chapter 35: The Contract 193

Chapter 36: Credentialing and Compliance.....................198

Chapter 37: Reporting to the Facility and Working Your Assignment 203

Chapter 38: Considerations for Future Assignments 214

Appendix 224

    Appendix A: Comprehensive Agency Checklist 224

    Appendix B: Sample Checklist for Company Provided Housing ... 226

    Appendix C: Sample List of Receipts for Records 228

    Appendix D: Questions to Ask During Hospital Interview 230

    Appendix E: Travel Nursing Resume 232

    Appendix F: List of helpful web sites 234

Resources 237

Introduction

Having worked in the healthcare staffing industry for close to 6 years, I've spoken to thousands of healthcare professionals. As a service oriented individual, the conversations routinely engaged in more than just the business at hand. Over the years, I've developed close personal relationships with many of my former clients. And I developed a profound respect for healthcare professionals overall. I don't know that there exists another field of practice that combines compassion, caring, personal achievement, commitment to excellence, integrity, innovation, and a quest for knowledge quite like the field of healthcare. I'm grateful that so many took the time to share their knowledge about their fields, jobs, and career goals.

Of course, we also discussed the business at hand, travel healthcare assignments. Within my first 6 months on the job, I had determined that a litany of misinformation and half-truths prevailed, in addition to an overall lack of information. I found the misinformation and half-truths everywhere I looked, from blogs to chat rooms. And while I always believed there to be a lack of information overall, I fully realized it when I started my own blog. At that point, I could see the search terms that were used to find my blog and realized that healthcare professionals are seeking information that just isn't readily available.

So, I decided to write this book. At the time, all of the books I could find about travel healthcare were written by traveling healthcare professionals. These are all great books. They're particularly good at offering information about the actual experience. They're great at detailing what to pack, what to expect on the job, and what to expect in your dealings with agencies.

However, I believe there's more to add to the conversation. Understanding what's going on behind the scenes can be greatly beneficial. I'm confident that such information can help travel healthcare professionals plan and negotiate to get the most out of their experience.

Furthermore, having worked in the industry for 6 years, I've experienced most of the pitfalls. I'd love to say I'd experienced them all, but not a week went by that I didn't experience something new. To put this in perspective, consider a travel healthcare professional

1

(traveler) with 10 years of travel experience. This traveler may have completed up to 40 contracts during that time. By contrast, a successful recruiter will have been through 60-100 contracts in a year. Moreover, each one would be unique in its own way. This exposes the recruiter to a broad range of successes, pitfalls, and unique scenarios.

Of course, not every detail can be shared in the span of a book. So, I'll focus on the overarching details that I believe will be most beneficial in helping you get the most out of your time as a travel healthcare professional. We'll begin with a brief look at the history of travel healthcare in America and a discussion of some of the advantages and disadvantages involved.

We'll then take an in depth look at healthcare staffing agencies. We'll define some general agency classifications and discuss how these classifications might affect the service you can expect from them. We'll also look at the various types of relationships that agencies can have with their client hospitals and how those relationships might affect the service you receive.

In the next section, we'll provide an overview of the methods that agencies employ to find interested candidates. Next, we'll provide an approach for you find agencies that can meet your needs. This approach is designed to minimize your input and maximize your results. We'll also take a look at recruiters, the people that most travelers identify as the most important person in the equation.

We'll then move on to a discussion of the compensation packages that healthcare staffing agencies offer. We'll point out why the compensation package should be viewed as a "pie." Additionally, a method for comparing compensation packages will be provided. And no discussion of travel compensation packages would complete without discussing tax-free money. So we'll take an in-depth look at why tax-free money exists, its advantages and disadvantages, and how you qualify to receive it.

With this solid base of knowledge, we'll then discuss each of the various compensation variables including lodging, benefits, 401Ks, travel stipends, etc. We'll point out the various factors you should consider when deciding which of these variables is important to you. We'll also provide suggestions for adequately handling each of the variables to ensure that all the bases are covered.

We'll then look at some of the additional travel assignment variables that you need to consider. We'll discuss some of the issues to to consider is whether or not you have the qualifications necessary to land travel assignments on an ongoing basis. Before we discuss this, I feel it's important to dispel with the myth that agencies are the ones setting the requirements. In fact, hospitals set the requirements. Sure, agencies may set a requirement here and there, but even an agency's requirements are driven by their hospitals' requirements. For example, if 70% of the hospitals that an agency works with require 2 years of experience, then the agency may require a minimum of 2 years of experience just to ensure that they are spending time with candidates that they have a higher likelihood of placing in an assignment.

Now, on to the qualifications which hospitals require. As I'm sure you are aware, hospitals want to keep their costs down. As a result, when it comes to contingent staff they're looking for individuals that will require limited resources to quickly become a functioning member of their organization. Essentially, hospitals would like to invest as little resources as possible into training and orienting. This means that they're looking for experience.

The level of experience that hospitals are looking for tends to fluctuate with employment conditions. If there is a dearth of potential candidates, then hospitals may reduce their experience requirements. If there is an abundance of candidates, then they will most likely increase their experience requirements. When hospitals are experiencing difficulty attracting the travel nurses they need, the standard requirement is 1 year of experience within the last 3 years in the specialty in question. When they're getting a lot of candidates, the standard requirement is 2 years of experience within the past 3 years in the specialty in question.

Again, these are minimum standards. Many hospitals maintain higher requirements. For example, some hospitals require 3-5 years of recent experience in the specialty in question and/or previous experience as a travel nurse. Trauma and teaching hospitals sometimes require recent experience in similar settings. Some hospital units require experience in similar settings. For example, L&D units taking high risk patients often require that travel nurses have experience with similar units. Sometimes hospitals require experience in hospitals with a similar number of licensed beds. Some hospitals require previous experience within the hospital system in question. For example, the Hospital Corporation of America (HCA), which is the largest private hospital corporation in the country,

9

regularly requires that candidates have previous experience in an HCA facility. Hospitals may also require experience with particular computer charting systems, specific patient populations, and/or specific equipment and procedures.

Hospitals also regularly require various certifications. The certification requirements tend to vary by specialty. As a travel nurse, it is highly recommended that you have all certifications that may be required for your specialty. Doing so maximizes the opportunities available to you. Some common certifications that often prevented travel nurses that I worked with from landing assignments they desired included: ACLS for MedSurg and TELE, PALS and TNCC for ER, AWHONN Advanced Fetal Heart Certification for L&D, and PALS for PACU. While we're on the subject, certain specialties tend to be more highly sought than others. Below is a list of specialties that are popular in travel nursing.

ICU, ER, MS, MS/TELE, TELE, OR, L&D, PACU, CVICU, Cath Lab, PEDS, PICU, NICU, Case Management, SDU, PCU, CVOR, PostPartum, Mother Baby, Home Health

In addition to experience, you must also consider if you have the desire to perform in the capacity that travel nurses are often asked to perform. This manifests itself on several levels. First, hospitals are seeking self-starters. You'll be walking into entirely new units that will most likely operate quite differently from the one you're used to, and you'll be doing so with a really limited orientation.   Travel nursing orientations tend to last 1 week, and much of them are spent with paperwork and class room training. It's very common for travel nurses to get 1 shift of orientation directly on the unit and sometimes less. In addition, there are often delays in getting travel nurses the access they need for medications and/or computer charting. This isn't because the hospital in question is a horrible place to work, but rather that they're trying to "onboard" a new nurse in a third of the time that they usually do. The point is that the travel nurse will have to roll with the punches in a productive way in order to be successful.

Second, hospitals are looking for candidates who are open to new methods, processes, and procedures. No two hospitals operate exactly the same way. There are multiple ways of accomplishing many of the tasks that hospitals are routinely faced with. Hospitals typically have very good reasons for utilizing their processes and procedures and they've typically been in place for years without incident. That doesn't mean that there is no room for improvement. There often is. However, your role as a travel nurse requires adaptability. I regularly had travel nurses say to me, "Once I got the hang of it." I say this to point out that things may seem horrific at first, but if you give yourself some time to adjust, everything may fall into place.

Third, you should be comfortable avoiding office politics. Every hospital has its internal strife, cliques, and enduring debates. Staying out of these matters is always best for the travel nurse. In fact, not having to deal with office politics was one of the most often cited reasons that I heard people give for being a travel nurse. Either way, you have to remember that you're a temporary employee. You can be easily dismissed for crossing the wrong person. I know this sounds harsh, but it is unfortunately true. Some might view this as a disadvantage, and others will view it as a huge advantage. The opportunity to not really care about anything other than your patients can be refreshing.

Fourth, you should be prepared to be flexible. Hospitals are typically beholden to some level of guaranteed hours for travel nurses. In order to meet these guarantees, floating to units in which you are qualified to work is often a requirement. Hospitals will sometimes make it a requirement for landing the assignment in the first place. How much and where you'll float will depend on several factors.

First, some specialties float more often than others. ICU and MS/TELE tend to be the ones that float most often. OR tends to float the least. Second, some hospitals work their travelers and permanent staff on different schedules. For example, the permanent staff may be working 8 hour shifts while the travel nurses are scheduled for 12 hour shifts. This results in an overlap for the travel nurse at some point during the 12 hour shift at which point floating is often the only option. Third, sometimes census drops in one unit and hospitals simply need to float their staff to units with higher need in order to keep their weekly hour guarantee. While it's true that you may find contracts that will guarantee that you never have to float, counting on them will be very difficult especially if you have limited to normal experience and are new to travel nursing.

Flexibility is also important when it comes to your goals as a traveler. For example, it's not always possible to get exactly what you want out of a contract. Sometimes there may not be any available assignments for your specialty in your desired location. Sometimes the only assignments that are available in your desired areas are at hospitals that might not be exactly what you're looking for. Sometimes the compensation package might be a little less than you were anticipating in a given location. Sometimes the available housing options aren't quite what you had in mind. It's true that you'll get exactly what you want most of the time, but flexibility is key for the rare occasions,

Finally, you should consider whether or not you're comfortable with some of the less glamorous aspects of the travel nursing lifestyle. You may be on the move every 3 months. I don't know about you, but I think moving is horrible. Of course, you'll only be moving your immediate belongings as opposed to an entire house, but there are other aspects of moving that aren't so desirable. You'll need to get acclimated to new surroundings each time you move. If you value a lifestyle of structure and routine, then this can be a difficult adjustment.

Also, the fact that you don't have a stable home can lead to a heightened state of homesickness. Of course, this can all lead to a feeling of loneliness as well. However, if you're generally independent and/or outgoing then you should be fine. There will never be a shortage of new experiences and people to meet while traveling.

Chapter 2: How the Business Works: The Short Story

In this chapter, I'll provide a very brief overview of how the healthcare staffing business works. This will undoubtedly be a pretty boring discussion for most of you. However, it is also one of the most important topics covered in this book. Understanding how the healthcare staffing business works will provide you with the foundation needed to truly understand your place within the system, enabling you to get the most out of your time as a traveler. I assure even the most experienced travelers will learn something they did not already know, something that will most certainly be beneficial.

Agency Client Services

Healthcare staffing agencies are at the center of the healthcare staffing industry, literally. Agencies are the "middle men" between the hospital and the healthcare clinician. There are hundreds, if not thousands, of healthcare staffing agencies in the United States. Unlike "middle men" in many other industries, healthcare staffing agencies seem to provide an invaluable service that cannot easily be cut out. There are some hospitals that attempt to cut out the middle man but such examples are few and far between, and typically require a unique set of circumstances.

Agencies provide many services to hospitals. For example, agencies provide sourcing services in that they seek out and find the qualified healthcare clinicians that hospitals need. It's important to keep in mind that contingent healthcare professionals are required to be experienced in the area in which they are going to practice. Ideally, hospitals are seeking candidates who will require no training at all and just a brief orientation to the unit. Candidates will need 1 year of experience within the last three years of work history at an absolute minimum. The majority of hospitals now require 2 years of experience in the unit to be worked. Experience as a traveler is also becoming a common requirement.

Finding such candidates can be quite a difficult task and most often requires casting a very wide net. Agencies accomplish this by several means. They undertake ad campaigns in various publications, and on the internet. They purchase lists of healthcare professional contact information and undertake aggressive phone and email campaigns. They advertise on internet job boards, and utilize social media tools. The cost of these activities can add up quickly.

Once contact is made and interest is expressed, agencies are required to vet the candidate. This includes evaluating the candidate's experience, and skills. Agencies will also check the candidate's employment references, and run background checks. As a result of their efforts, agencies build large databases of qualified healthcare professionals who have expressed an interest in contingent work. These healthcare professionals can then be quickly informed about potential employment opportunities.

It's important to point out that agencies realize economies of scale in their recruiting and vetting processes relative to what an individual hospital could achieve. Agencies typically have hundreds of hospital clients. As a result, agencies typically have hundreds and sometimes thousands of open travel assignment opportunities at any given time. A single hospital on the other hand has far fewer travel assignment opportunities. Therefore, agencies have a higher likelihood of being able to match the candidates they find and vet with assignments the candidates are interested in.

Healthcare staffing agencies also provide credentialing and compliance services. In this regard, agencies ensure that the required licenses and certifications are active and in good standing. Agencies are required to ensure that such credentials do not expire during the healthcare professional's tenure. Agencies must also ensure that all required medical tests and physical screenings are current and in compliance with the hospital's standards. This includes items like physical exams, immunization records, and drug screens, in addition to any and all documentation requirements specific to the hospital. For example, hospitals often have their own tests, standard hygiene forms, and other documents that must be completed prior to starting work.

Agencies also realize economies of scale in the credentialing and compliance process. A hospital might need an employee for 3 months only. In addition, travelers tend to enjoy moving on to the next opportunity and experiencing new things, so it's typical for them to stay in one location for only one 13 week contract. However, travelers will often stay with the agency if they've had a positive experience and the agency is able to find them a desirable contract. As a result, it's common for travelers to complete multiple contracts through the same agency. The credentialing and compliance process can be quite expensive. Spreading this cost over multiple contracts represents a savings that agencies are able to realize relative to the hospital.

While sourcing, compliance, and credentialing are all very valuable services, human resource services are perhaps the most valuable set of services that agencies provide to hospitals. Technically, the healthcare professional works for the agency, not for the hospital. The agency is the employer and as such, they are responsible for all of the responsibilities and requirements involved with employing someone, thereby removing these burdens from the hospital. The agency is responsible for payroll processing, payroll taxes, worker compensation claims, disability insurance, unemployment insurance, liability insurance, disciplinary actions, and benefits management.

Outsourcing human resource services results in huge cost savings for hospitals. Take unemployment insurance, for example. If a hospital were to directly hire employees for temporary positions, their unemployment costs would increase dramatically. When the temporary need expired, the hospital would have to lay off the worker.

The individual could then collect unemployment. The hospital avoids this dilemma by utilizing a staffing agency.

Meanwhile, the agency is in a better position to avoid unemployment costs. Agencies will almost always have work to offer the employee. It may not be work that the employee wants, but that doesn't really matter in most cases. In most cases unemployment benefits can only be collected when one is laid off, and no other similar work has been offered. When someone goes to work for a travel staffing company, the understanding is that they are agreeing to travel for work. The travel staffing company will almost always have work to offer its employees. An employee's refusal will almost always result in a refusal of unemployment claims.

In addition to all of these traditionally required human resource services, agencies also provide benefits and other services that are unique to traveling professionals. In this regard, agencies may provide medical benefits, 401Ks, travel arrangement services, housing services, rental car services, and any number of other related services. When it comes to these services, you'll find that agencies offer these services in varying degrees. However, the important thing, as it pertains to the relationship between the agency and the hospital, is that the hospital is not responsible for these services.

You'll find many people who will argue that agencies can indeed be cut out as middle men in this process. They assert that healthcare professionals can work as independent contractors which would allow the hospital to avoid the costs and resources associated with hiring workers as employees. Unfortunately, hospitals would still be faced with the burden and cost of finding and vetting candidates. More importantly, the vast majority of healthcare professionals do not meet the legal requirements to qualify as independent contractors. We'll discuss this in greater detail in the section on taxes.

All together, the services provided by healthcare staffing agencies represent a valuable resource for entities in need of contingent healthcare staff. These services, and the cost savings they represent, constitute the agency's sales pitch to prospective hospital clients.

Agency Client Contracts

An agency must have a contract with a facility in order to send its employees to work there. No one agency has contracts with every healthcare provider utilizing contingent staff. In fact, you'd be hard pressed to find an agency that has contracts with every hospital in a major metropolitan region. Some agencies focus on particular regions or states. Others cast a broader net and work with facilities across the country.

Contract provisions differ from contract to contract. However, it is standard for the contracts to contain a common set of provisions. These provisions include things like the bill rate, solicitation clauses, liability insurance requirements, contract termination rules, shift guarantee and cancellation policies, compliance and record management policies, billing and collection policies, and a host of others.

It's important to understand one of these provisions at the outset, the bill rate. The bill rate is the hourly rate that the agency charges the hospital for its employees' time at the hospital. Typically, the contract will include a bill rate schedule that defines the rates for various licenses, specialties, shifts, holidays, and other distinctions. We will expand on this and other provisions that have a direct impact on the employee where applicable throughout the book.

The most important thing to understand at this point is that agencies need to have a contract with a facility in order to work with the facility. For the traveler, this means you shouldn't rely on an agency to get you work at a specific facility unless the agency already has a contract with the facility. If you're attempting to work in a specific state, or in a specific city, or in a specific hospital, you must be certain that the agency has the contracts necessary to get you there. Do not rely on an agency that does not have the contracts already in place.

Landing these contracts is a priority for agencies. In larger agencies, they have teams of Account Managers and high level sales executives engaged strictly in landing new contracts. In smaller agencies, this responsibility may fall to a single Account Manager or the agency's top level leaders. In years past, landing these contracts was far less difficult than it is today. There was less competition in the early days of the industry. There were simply fewer agencies providing the service. Hospitals received calls less frequently. As a result, they were more likely to entertain the notion of a new service provider, and working with multiple service providers, sometimes 100 or more, was the norm. Additionally, there was far less bureaucratic red tape in the early years of the industry. Contracts included fewer provisions and details. The decision making process was streamlined and often times required a lower level of approval within the healthcare organization.

These days, landing a new contract directly with a hospital can be quite difficult for an agency. There is far more competition because there are far more agencies in the business. Hospitals receive multiple calls daily from agencies seeking to land contracts. Hospitals are much less enthused to take those calls as a result. And perhaps the most profound change has been the proliferation of the Vendor Management Service model.

The Vendor Management Service offers a very attractive service proposition for hospitals. The Vendor Management Service provides a central source for managing the hospital's contingent staffing needs. There are several different Vendor Management Service models and we'll discuss them in detail later. Essentially, utilizing a Vendor Management Service means that the hospital no longer needs to work with multiple staffing agencies on an individual basis. Instead, the entire operation is centralized, making it far more efficient.

When a hospital utilizes a Vendor Management Service, the agency must try to land a contract through the Vendor Management Service to do business with the hospital. Sometimes these contracts are very easy to land, and other times they're extremely difficult to land. Again, the important thing to remember for now is that it's important to establish the agency's contract status with hospitals and or regions that you're interested in. Relying on an agency that doesn't already have contracts in your desired locations is risky at best and futile at worst.

Revenue Generation

Once the contract is in place, the agency can begin staffing the hospital's contingent staffing needs. The revenue generation process starts when an agency employee submits a time card. For example, let's say an agency sends an employee to a hospital for a 13 week contract. The employee will typically keep a weekly time record which may be paper, electronic, or both. That time record will typically be transmitted weekly to the agency by the employee, the hospital, or both. The agency will process a paycheck for the employee based on the contract agreement between the agency and the employee. The agency will also use the time record as a bill of sale to collect the money due the agency per the contract between the agency and the hospital. In most cases, hospitals will take 60 to 90 days to make payment which is a standard billing practice. As a result, agencies typically have a line of credit for meeting their payroll requirements.

Conclusion

In this section a very general overview of the healthcare staffing industry was provided. We briefly discussed the history of contingent staffing and the reasons that hospitals require contingent staffing. We defined the different types of contingent staffing. We also discussed many of the considerations in determining if travel healthcare is right for you. We learned about the value proposition that healthcare staffing agencies offer to hospitals that need contingent staffing. We briefly touched on hospital-agency contracts. Finally, we touched on the financial transaction that takes place between the hospital and agency. In the next section, we'll take a much closer look at healthcare staffing agencies and how their varying operations can affect you.

Section 2: Agencies in Depth

Chapter 3: Agencies: Differentiating by Size

Understanding Agencies

There are hundreds, if not thousands of agencies in operation today. In a general sense, they all operate the same exact way. They have contracts with hospitals. They send contingent healthcare staff to the hospitals. They bill the hospitals for their contingent staff's time. They pay their contingent staff, cover the associated costs, and keep a cut to cover their own pay and associated business expenses. However, there are differences between agencies that can have an impact on you. In this section, we'll categorize and analyze the agencies, and we'll take a close look at how some of their operational differences can affect the service that you receive from them.

Now I'll admit that fitting agencies into categories can be a bit unfair to them. The categories characterize the agencies, and these characterizations may not always be 100% accurate. However, categorizing the agencies provides a framework that helps us understand their challenges, advantages, disadvantages, and organizational differences. Understanding these issues will assist you in getting the most out of your contingent staffing experience.

Perhaps the most common method of categorizing agencies is by size. For all intents and purposes, there are large, medium, and small agencies. I'm not going to demarcate these agencies using some sort of arbitrary aspect of the industry like annual revenue, or number of employees. Instead, we'll focus on describing the organizational and operational differences, and how those differences will impact you as a customer.

LARGE AGENCIES

The largest agencies in the business include companies like American Mobile, Cross Country, and On Assignment. Some of these companies are publicly traded on stock exchanges, and others remain privately held. Some of them have annual revenues near or above $1 billion. Despite all of the negative press they receive, they're big for a reason. They're good at what they do.

Almost all large companies have highly structured internal staff organizations with specific teams responsible for handling each aspect of the business. Account Management teams are responsible for serving current client (i.e. hospital) needs, and signing up new clients. Housing departments are responsible for finding and securing housing for all travel staff requiring this service. Travel departments handle any flight arrangements or transportation details. Compliance and credentialing departments handle all issues pertaining to required documentation. Payroll teams handle all issues pertaining to payroll. Benefits teams handle all issues pertaining to company provided benefits. Recruiters are responsible for contacting and signing up new travelers. And often times there are even customer service teams to handle all inquiries from current travelers. The important thing is that everyone stays in their lanes in an effort to achieve maximum operational efficiency.

SMALL AGENCIES

Organizationally, small agencies are almost the exact opposite of large agencies. They typically have less than ten internal employees, and often times less than five. They can be managed from a home office or a tiny 100 square foot office space. Duties often overlap. Sometimes, your recruiter may be responsible for everything including credentialing, housing, benefits, and certain aspects of payroll like time card collection. It's also common for the owner of a small staffing company to maintain responsibility of the recruiting and account management aspects of the business, while employing one or more assistants to handle the various other details.

MEDIUM AGENCIES

There's a reason that medium agencies are being described last. They're kind of a cross between the large and small agency. Medium agencies may have anywhere from 10 to 50 internal employees. Organizationally, they may have a structure that is very similar to a large agency. However, they may be unable to adequately manage spikes in volume so, like the small agency, duties can often overlap. For example, let's say a medium sized agency brings on 10 new travelers in a 2 week period. Their credentialing team may become overwhelmed, which would require recruiters to step in and provide assistance. All that said, some medium agencies may also have an organizational structure similar to that of small agencies. In this case, the recruiter is typically responsible for everything, but may have an assistant or two to help with all of the clerical, scheduling and research issues.

Assignment Volume

The size of the agency will most certainly have an impact on the volume and selection of available assignments that the agency has to offer. Simply put, large agencies have the largest selection of available assignments. This is because they have contracts with more hospitals than smaller agencies. That's part of what makes them large. You see, in order for an agency to grow, it has to do a very good job at retaining its current contingent staff. And retaining staff requires that the agency has options for their staff when a contract ends without an extension offer. The agency must be able to offer options for the traveler's next contract.

Meanwhile, landing contracts with hospitals these days often requires that agencies have a documented ability to fill openings quickly and effectively. Larger agencies are better able to do this because they have more recruiters and more contingent workers working for them already. And even when agencies are able to land contracts, maintaining them often requires that agencies provide the needed travelers on an ongoing basis. An agency can lose a contract with a hospital because it has been unable to fill any openings for the hospital in a long period of time. The hospital will view the agency as dead weight, and cut them off at some point, or the relationship will go stale.

Large agencies do an excellent job at managing their contracts, landing new contracts, and retaining their travelers. This translates into a larger selection of available options for the traveler. And I'm not just talking about more options in a given region. Large agencies have more options nationwide. They also have more options in terms of facility types. Large agencies are more apt to work with surgery centers, chemotherapy centers, home health providers and other niche providers. Large agencies are also more likely to work with the most prestigious hospitals in the country, and university hospitals. These hospitals typically sign exclusive contracts with one of the larger agencies. For example, as of the writing of this book Stanford Medical Center and Lucille Packard Children's Hospital go through American Mobile, while Cedars Sinai goes through Cross Country.

You can expect medium agencies to have fewer contracts and small agencies to have even fewer. This is not to say that all is lost for these agencies when it comes to providing you with the options you need. Some medium and small agencies do an excellent job of focusing on a specific niche, or region. For example, there are agencies that specialize in working with Operating Room Registered Nurses, or Ultrasound Technicians. Other agencies may focus on a specific region, or market. For example, some agencies provide services only for California, or only for Florida, or only for some large metropolitan area like Chicago. Such agencies may have selections for their specific area of focus which can be comparable to the offerings of even the largest agencies, or better.

Service

The size of the agency may have an impact on the type of service you receive. On the message boards and blogs dedicated to travel nursing, it seems to be fairly well established that small and mid-sized agencies tend to offer a personalized and personable approach. As the story goes, at small and mid-sized agencies, you'll often have only one point of contact, your recruiter. You'll contact your recruiter for anything and everything, and your recruiter will know everything there is to know about all aspects of your contract and your personal circumstances. In addition, you'll work with only one recruiter no matter where you take an assignment, or what specialty the assignment is for. All of this tends to ensure continuity of service.

When it comes to large agencies, the conventional wisdom contends that you're just a number. As the story goes, large agencies deal in volume at the sacrifice of service. You'll have to talk to the benefits department for any problems with your benefits, and to the housing department for any problems with your housing, and to the payroll department for any problems with your pay. You'll find that these departments may be unaware of the conversations you've had with your recruiter regarding these issues, so you'll have to explain them again. As a result, resolving issues can be far more tedious. In addition, the recruiters at large agencies may be assigned to geographic territories or have particular specialties that they work with. As a result, if you move from the east coast to the west coast, or accept a contract for a different specialty than before, you may have to work with a different recruiter. All of this combines to reduce service levels.

These narratives exist because there's some truth to them and when working with agencies you'll definitely want to ask questions that are geared toward determining how they operate from a service standpoint. However, I have a different take on the issue of service. I believe that you'll receive different levels of service depending on the agency and the issue.

For example, I agree that you stand a better chance of receiving more personalized service from a smaller agency. You may indeed have one point of contact that is responsible for every aspect of the service you receive. However, that recruiter is also responsible for every aspect of service for every other traveler that he or she works with. At some point, providing that level of service can become overwhelming. During these periods, you may not recognize that your recruiter is failing you in other ways.

For example, the recruiter may be failing you on finding your next contract. This is one of the reasons that larger agencies tend to have higher retention rates. You may be just a number, but you're a number that they really want to keep. The Recruiters and Account Managers at large agencies tend to be laser focused on making sure that you'll have your next contract lined up in advance.

While retention is also a top priority at small and mid-sized agencies, there are times when they have a more difficult time managing it. It becomes a balancing act between new business and current business. Recruiters are always in the process of recruiting new candidates and retaining current ones. When recruiters are pulled away to handle other tasks like compliance, housing, benefits, or payroll, then they may miss an opportunity to provide other aspects of service.

Compensation

I often times read or hear it stated that smaller agencies can provide better compensation because they have lower overhead costs. I've discussed this with many of the travelers that I've worked with and I've read it in chat rooms and on blogs. The logic seems sound. Larger companies have larger offices, more internal staff, larger advertising budgets, and so on. As a result, they have to keep a higher percentage of the bill rate to cover the costs, which results in less pay for the traveler. While this may be true to some degree, my experience has proven that there is much more going on than this simple logic accounts for. And besides, if this were always true, then WalMart would be the most expensive retail store on the planet.

I would argue that there is a curve of sorts. For the smallest of companies, this conventional logic may be true. These companies are so small, and their overhead is so low, that they do indeed have a competitive advantage. However, once a company begins to realize any sort of growth they begin to lose this advantage. You see, large companies realize economies of scale that small to mid-sized companies are unable to realize. For example, if a small company wants to offer medical benefits, they are going to be burdened with much higher costs than a large company. Like almost every industry in the world, the health insurance industry gives price breaks for buying in bulk. Additionally, large agencies may realize advantages in their worker compensation, disability, and unemployment insurance costs.

Large agencies may be able to negotiate discounts with organizations that provide some of the standard amenities that comprise a traveler's compensation package. For example, larger agencies can get a better deal on rental cars because they use them more. Larger agencies can also get great deals on apartments and hotels. Large agencies may work out a deal with a large national property management company that manages apartment complexes throughout the nation. Large agencies will sometimes sign long term leases on apartments in major markets where they know that they will regularly have travelers to occupy the space. Meanwhile, smaller and mid-sized agencies are stuck paying premium prices for short term leases. These short term leases can often times costs 10%-15% more than a standard lease.

Large agencies also realize economies of scale when it comes to recruitment costs. For starters, large agencies have much higher contingent staff retention rates. This is because they have contracts with more hospitals than smaller agencies, which results in a larger selection of travel contracts at a higher number of locations throughout the country. So, when a traveler is finished with one contract, the larger agencies will have many more options available than smaller and mid-sized agencies for the next contract. This is a huge cost reduction because bringing on new employees is much more expensive than retaining current employees.

Large agencies also do an excellent job of attracting talent with advertising campaigns and, better yet, with referral campaigns. While advertising may seem like an overhead cost, the simple truth is that advertising exists because it works. It works to generate enough revenue that the costs are more than made up for. And large agencies are able to advertise nationally, because they are able to staff nationally, because they have more hospital contracts. Additionally, because they have more nurses working for them, large agencies receive more referrals.

This all translates into lower recruitment costs. The recruiters at a large agency are spending less time finding interested candidates because the company, and the company's success, is driving candidates to them. As a result, they have more time to work with candidates. Meanwhile, recruiters at small and mid-sized agencies are spending much more time finding candidates, which results in higher recruitment costs.

Finally, large agencies may be generating revenue in other ways that they can then divert to their travel nursing operations should they so choose. For example, American Mobile has a continuing education site called RN.com. Other companies have highly successful blogs or job posting sites that also generate revenue. I can't be certain about this, but I suspect that all of this revenue makes its way to the bottom line, and could possibly afford these large agencies the leeway to offer better rates.

Smaller agencies may have one advantage over their larger counterparts when it comes to compensation. They often times offer much more flexible compensation packages. Larger agencies have a tendency to maintain boiler plate type compensation packages. They'll offer the same stipends no matter where you go. For example, Cross Country offers $250 per week for Meals and Incidental Expenditures (M&IE) whether you're in San Francisco, or Bakersfield. You may find a little wiggle room, but not much. In contrast, a smaller company might offer the maximum stipends for any given location. For example, a smaller company might give you $500 per week for San Francisco and $300 per week in Bakersfield. This is not to say that the smaller agency is giving you more money overall, but they are willing to divvy the money up in a way that may result in higher net pay for you. We'll discuss this in greater detail in the section on compensation.

Smaller agencies may also exhibit greater flexibility with housing options. Large agencies often have specific housing locations in any given area. Also, with larger agencies you may have no say at all in the housing choice. They will put you where they have availability. In contrast, smaller agencies may be willing to provide you with several housing options, each with different prices. You can then select the option that best suits your needs. This can come in handy when traveling with loved ones or pets. A smaller agency may be better able to accommodate pets because they're willing to search for a housing option that accepts pets.

Now, I'm not saying that large agencies will pay you more. All I'm saying is that you can't assume that they will pay you less. There are many advantages to being large. Many of these advantages involve significant cost savings. As a result, a large agency may be able to pay you the same as, or more, than a smaller competitor. In order to know for sure, you'll need to conduct an apples-to-apples comparison between agencies. I'll provide everything you need to accomplish this in the section on compensation packages.

Chapter 4: Hospital-Agency Relationships: Direct Relationship and Vendor Management Services

Direct Relationship

It's useful for travel healthcare professionals to be informed about hospital-agency relationships. Remember, an agency can only work with a hospital if it has a contract to do so. These contracts exist under several different arrangements. Each arrangement results in different outcomes for the hospital, the agency, and the travel healthcare professional. There are essentially two relationship categories, Direct Relationships and Vendor Management Service relationships.

A Direct Relationship exists when the agency has a contract directly with the hospital to provide staffing services and communication between the two parties is direct, without any intermediaries. Direct Relationships are the traditional/original type of relationship in healthcare staffing. Typically, hospitals that engage in direct relationships will work with a fairly large number of agencies depending on how much they utilize contingent staffing and how difficult it is for the hospital to get their openings filled. There are some hospitals that work directly with over 100 different agencies. However, others are able to have their needs met by far fewer agencies and may work with less than 10.

Hospitals typically have designated contacts for their contracted agencies to communicate with. These contacts are typically staffing office representatives. Hospitals may or may not have policies in place that govern how their representatives engage with agencies to handle the talent acquisition process. Those that do have policies in place are seeking to achieve what is commonly referred to as "vendor neutrality." Vendor neutrality policies seek to ensure that all vendors (healthcare staffing agencies) are treated equally in an effort to ensure that the hospital gets the best talent as opposed to talent only from favored agencies.

Typically, when vendor neutrality policies are in place, the hospital's staffing office representatives will receive requests for travelers, otherwise known as orders or requisitions, from Unit Managers, Chief Nursing Officers, or someone in the finance department who has approved the order. The orders should then be released to all of the agencies that have a contract with the hospital. To accomplish this, the hospital typically sends out a mass email with the necessary details to all of the contracted agencies.

Typically, agencies receive only the most basic information such as License, Specialty, Shift, Start Date, and Contract Length. Specific details about the unit or qualifications sought will sometimes be included as well. So the agency may receive an email from Hospital X that says, "RN, PICU, 7p-7a, 4/18 Start, 13 weeks." Agencies will then survey their available candidates and reply with the profiles of any interested candidates. These profiles will be reviewed by the staffing office to ensure that the basic requirements are included. If the staffing office deems that all the basic requirements are met, then the profile will be forwarded to the Unit Manager, or someone designated in the unit, who will review the profile and decide whether or not to contact the candidate for an interview.

This scenario represents the way things should work with a direct relationship model when the hospital has vendor neutrality policies in place. It ensures that all agencies who are contracted with the facility receive a fair shot at submitting any candidates they might have. It also ensures that the hospital receives the largest possible selection of candidates, thereby increasing the chances that the hospital receives more highly qualified candidates from which to select. Despite these advantages, some hospitals choose not to institute vendor neutrality policies and sometimes their vendor neutrality policies are disobeyed.

Sometimes, the staffing office representatives play favorites or enter into side agreements with agencies. For example, the hospital's staffing office representative responsible for handling the contingent staffing requirements may develop a strong relationship with particular agencies, or worse, accept gifts or kickbacks from agencies in exchange for favorable treatment. Other times, agency representatives will somehow develop close personal relationships with Unit Managers, or other individuals who can trump the staffing office. In this case, the agency representative may be able to bypass the staffing office and learn of openings from the Unit Manager before the staffing office is made aware.

I have experienced such cases even when the facility has vendor neutrality policies in place. For example, one facility I worked with had a very stringent vendor neutrality policy that went so far as to require that the profiles sent by agencies include absolutely no mention of the agency, whether in writing or logo form. They were aiming to ensure that people at the facility would not even know where the profile was from. The only person who could possibly know was the staffing office representative who originally received the profile, and that's where the breakdown originated. It became well known that the representative developed a very close relationship with a single agency, and was forwarding all of that agency's profiles to the hiring managers first, before sending any others. This ultimately resulted in one, pretty small agency having 18 to 20 travelers at the facility at one time.

In another instance, a county hospital I worked with had strict vendor neutrality policies, which most municipal facilities do. I was working with a traveling couple, he an OR nurse and she a Cath Lab nurse. The couple was also working with another agency, and both agencies submitted him to an open OR position at the county facility. He interviewed, was offered the position, and selected to work through us. We were told there were no Cath Lab openings, nor would there be any time soon. Then, the other agency called the couple and told them they had secured her a position in the Cath Lab, and could get them both a contract if they both agreed to work with the other agency. We called our contact in the staffing office who knew nothing of the Cath Lab opening. The other agency had clearly bypassed the staffing office, perhaps directly to the hiring manager, and the couple was forced to go with the other agency to ensure that they were able to lock down contracts at the same hospital.

What does this all mean for you? Well, there are a few important things to take away from all of this. First, if the hospital works with many agencies, and things are working like they should, it's possible that landing a spot will be quite competitive. The orders will be released to many agencies, and the facility may immediately receive a large number of profiles. I've seen openings filled in less than an hour. I've also seen emails from hospital staff indicating that they had received 50 or more profiles in less than hour. However, this is just the name of the game in today's market.

Second, if the hospital engages in direct relationships with relatively few agencies, then you'll stand a much better chance at getting an interview. The hospital will still receive many candidates, but there will be fewer candidates to compete against. Additionally, there is a good chance that the few agencies who are working with the hospital have developed a strong working relationship with the key players at the hospital. This will result in the agency having more information about the hospital, the unit, and the assignment overall.

Finally, if the hospital is working with many agencies, but is giving preferential treatment to a few agencies, you'll have a difficult time navigating the system unless you happen to be working with an agency that is receiving preferential treatment. If you're working with an agency that is not receiving preferential treatment, you'll have a very difficult time landing an assignment. Your agency may not even receive word that an opening exists, and even if they do, your profile may be passed over in favor of others from preferred agencies.

Vendor Management Services

The Vendor Management Service relationship is a little more complex. This type of relationship is becoming more and more prevalent in the healthcare staffing industry. I have seen estimates claiming that over 90% of hospitals use Vendor Management Services to meet their contingent staffing needs. We previously discussed why hospitals are migrating to this model in droves, and here we'll discuss the intricacies and how these relationships affect you. To recap, a Vendor Management Service relationship exists when a hospital, or hospital corporation, signs a contract with an organization to be the central source for the hospital's contingent staffing needs. There are 3 types of Vendor Management Services prevalent in the healthcare staffing industry.

The first is known as the Vendor Management System (VMS). A VMS is a web-based software application that provides a range of tools designed to allow hospitals to centrally manage their contingent staffing suppliers (healthcare staffing agencies). Hospitals and their contracted agencies are able to log on to the website where they utilize the tools to conduct their business. The software can include job requisition management, interview scheduling, notification systems, credential management, invoice/billing management, timekeeping management, and other tools. The companies that design and market the VMS typically offer training, customer service, and on-going support. Simply put, the hospital's staff receives training on the software and puts it to use with customer service assistance from the VMS provider.

Such arrangements are routinely referred to as "vendor neutral." This is the most important point for the travel healthcare professional regarding this arrangement. Again, the idea is that all the healthcare staffing agencies that are contracted with the hospital through the VMS are supposed to receive equal treatment. For you, this means that you have got the same chance to land an assignment no matter which agency you choose. For the hospital, this means that they stand the best chance of hiring the top available talent because bias favoring certain agencies over others is removed. Examples of VMS companies include ShiftWise, Medefis, FieldGlass, and PeopleFluent. As of the writing of this book, it is estimated that over 1500 hospitals in the United States use a VMS.

The second type of Vendor Management Service prevalent in the healthcare staffing industry is called a Managed Service Provider (MSP). An MSP manages virtually everything related to the hospital's contingent staffing needs. The MSP will manage all of the billing, timekeeping, credentialing, supplier management, on-boarding, and orientation. The MSP may also offer a guarantee on meeting the hospital's staffing needs. So essentially, a VMS provides the hospital with the tools to manage all of these things on their own, whereas the MSP manages everything for the hospital.

In order to land such a contract, the MSP typically offers a very attractive Service Level Agreement that guarantees high staffing levels and lower costs. Consider how attractive this offer is. The MSP is offering to be the single point of contact for the hospital, as opposed to the hospital dealing with multiple, sometimes 50 to 100 agencies. In addition, the MSP is guaranteeing that they will staff a very high percentage of the hospital's contingent staffing needs. For example, they might guarantee that 98% of all staffing needs will be filled at all times. If not, all payments for services are held in escrow until minimum levels are met, at which point, the payments are released to the MSP. The MSP also offers the hospital standardized and often times much lower bill rates which saves the hospital money.

Moreover, the MSP will take care of interviewing, credentialing, and on-boarding all contingent staff.

In return, the MSP typically receives a guarantee that all contingent staffing needs will be handled through them. This is commonly referred to as exclusivity, or an exclusive agreement. And this is where we get to the key difference between the VMS and MSP as far as it pertains to the travel healthcare professional. Unlike the VMS, the MSP is never "vendor neutral." This is because the MSP is itself a staffing agency. These are typically larger companies like American Mobile Network (AMN), Cross Country, and Medical Staffing Network (MSN). To provide their services efficiently, MSPs will routinely utilize the services of a VMS. For example, as of the writing of this book, AMN is the MSP for Kaiser Permanente and AMN uses FieldGlass, a VMS, to manage their services.

But because even the largest of agencies may have difficulty meeting the staffing levels that are required by their contract with the hospital, the MSP will enlist the services of "Sub Vendors." Sub Vendors are just staffing agencies that obtain a contract with the MSP to provide contingent staffing to the hospital. However, they can do so only through the MSP. In exchange, the MSP charges a fee that is typically between 1.5% and 4% of the MSP's bill rate with the hospital.

Obviously, the MSP would prefer to staff every opening themselves. If they do, they'll make 15%-25% of the bill rate versus the 1.5%-4% they'll receive if a sub-vendor fills an opening. Therefore, the MSP is incentivized to favor its own candidates over those of their sub-vendors, hence the reason that this system is not vendor neutral.

Group Purchasing Organizations (GPO) and Hospital Associations (HA) represent the third type of Vendor Management Service prevalent in the healthcare staffing industry. GPOs and HAs have differences from the hospital's perspective. GPOs are organizations that have traditionally purchased goods and supplies in bulk in order to qualify for large price discounts from suppliers. The GPO then passes a percentage of the savings on to the hospital. At some point GPOs began applying this same model to the services that hospitals utilize, including contingent staffing.

HAs operate more like advocacy groups. Every state has HAs that hospitals can choose to be a member of. HAs offer legislative advocacy and information services to their member hospitals. Many HAs also provide services similar to that of a GPO either directly or through separate private organizations established by the HA. Contingent staffing management is one of the services that some HAs offer. For example, a large number of hospitals in Arizona utilize HAs to meet their contingent staffing needs.

Many HAs and GPOs have developed their own VMS technology to help them manage contingent staffing services. Broadlane is one such example. Others partner with VMS providers to help them manage their contingent staffing services. The most important thing for the travel healthcare professional to understand is that GPOs, HAs, and VMSs are all fairly similar from the travel healthcare professional's perspective. In other words, MSPs are different than VMSs, GPOs, and HAs.

Vendor Management Services and Vendor Neutrality

So, what does all this jargon mean for the travel healthcare professional? The two most important aspects of Vendor Management Services as they pertain to travel healthcare professionals are vendor neutrality, and bill rates. These aspects differ for the travel healthcare professional depending on whether the Vendor Management Service is an MSP or VMS/GPO/HA.

The VMS/GPO/HA model offers vendor neutrality. Again, this means that all agencies that have a contract with the hospital should be treated equally. All agencies should receive notification of openings at the same time. All agencies should have to jump through the same hoops and be subject to the same policies and procedures. Vendor neutrality is designed to ensure that the best candidates at the best price are selected rather than the candidates of the most favored agencies.

It's important to note that there are those who contend that breakdowns in vendor neutrality can occur with the VMS/GPO/HA model just as they can with Direct Relationships as described previously. For example, Medefis, a VMS, is owned by the private equity group Welsh, Carson, Anderson, and Stowe which also owns Onward Healthcare, a large healthcare staffing agency. This relationship leads some to contend that Medefis can't be vendor neutral in the strictest sense. However, Medefis maintains that it is vendor neutral. Additionally, there is no question that the prospect of vendor neutrality it greatest with the VMS/GPO/HA model.

In a simple VMS scenario, the hospital's staffing representatives will submit a job requisition using the VMS. All contracted agencies will then receive an email update from the VMS that a new job order has been entered. Agencies must then submit candidate profiles through the VMS. It's possible for the VMS to be circumvented but it is far less likely than vendor neutrality policies in a direct relationship being circumvented.

By contrast, MSPs are never vendor neutral. Therefore, the processes and mechanisms at work are much different. In a simple scenario, the hospital will contact the MSP to let them know that they need a traveler. The MSP will keep the order for themselves, typically for a period of 3 days to 2 weeks. During this time, the MSP's recruiters will attempt to recruit candidates for the opening. If they are unsuccessful, the order will be released to the Sub Vendors who will recruit and submit any candidates they may have. At this point, both the MSP and the Sub Vendors attempt to recruit for the order until it is filled.

Sometimes, MSP's have preferred Sub Vendors, or they may have tiers of Sub Vendors. This means that when the MSP decides to release the order, they might release it to a preferred group first, and then to others if the order is not filled in a certain period of time. Remember, by the time the opening gets released to Sub Vendors, the MSP's recruiters have a head start. In addition, when the order gets released to Sub Vendors, the MSP may be flooded with profiles due to the large number of Sub Vendors. In any case, your competition to land the assignment becomes fierce.

Essentially, the MSP is the agency with first crack at the orders. If you're not working with the MSP, then you stand less of a chance at even knowing an opening exists, let alone landing an interview. An opening may get filled by the MSP without your agency ever knowing about it. In addition, even after the order gets released to the Sub Vendors, the MSP still has an incentive to give preferential treatment to any of its candidates because the MSP stands to make more money placing its own candidate as opposed to a Sub Vendor's candidate. Add to this the fact that the MSP charges the Sub Vendors a fee for doing business, which lowers the bill rate for the Sub Vendor thereby potentially lowering the pay for the traveler, and the MSP starts looking like the most attractive option for you to work with.

Vendor Management Services and the Bill Rate

In addition to differences in vendor neutrality, the MSP model can also differ from the VMS/GPO/HA models when it comes to bill rates. Again, a bill rate is the hourly dollar amount that the agency charges for an hour of their employees' time at work. The bill rate is the single most important variable in determining how much the agency can pay the employee.

MSPs offer "standardized" bill rates. This means that there is one rate for all workers with any given license covered by the contract. For example, all Registered Nurses have the same bill rate, all Physical Therapists have the same bill rate, and so on. It's also possible for the licenses to be broken down by specialty and every so often by level of experience. For example, Medical Surgical and Telemetry Registered Nurses have one rate while all other Registered Nurses have another. Or, Registered Nurses with 1-3 years of experience get one rate, while those with more than 3 years of experience get a slightly higher rate. The important thing to understand is that the rates are set in stone by the contract for all intents and purposes. There is no possibility of negotiating a higher rate based on a candidate's salary history or work experience.

With the VMS/GPO/HA models it's at least remotely possible that a higher bill rate be negotiated on a case by case basis. I say "remotely possible" because many VMS/GPO/HA models may also have standardized bill rates and the trend in the industry strongly prefers standardized bill rates. In addition, these models provide hospitals with the tools to efficiently manage a large number of staffing agencies. Therefore, the competition for open jobs can be fierce. In this case, agencies and their candidates can expect to have great difficulty negotiating higher bill rates in a slack labor market, and a better chance at negotiating higher bill rates in a tight labor market.

The level of flexibility for the agency to negotiate a higher bill rate depends on the specific VMS/GPO/HA. Some services allow the hospital to specify a bill rate range for a specific job opening. Other services allow agencies to place a bid for the bill rate. Again though, these systems are typically designed to help hospitals reduce costs, so it's difficult to bid the rates up, especially in a slack labor market.

In any case, I recommend against being overly concerned about the bill rates and trying to negotiate higher bill rates as a travel healthcare professional. It has become nearly impossible. This is why I call "bill rate negotiation" a myth later in the book. However, I do think it's important for travel healthcare professionals to understand the mechanisms at play. And it never hurts to ask your recruiter if there's a chance that a higher bill rate can be negotiated if you feel it's deserved and you are truly interested in the assignment.

Also, please note the difference between "a higher bill rate" and "a higher pay rate." You should always try to negotiate a higher pay rate for yourself. This would mean that the agency is taking less money out of the bill rate and giving you more. Again, if you really want the assignment and are at an impasse in negotiations regarding the pay rate, then you could potentially ask the agency if negotiating a higher bill rate with the hospital is possible.

Relationships: The When and How

Putting the hospital-agency relationship information to use in a practical sense means determining the best agency to work with at any given hospital based on the hospital-agency relationship. Accomplishing this can be difficult. It could potentially take hours of your time. If you're like me, you don't want to spend countless hours with minutia only to achieve limited benefits. So, when and how do you put this information to use?

I have two recommendations for determining when to put this information to use. First, the narrower your travel assignment search is, the more you should put this information to use. The broader your travel assignment search is, the less you should put this information to use. This is because it's much easier to determine the exact relationship scenario occurring with one hospital, or with all the hospitals in a given city, versus finding out the exact relationship scenario for all the hospitals in a given state, or across several states.

Second, you should always be at least interested in whether or not an MSP relationship exists for a hospital that you're considering. Again, this is especially true if you're interested in working at a particular hospital, or even in a particular city. Remember, it's highly likely that the MSP's candidates get preferential treatment. If you know that there is an MSP, then you can at least contact the MSP to find out what they have to offer and compare it to your agency and/or a Sub Vendor or two to determine who has the better overall combination of compensation and service, and then make a decision as to which agency is best for you.

There are many ways of determining hospital-agency relationships. The easiest way is to ask the agencies you speak with. If you're targeting a specific hospital or city, then you should ask agencies if they work with the particular hospital, or which hospitals they work with in a particular city. And you can always ask what type of relationship agencies have with a given hospital. Ask if the hospital uses an MSP or VMS. And ask if the agency has many travelers at the hospital, or if they've had many in the past.

The sad thing is that your recruiter may not know what any of this means. If your recruiter is unable to answer, then you should first try to determine if the hospital in question is independent or part of a larger organization. This is because MSP relationships typically exist for the entire hospital organization rather than just one hospital within the organization. For example, Kaiser Permanente in California uses American Mobile Network (AMN) as its MSP, and the Hospital Corporation of America (HCA) uses Parallon (formerly All About Staffing) as its MSP. In fact, Parallon is actually a subsidiary of HCA. The first indication that the hospital is part of a larger organization can be the name. For example, Kaiser San Francisco is obviously a Kaiser hospital. If the name isn't an indication, then you can also check the hospital's web site where you should find reference to its affiliations.

Once you've determined if the hospital is independent or part of a larger organization, you can begin with an internet search to see if you can determine a hospital-agency relationship. If the hospital is independent, you can search using the hospital's name. If the hospital is part of a larger organization, you can search using the organization's name.

You may find that other travelers have written about their experience on a message board which may give an indication regarding a hospital-agency relationship. For example, a traveler may write that they had to go through an AMN representative to get a Kaiser contract, which would be an indication that an MSP relationship exists. A traveler may also write that they worked at a particular hospital through a particular agency. You can contact that agency and inquire about the relationship status with that particular hospital. You may also find articles written by an industry organization, business journal, or local news agency that highlights hospital-agency relationships.

If you're still unable to determine the hospital-agency relationship prior to being submitted for an assignment, then you can look for clues during the process. For example, you may have to schedule an interview with someone from the MSP. This is because interviewing and screening services are part of what the MSP offers the facility. Typically, your agency will submit your profile to the MSP and a representative from the MSP will contact you to either ask some preliminary questions, or schedule an interview with one of the MSP's clinical interviewers, or both. This is a dead give-away that there is an MSP.

Furthermore, if you're interested in specific hospitals and all else has failed, then you can try contacting the hospitals directly to try to determine if there is an MSP or even if they would recommend a particular agency. I'm not going to lie, some hospitals don't like this. But you can call the facility, ask for the staffing office, then ask for someone who handles travel contracts (or PRN staffing), then ask which agency or agencies they would recommend. You may have a difficult time getting to the right person, but if you're persistent, you'll succeed.

Conclusion

The size of travel healthcare staffing agencies impacts the services they provide. Size tends to affect organizational structure which can impact the customer service you receive. Size also tends to affect the compensation packages that agencies offer. And size certainly has an impact on the number of hospitals that agencies are contracted with, which has an impact on the number of assignments they have available.

Meanwhile, hospital-agency relationships also have an impact on the travel healthcare professional. Traditionally, hospitals utilized direct relationship contracts with agencies in an effort to quickly and efficiently meet their contingent staffing needs. Working with a few agencies typically doesn't cut it, so hospitals had to work with more and more agencies to get their needs met. But managing all of these agencies becomes exceedingly difficult. While direct relationships still exist, Vendor Management Services saw the difficulties posed by managing multiple agencies as a business opportunity and are now utilized by over 90% of all hospitals in America.

Knowing about the different relationships that exist between agencies and their client hospitals is useful in a general sense even if you find yourself unable to put it to use in a practical sense. Having read this, you may know more about how the industry works than many recruiters. This alone will help you have informed conversations with your recruiters which will let them know they're not dealing with a rookie. This can be beneficial in negotiations and it can have a positive impact on the service you receive.

Moreover, you'll be better prepared to navigate the system. You'll understand that the level of competition is high because Vendor Management Services allow hospitals to efficiently utilize far more agencies which results in more candidates. You'll also understand that there's a gatekeeper between your agency and the hospital which tends to complicate communication between the two. You'll find that all of this knowledge will come in handy at different points throughout the process, helping you to realize a better travel healthcare experience.

Section 3: Working with the Agencies

Chapter 5: Finding Agencies Finding You

With literally hundreds of agencies in business, determining which agencies you're going to work with can be daunting. In addition, there are so many different ways to find agencies. There are many businesses that essentially act as referral services. I refer to them as rating services and broadcast services. You could also receive information from current and former travelers whether in person, or via blogs, and message boards. Agencies are also going to do their best to find you. They engage in huge advertising campaigns, utilize social media, invest in Search Engine Optimization, post jobs on job boards, and engage in aggressive email and telemarketing campaigns. In this section, we'll discuss the various ways of finding agencies and the ways that find you.

Broadcast Services and Rating Services

Let's start with the businesses that are aimed at guiding you to particular agencies, and those that provide some sort of referral, review, or rating service. One of the newer models is what I refer to as the "Broadcast Service." The "Broadcast Service" is a service that offers to broadcast your interest in travel nursing to travel nursing companies. These web sites all have the same basic pitch, "Provide us with your contact information and some basic details about what you're looking for, and we'll send your information to the top 20 agencies in the industry!" Or, "Make agencies compete for you, provide your information and we'll have the top agencies contact you!" Or, "Complete one profile for multiple agencies!" Like all sales pitches, these sound amazing! The reality is a bit different.

Broadcast Services come in two distinct forms. The first is essentially a shell company. A large healthcare staffing agency that has multiple subsidiary agencies puts up a web site that makes this great claim, "Fill out one application for the top companies in the business." It provides a list of those companies, maybe 5 to 10 companies in total. What you don't know is that they're all part of the same company. For example, American Mobile and Cross Country both have sites that do this. American Mobile's is called travelnursing.com and Cross Country's is called rntravelspace.com. You will indeed fill out one profile at each of these sites, which will be transmitted to the respective travel nursing company and its subsidiaries. However, the insinuations that your information is going to be sent to the "top" agencies or that you're filling out "one application for multiple agencies" are a bit disingenuous.

The second type of Broadcast Service is essentially an information broker. Examples include companies like travelnursesource.com and rnvip.com. These services collect your information and sell it. They tell you they are sending it to "the top agencies." However, they're sending it to essentially any agency, or anyone claiming to be involved with employment, who will pay for it. If you don't believe me, closely read their terms of use. They reserve the right to sell your information, and your information is valuable! They obviously don't use the term "sell" when describing their practices. They prefer terms like "release" and "transfer".

One of the claims they often make is that they'll send your information to the top 15 or 20 agencies. They cap the number of agencies because it makes your information more valuable, not because the broadcast service has conducted research to determine the top agencies. Companies are willing to pay a higher price for the information if they are assured to be 1 of 20 companies receiving the information as opposed to 1 of 100 companies receiving the information. The travel nursing company has a better shot at landing your business if there is less competition.

The typical guarantee that the agency receives for being one of "the top companies", is that your information will be released to only "the top companies" for a period of 1 month. So the agency receives hot leads and is assured to be one of a certain number of companies receiving the information. After 1 month, the Broadcast Service is free to sell your contact information to anyone who will pay for it. Companies who are not currently part of the top group can then purchase the leads.

The insinuation of their claim to "send your information to the top agencies" is that they have somehow determined which agencies are "the top." They don't come right out and say this, but it is certainly insinuated by their claims. Again, the truth is that they'll sell your information to anyone who will pay for it. These companies may take exception to this claim and point out that there are some companies that they will never sell your information to. For example, they may not sell your information American Mobile, or any of the other very large agencies in the industry. However, this is again due to the fact that not selling your information to the largest of agencies makes the leads more valuable to everyone else. This is due to the fact that mid and small sized agencies do not like competing with the largest agencies. So one of the first questions that agencies might ask a Broadcast Service is, "Do you sell your leads to American Mobile?" Not selling to the large agencies ensures the Broadcast Service a larger pool of potential clients.

Now I've gone and made these Broadcast Services sound evil. But they're not all that bad. I just want you to know what you're in for. These services do indeed deliver on their claim. If you provide them with your information, you will get calls and emails from many different agencies interested in your business. You won't have to do any digging around to find agencies to call. However, you can't be assured that the agencies that call are great and wonderful agencies to work with. But this is also ok. You can simply do some internet research on any agency that contacts you and determine if you'd like to move forward them. The one negative that you can't avoid with the Broadcast Service is the spam and onslaught of calls you will most certainly receive. If you meet the minimum criteria for a travel health care professional in a sought after area of expertise, you'll receive more calls and emails than you could possibly handle alone. You may end up changing your telephone number and getting a new email address just to get out of the loop.

Rating services are another type of business that has sprung up as a result of the contingent healthcare staffing boom. These services are typically engaged in ranking agencies based on some criteria that they've deemed useful in making such a determination. There are so many of these services that discussing the nuances of each would be more trouble than it's worth for you. Instead, we'll focus on a few themes that will help you interpret the usefulness and validity of these services.

Some of these services employ an open forum rating system that allows members of the site, or sometimes anyone, to complete a survey designed to rate an agency they've worked with. Some sites will then assign a cumulative score based on a tally of all surveys, or the number of positive versus negative ratings is highlighted. There are three important factors to keep in mind for this type of service. First, research indicates that all else being equal people are much more incentivized to complete these surveys when they feel disappointed in some way. So these systems may be biased on the negative side. Second, and in contrast, some agencies give their travelers an incentive to complete these surveys when they know that the traveler has had a good experience with them. Agency employees may also log on to the site posing as a traveler. It's not possible for agencies to do this for every single service. They may focus on one or two, so they'll have a high rating on just those sites. Your task is to cross reference the ratings with multiple sites to get a better idea. Third, an agency may receive a high or low score based on some criteria that is meaningless to you. For example, the agency may have a reputation for providing sub-standard housing. But if you don't take agency provided housing, then this shouldn't matter to you. You'll want to check the details of the surveys to determine these issues.

Another type of rating service provides its own ratings based on a set of criteria. For example, one popular site assigns points based on various aspects that comprise the overall service provided by an agency. For example, company provided medical benefits, pay check frequency, rental car availability, maximized tax advantage pay, company provided housing, etc, are scored based on their availability. If an agency can provide medical benefits, then they get a point. If they can provide a 401k benefit, then they get a point. Again, you'll need to look at the criteria to determine if the various services are of any importance to you. I must also point out that the information on these sites isn't always accurate. I know for a fact that some agencies have been reported as having medical benefits and a 401K for company employees when they most certainly did not have these services.

This brings me to my final point on rating services. My experience has revealed that rating services are suspect, but useful. As mentioned previously, you'll need to cross reference what you find on one site versus another in order to really get a good picture. I know from firsthand experience that even the most trusted sites have inconsistencies and/or false information. Some sites rate agencies higher because the agency pays them in some way to do so, either directly or through advertising. Some of these sites are biased by their own personal feelings on the subject. For example, they may have an obvious bias against large companies based on their own personal beliefs rather than anything substantive. Some sites have a very limited number of reviews per agency which isn't a good sample size based on the fact that most agencies engage in hundreds of contracts per year. Again, these sites are very useful, but be sure to cross reference what you find if you plan on relying on them to make your choice.

Blogs, Message Boards, and Word of Mouth

You can obtain some great information from experienced travelers. There are tons of blogs, and message boards devoted to travel nursing. With these services, you can read about first hand experiences and obtain some very useful information (just be sure it's not a blog or chat room owned by a travel nursing agency!). However, I believe that the most useful information you can get from these sources is the information that relates to the job itself, and the experience of traveling. In my opinion, travelers know much more than their recruiters about what you can expect on a day to day basis while actually working your assignment. They also know much more about the actual experience of traveling. For example, what to pack, what to expect while on the road, useful tools to help make traveling easier, and related items are all best gotten from the travelers themselves. While they can certainly provide information about agencies, and dealing with agencies, the information is going to be limited in scope.

Consider a traveler with 10 years of travel experience. Even if they've worked with 2 different agencies every year, they've only worked with 20 agencies. While that is no doubt a large number of agencies for one person to have worked with, it's a small number relative to the number of agencies out there. Additionally, the traveler whose blog or message you're reading may have been utilizing an agency that wouldn't meet your needs. As a result, their recommendation or condemnation may or may not be pertinent to you. For example, if someone condemns American Mobile for an experience they had while traveling in Texas, and you wanted to travel to San Diego, you'd be wise to keep American Mobile in consideration despite what you've read as American Mobile has a very large footprint in the San Diego market. At the same time, if someone exalts an agency they worked with in New York, and you want to go to Colorado, it might be worth calling the agency, but your first question should be whether or not they service Colorado.

You must also take with a grain of salt the information from these sources pertaining to how the contingent staffing industry works. When it comes to issues like contracts, compensation packages, tax free money, guaranteed shifts, and other such issues, travelers often know what they've been told by their recruiters or agencies. Recruiters and agencies often times spin the information, or just flat out lie, to make things sound better, or worse, than they actually are. I've seen the most reputable travel nursing bloggers and authors make claims that sounded as if they came directly from the week 1 sales training seminar titled "How to Sell It!" provided to newly hired contingent healthcare staffing recruiters. Again, I firmly believe that experienced travelers are among the most valuable resources for you to utilize. Just be sure to approach the information critically, with an eye toward your specific goals.

Agencies Finding You

Travel nursing agencies spend a lot of resources and utilize many methods trying to find interested candidates. They engage in advertising campaigns and attend conferences and job fairs. They utilize all facets of internet media including job boards, social networking, targeted advertisements, ad words, informational offerings, blogs, and even Continuing Education Unit web sites. I assure you that at least a couple of these methods will blow your mind.

Advertising campaigns, conferences, and job fairs are all quite overt. Agencies commonly purchase advertisements in trade publications as well as niche publications, like Healthcare Traveler, that are obvious places for them to advertise. During peak times, when there are many more jobs to be filled than usual, it's not uncommon to find agencies shelling out the cash to attend conferences of various types as well as job fairs. I call these "overt" because there's nothing surprising or unusual here, just good old-fashioned marketing.

The rest of the methods are all quite interesting, and some are just down right shady. Take the job board for example. It seems innocent enough; travel nursing agencies post their open jobs and people apply for them. Not so fast. Yes, agencies do post jobs. However, travel healthcare assignments get filled very quickly. As mentioned previously, Vendor Management Services allow hospitals to work efficiently with many different agencies to fill the hospital's contingent staffing needs quickly.

Now, that's not the shady part. The shady part results from this reality. You see travel nursing agencies know that they need to have candidates ready to submit as quickly as possible, so they often post ghost jobs just to get people to apply. For example, if an agency knows that they have a pretty consistent need for ICU nurses in Boston, then they may post a job advertisement to lure potential candidates to complete the necessary paperwork. Then they'll contact those candidates if/when an assignment opens up.

Job boards can also be a great source for agencies to obtain your personal contact information. "I set the privacy setting", you say? Not so fast, there are tricks! There are two types of information that are entered on most job boards. The first is the information that the job board captures through its profile and resume building services. These services are capable of capturing your personal contact information, work history, education history, and other pertinent information. The information gathered by these services can typically be kept private with the job board's privacy settings, but sometimes it can't be kept private. You'll need to check each job board's Privacy Policy or Terms of Use to see exactly what their policies are if you value your privacy.

The second type of information captured by the job board is the resume upload. This is where they provide you with the capability to upload your resume. A significant percentage of people do this because it's easier than completing the job board's profile. A significant percentage of the job boards I've visited do not offer the capability to keep your uploaded resume private. They often times have specific language in their privacy statement indicating that they cannot keep this private. So, agencies, or anyone who has subscribed to the site, can just come along and dump the job board's uploaded resumes into their own database. Many job boards even have useful tools for facilitating the transfer of information. I suspect that there are even information brokers out there who use job boards to obtain contact information and then sell it to third parties. If you've posted your contact information on a job board, and are wondering why you receive 10-20 calls per week, this is perhaps the reason.

Social networking is another method travel nursing agencies use to find and recruit potential candidates. On the surface, social networking seems to be an obvious and above board method of contacting you. However, the ways these services are exploited is quite interesting. For example, you might use services like LinkedIn or Facebook and there's nothing too intriguing about these services on the surface. However, these services may know an awful lot about who you are depending on the amount of information you've shared about yourself. Agencies can purchase targeted advertising that assures the agency a very specific audience. Facebook may have been able to determine that you're a PACU RN between the ages of 25 and 35 who likes to travel and loves the beach. If you suddenly see an advertisement for PACU travel assignments in San Diego, CA, don't be surprised.

Informational offerings are one of the more interesting uses of social media. In this scenario, you might be looking into travel nursing on the internet one day. A cookie in your browser captures this information and it's sold to an advertiser. The next day, you see an advertisement that might say something like, "Top 10 Questions to Ask Your Travel Nurse Recruiter: Free information guide to getting the most out of travel nursing." Awesome! You click on the link and it asks you to enter some information about yourself to receive your free information. You find out that the 10 questions could have been written by a third grader, and the next day, you receive a call from a travel nursing agency...or 10. This fancy trick can also be pulled off using social media services and chat rooms. You'll see something like, "Download Our Free White Paper on Travel Nursing Salaries." They'll ask for your contact information and the next day you'll receive a call from a travel nursing company...or 10.

Agencies also operate their own blogs. Blogs can be a great way for agencies to achieve "Search Engine Optimization" (SEO) when agencies attach them to their company web site. SEO is an internet buzzword that basically means that a web site is fine tuned to show up higher in the search results of Google, Bing, and other search engines than other web pages when someone conducts an internet search on terms relevant to the site's subject matter. The trick is that some of these blogs aren't so obviously run by an agency. While they do indeed provide an informational service, they are designed and written for the purpose of guiding internet traffic to the site in an attempt to find people interested in travel nursing. This is accomplished by making many mentions of the key search terms and buzz words used in web searches for information on travel healthcare. As a result, when you conduct a search on terms like "travel nursing" or "travel nursing jobs", the agency's blog shows up higher in the rankings. When you arrive at these sites, you have no idea that you're on a web site owned and operated by a travel nursing agency. Then, they ask you to join their community to receive all of the great benefits. You provide your contact information, and the next day you receive a call from a recruiter...or 10.

Agencies will also use Continuing Education Unit (CEU) web sites to draw in potential candidates. These web sites obviously provide a service to you, CEUs. But did you know that some of these sites are owned and operated by travel nursing agencies? One such example is rn.com. This website offers a massive library of CEU courses, and offers an annual unlimited CEU package for a pretty good price, currently $34.95. It's also owned and operated by American Mobile, one of the nation's largest healthcare staffing agencies. So they not only collect a fee from you, but you provide them with your contact information to boot, as well as some basic information about your career. To be fair, I can't be certain as to how they utilize this information, but their privacy statement is certainly worded in a way that gives them the authority to use it for recruitment purposes.

The point here is to simply point out that it's best to be cautious with such services if you value your privacy and/or don't want to be contacted on a regular basis by telemarketers.

Recruitment

As you can see, agencies have many different methods for collecting the contact information of people in the healthcare industry. Once they have the information, it goes into a data base where it is put to use by the agency's recruiters. The recruiters' primary focus is to sort through the leads to find interested travel nursing candidates, determine and package their qualifications, and sell them on assignments that the agency has access to.

The primary methods for finding interested candidates out of the agency's database are email campaigns and call campaigns. This is where all of that information that gets collected really comes into play. Recruiters will utilize the email addresses collected by the agency to engage in "email blasts." Essentially, they send an email out to hundreds or even thousands of potential candidates in one blast. They may even use email blast software that allows them to give the appearance that the email was sent specifically to you, even though it was a mass email. It's a nice touch and a great way to reach many potential candidates quickly and efficiently.

However, in the agency's eyes, nothing beats the phone. Call campaigns reign supreme at healthcare staffing agencies. At most agencies, recruiters have to make a minimum number of calls per day. At some agencies, this minimum number can be 100 or higher. When you stop and consider that there are tons of agencies, with tons of recruiters, you realize why you receive so many calls per week once your information is compromised.

Now I don't know how other recruiters handled their minimum call requirements, but I can tell you that if you put a resume, or anything for that matter, in front of me, the first thing I'd do is call the telephone number. That's right; I'd call before I even knew anything about who I was calling. 8.5 out of 10 times, the number is going to be disconnected, or the call is going to voice mail where I can leave a quick message. While the phone is ringing, I can quickly peruse the resume, or any other data I might have. If someone answers, I can determine whether or not I'm able to help them in far less time than had I sat and reviewed the information in detail. The point is, you will get called if you let your information get out there, you can count on it.

Finding the Right Agencies

When you put all of these factors together, from the lead generation services to the recruiters, the question really becomes, "Are you finding the agency, or is the agency finding you?" I mean, when you stop and think about it, many of the ways that you might use to find the agency, are really just sneaky ways for the agency to find you. This isn't necessarily a bad thing. However, you do need to be prepared to deal with it.

I have noticed that travel nurses make two key mistakes in their approach to finding the right agency. First, there's a tendency to approach a search for a travel assignment in the same way as a search for a permanent job. In this regard, the candidate will search for jobs and complete the agency's application process only when they've found an agency claiming to have a job opening that the candidate is interested in. The problem with this approach is that travel nursing assignments are filled much faster than permanent assignments. Your chances of landing an assignment are greatly diminished if you are not submitted within the first few days of its opening, and even within the first few hours depending on the location.

Second, candidates tend to rely on rating services and positive reviews to the detriment of finding agencies that can provide the services they want and/or have contracts with hospitals in areas they're interested in. Again, I'm not bashing rating services. They can be quite useful. However, if you want to go to Minneapolis,

Minnesota, then you need to find an agency that has contracts there. If the highest rated agency doesn't have contracts there, then they're of no use to you.

You should have a strategy for actually finding the right agencies to work with. The approach that I propose involves two mandatory steps and an optional third step. First, determine exactly what you want. Second, immediately determine if agencies that contact you can meet your needs. Third, target agencies that can potentially meet your needs and contact them.

So, step 1 is to determine exactly what you want. Of course, you'll need much more information in order to determine exactly what you want. Therefore, you should read the entire book before coming to any decisions as we'll cover all of the information you need. Once the information is covered, we'll provide a comprehensive checklist that can be used as a quick reference.

You will use the information in this book and the comprehensive checklist provided in Appendix A to develop a list of preferences that will guide your interactions with agencies. I recommend categorizing your preferences into three categories: 1) "Requirements" 2) "Preferences" and 3) "Irrelevant" The resulting list will allow you to control the discussions you have with travel nursing agencies in order to minimize your time and maximize your results. For now, a sample list of preferences is provided below to give you an idea of what we're talking about.

Requirements

Medical Benefits

Company Provided Apartment

401K

Assignment in Texas (Austin, San Antonio, Houston, or Dallas)

Preferences

Weekly pay

On-line pay stubs

Maximized tax-free stipends

Irrelevant

Everything else!

Once you have your list developed, you're on to step 2: immediately determine if agencies can meet your needs. For example, if you must have medical benefits, a company provided apartment, and a 401K, then the first 3 questions for every new agency you speak with should be on these topics. If the agency can't provide them, then kindly ask to be removed from their list, or to be contacted only when they are able to provide these items. Why discuss anything else? It would be a waste of your time if the agency is unable to provide your requirements. Rather than letting the travel nursing recruiter control the conversation, which could take a ton of your valuable time, you'll be able to quickly determine if the agency is a fit for you. Most importantly, don't complete any paperwork for an agency until you are able to determine if they can meet your needs.

Also, I recommend registering all your contact phone numbers on the National Do Not Call Registry. Then, you can tell agencies that do not provide the services you require that you are on the Do Not Call Registry and will report them for violations. This may sound harsh, but it will also save you from regular telemarketing calls that you are not interested in fielding.

Now, you'll need to determine how you want to initiate communication with agencies. As we've discussed previously, to let agencies find you, simply submit your contact information with a couple of broadcast services, or post your resume with the words "travel nursing" on a couple of job boards. Trust me, you'll start receiving calls. This is obviously a passive approach. As a result, you'll have a lower chance of speaking with agencies who can truly meet your needs, especially in terms of location. I'm not saying that this approach won't work, but it may not generate the best results in the least amount of time.

This brings us to the optional third step in the recommended method for finding the right agencies: target agencies that can meet your needs and contact them. This is a more aggressive approach and may seem like a daunting task considering that there are at least 300 travel nursing agencies. There are two ways that you can approach this step. First, you can contact agencies and utilize your checklist to quickly knock them off your list of potential agencies. You can find a list of over 200 agencies on my blog, thetruthabouttravelnursing.com. I would recommend some sites where you could get ratings and reviews on travel nursing agencies, but I'm concerned that the sites would ask for your contact information before providing the ratings and then sell your information to agencies, and I'd prefer not to lead you down that path. However, you can cross reference the agencies on the list with the rating services of your choice to prioritize the process.

The second way to approach this process is to seek out agencies that operate in your desired locations. This is the recommended approach. Most people have a single desired location, or several desired locations where they want to travel. Say for example that you are interested in San Diego, Los Angeles, San Francisco, and Seattle. Obviously, you only want to work with agencies that can staff in one, if not all, of these locations. There are two good ways to go about determining where various agencies are able to staff.

First, agencies post jobs on many job boards and other web sites. Agencies love free job posting services like eBay, and jobspider. They also post jobs on healthcare niche sites like allhealthcarejobs.com and travel nurse niche sites like travelnursesource.com as well as many other job boards. I highly recommend the web sites indeed.com and simplyhired.com. These sites are job-board-aggregators, which means they collect jobs from other sites and post them in one location. You can search sites like this for "travel nurse" in your desired location.

Chances are very strong that if an agency is advertising a job in a particular city, then the agency has contracts in that city. These job postings may not actually be openings that are available at this time, but the fact that the agency is advertising in a particular location indicates that they work with hospitals there. Don't be concerned about the specialty; you're only interested in finding advertisements for your license. For example, if you're an Operating Room Registered Nurse, and you see an advertisement for Labor and Delivery Registered Nurses in your desired location, that's ok. You're not looking for jobs at this point. You're looking for agencies that provide service in your desired locations. Take note of the agency's name and any contact information, or look the name up on the internet to obtain the contact information. Then contact them and use your checklist to determine whether or not they'd be a good fit for you.

Another way to find agencies that have contracts in a particular state or city is to target the hospitals in that state or city. This could be daunting for an entire state, but if you're able to narrow your desired locations to specific cities, or metropolitan areas, then you can accomplish this quite easily. For example, let's say you wanted to go to Charlotte, North Carolina. You could use the American Hospital Directory (AHD) to find the hospitals in the area, as well as their general contact information.

AHD's web address is ahd.com. When you get there, you'll see a link for "Free Hospital Search." On the next page, you'll see a link for an "Advanced Search." On the next page, you'll be able to enter the city and state of your choice. The web site will return all of the hospitals registered in that city. You can then contact the hospital's main line, ask to speak with the staffing office, and then try to be connected with someone who handles travel nursing, or Registry/PRN/PerDiem. You can then ask if they use travel nurses, and if they do, ask which agencies they recommend. You may get rebuffed, but if you're persistent, you will succeed. When using AHD, be sure to also check the surrounding cities in the metro area you're interested in because AHD is very specific with its search results.

This is a great way to maximize your exposure to the travel job market in a given city. As mentioned previously, it's unlikely for one agency to work with every hospital in a given metro area...possible, but unlikely. Agencies often give the impression that they work with every hospital in the area, and they may assure you that they will definitely get you an assignment in the area. But they have an incentive to make these claims and assurances. By calling the hospitals, you'll ensure that you receive accurate information. By working with the agencies recommended by each hospital, you'll increase the odds that you're working with a favored agency. Again, hospitals may not provide this information, but it doesn't hurt to try if you have the time. This method may likely take less time than wading through the sea of agencies to find the right one, and I've had many travelers tell me they were successful with this approach.

As you can see, there are many ways to find agencies or have them find you. You can use broadcast services, referral services, and job boards. However, be aware that your contact information stands a chance of being spread throughout the industry resulting in a glut of calls and emails. Your contact information can also be compromised unknowingly by free informational offerings that request your contact information in exchange for their "free" information. As an alternative, you can take a strategic approach by utilizing the method

I've just described. Each approach works in different ways, but they both work effectively. In any case, you should always ask questions about your "Requirements" immediately in an effort to find the agencies that can meet your needs, thereby mitigating wasted time.

Chapter 6: Recruiters: The X Factor

Chances are good that you'll be able to find multiple agencies that can meet your needs. So you'll still be stuck figuring out which agencies to work with. Almost every traveler will mention how important it is to have a good recruiter. The recruiter really can be the X Factor in choosing an agency. Recruiters can make bad agencies good and good agencies bad. It's tough to come by a really good recruiter. My experience indicates that it's a position with a fairly high turnover rate, so coming by a recruiter with more than 2 years of experience can be tough. In addition, evaluating a recruiter can also be a difficult task.

First, you need to understand the role of the recruiter in the agency. From the outside, it may appear that the recruiter is a service representative seeking to match candidates with ideal jobs. After all, that's how agencies advertise it. But on the inside, recruiters are revenue generators, also known as sales representatives, and they are treated as such. Every recruiter I know, from agencies large and small, is treated as a sales representative. This means that they are measured by "Key Performance Indicators." You can think of Key Performance Indicators as actions and results. Actions include things like the number of telephone calls per day, the length of time on the phone, the number of completed job applications obtained, and the number of candidates submitted to open assignments. Results pretty much boil down to money...gross revenue and gross profit.

These key performance indicators are typically wound pretty tight. For example, the recruiter may be responsible for making and/or taking 100 calls per day, or being on the phone for 4 hours per day, or a combination of both. They may be required to submit a minimum of 2 to 5 new candidates per week. They may be required to close 1 or more deals per week. Meanwhile, they're providing customer service to existing travelers, getting candidate profiles ready to submit, matching candidates with potential assignments, and discussing compensation and contract details. Add to this the fact that it's an extremely competitive market place with little customer loyalty, and it can be quite overwhelming at times. Successful recruiters typically work a minimum of 50 hours per week as they derive the majority of their pay from commissions, and every day is a very busy day.

Now, most of what you'll read on the internet and in books written by travelers regarding what makes a good recruiter tends to focus on whether or not the recruiter is available to meet any need the traveler may have, at any time of the day, every day of the week. You'll read stories about a recruiter who saved someone during a hurricane by coordinating travel plans and securing accommodations at 3am on a Tuesday morning. Or you may read the story about the recruiter who was always there when the traveler had a particularly rough day at work and needed someone to discuss it with at 8:30pm on a Thursday. While I believe that this type of accessibility is important, I also believe that expectations should be realistic, and that there are far more important considerations when evaluating a recruiter.

Don't get me wrong, I do believe that travelers should be able to build a good rapport with their recruiters. I've had travelers spend the holidays with my family. I've volunteered to watch their pets while they were on vacation. I've had them stay in my spare room for free while they were on assignment with another agency no less! And there are many travelers that I've kept in touch with long after they stopped traveling. They've become some of my closest friends.

You should also be able to rely on your recruiter in time of need and in emergencies. However, this is where it gets a little gray. As mentioned previously, successful recruiters typically put in at least 50 hours per week. They must effectively balance their time between servicing current clients and recruiting new ones. As mentioned previously, recruiting new clients is a time consuming endeavor. As recruiters build their client lists, the amount of time they spend recruiting diminishes while the amount of time they spend servicing clients increases. But remember, contracts last 3 months, and people are always moving on. So the recruiter must constantly be focused on recruiting in order to stay ahead of the game and maintain productivity.

The number of clients that a recruiter can handle depends on their agency's structure. If the recruiter has a lot of support, then they can handle more clients. If a recruiter has no support, then they can handle fewer clients. Moreover, if a recruiter works for a company that has tons of hospital contracts and available jobs, then they will achieve better results for their recruiting time because they have more options to offer the candidates they connect with. Recruiters that work with companies that have fewer contracts and fewer available jobs will spend more time recruiting because they will have to reach more candidates to find those that are interested in the few jobs they have available. Essentially, "fewer jobs" means a "tougher sell".

Recruiters at smaller companies will typically need to have a minimum of 15 full time staff working at all times in order to make the job worthwhile. At larger companies the minimum is more like 25. In order to be successful, the range is anywhere from 25 to 60 clients per recruiter. I've heard of recruiters with larger agencies having as many as 70 clients at a time. Remember, all the while these recruiters must be actively engaged in the recruitment process as well servicing their clients.

That said, emergencies should be classified as emergencies only if they are genuine emergencies. I had a traveler call me on my cell phone before 6am to demand a new toaster immediately because the one they had was only cooking the toast on one side. I was called on a Sunday morning when a traveler's paycheck was $4 short of what it should have been. These are certainly valid concerns that should be addressed promptly. However, maintaining realistic expectations will ensure that you're able to maintain a strong relationship with what may be an excellent recruiter.

So what makes an excellent recruiter? In my opinion, honesty, experience, and customer service are the most important characteristics of a good recruiter. I do believe that the vast majority of healthcare recruiters are honest individuals. However, as mentioned previously, recruiting is essentially a sales job. Recruiters are selling you on the services and products they have to offer. It's no secret that there are a lot of sales people out there who utilize disingenuous tactics to close a deal. Recruiting is no different. I've heard so many stories from travelers who feel they were misinformed I couldn't even begin to describe them all here. I've heard from people who were told they would receive free medical benefits, only to later find that they were charged for them. I've heard from people whose pay was dramatically less than what they were led to believe it would be.

There's no perfect method for determining whether or not a recruiter is being honest with you. However, you can improve your chances of finding an honest recruiter by determining whether or not they're willing to provide you with both sides of the story. It's pretty rare for something to have absolutely no downfalls. An honest recruiter should be willing to share the positive, as well as the negative. There are negatives to almost every aspect of contingent staffing, so there are plenty of opportunities for the recruiter to reveal their honesty. At the same time, sales people typically don't provide such information, but you can tease it out of them by asking the right questions. For example: What's the downside of taking tax free money? Or, you can just ask them point blank to provide you with some negative aspects of travel nursing in general, or a specific assignment that they are trying to sell you.

Experience is probably the single most important variable to consider when determining the value of a recruiter. There is a ton of information that a recruiter must know in order to provide you with outstanding service. Additionally, there is a ton going on behind the scenes to ensure that you're taken care of. It's far too much for any individual to soak up in even the most comprehensive of training programs. Experience ensures that your recruiter has the knowledge and know-how necessary to guide you through a metaphorical minefield.

Recruiters must be very knowledgeable regarding all aspects of contingent staffing requirements and expectations. This includes experience requirements, both general and facility specific. It includes compliance and credentialing requirements, both general and facility specific. It includes experience with your specific area or areas of expertise. It includes knowledge of trends and cycles in contingent staffing, both nationally and regionally. It includes knowledge of the on-boarding processes and procedures of the facilities they work with, often times numbering in the thousands.

This may all seem rather unimportant, or perhaps a given. However, if the recruiter is not knowledgeable in all of these aspects, then he/she could end up getting you into a bind, or selling you on an opportunity that will never come to fruition. I know this to be true from firsthand experience.

When I was starting out as a recruiter, I submitted an ICU RN who had graduated from nursing school 15 months earlier. She had also worked at her current hospital for a little over 2 years. I submitted her for a Kaiser assignment in Redwood City, CA. At the time, Kaiser required 1 year of experience in the specialty being submitted for, so I figured all was well. However, I didn't realize that they required that the nurse's license needed to be active for more than 1 year. This nurse had obtained her RN license 6 months after graduating, making her license only 9 months old at the time of submission. As a result, she was disqualified at which time I learned about another of Kaiser's policies. When someone is disqualified, they have to wait for 6 months to be considered again. Needless to say, I never heard from the nurse again, despite my impassioned apologies.

Shortly after this incident, an L&D nurse and I decided that we'd tell a facility that we already had her scheduled to take an AWHONN Advanced Fetal Heart Monitoring course in an effort to get her an interview. She was highly experienced and of course got the interview and the offer which we accepted. Then we both found out the hard way that getting this AWHONN certification wasn't going to be as easy as getting a BLS certification.

Despite the fact that she lived in Chicago, the second largest city in the United States, we were unable to locate a course. We were even unable to locate a course anywhere in the country in time for the assignment's start date. Ultimately, my agency had to back out. While the nurse and I continued to work together for nearly 2 years, my agency was fined by the hospital per our contract with them, and while we can't be certain, we believe the nurse was made a "DNU" (do not use) at this particular facility. So you can see that these things matter, and they matter a lot.

There are also things going on behind the scenes that you may never really know about, but that are none the less extremely important. Your "submission profile" is one example. It's fairly standard for hospitals to require that an agency provide an application, a skills checklist, and two references in order to have a candidate submitted for an opening. Together, these items are commonly called a "submission profile." No offense to anyone out there, but candidates typically do a very poor job at filling these out. Therefore, an experienced recruiter will most certainly revise your profile to ensure that it's professional and includes all the information that the facilities are seeking. In addition, they will take every opportunity to make that profile shine. The profile can make or break your chances of landing an assignment. There is ALWAYS competition for the job, and the profile is the first consideration in determining who will win. Knowing what to look for, how to present the information, and how to gloss over any negatives comes from experience.

To determine a recruiter's level of experience you should first ask them how long they've been a recruiter. Of course, they could provide you with false information, but you could always try and look them up on LinkedIn to see if you can find a profile which would most likely reveal the true nature of their experience. You can even ask them to connect on LinkedIn instead of looking them up. Short of that, you will most likely be able to tell by the speed with which they answer your questions. An experienced recruiter should be quick to respond and sound comfortable and confident during your discussion. They should be able to provide highly informative and thorough answers to any questions you may have.

Finally, you'll want to make sure that the recruiter has excellent customer service skills. Of course, "customer service" is a broad term. Specifically, you want to make sure that the recruiter takes an interest in finding out about you and your goals as a traveler. From the outset, they should be asking you insightful and probing questions aimed at determining what type of experience you have, and what type of assignments you're looking for. Remember, all recruiters are sales people so they're going to try and sell you what they have available. However, you want to make sure they're also interested in helping you achieve your goals.

Getting the Most Out of Your Recruiter

Once you've found a good recruiter, there are steps you can take to get the most out them. Remember, recruiters are constantly juggling multiple candidates. They often need to determine which candidates merit the most value for the recruiter's time. You want to make sure that you're at the top of that list.

First, be decisive and clearly communicate your circumstances and priorities. Be sure to disclose important information at the outset. Let your recruiter know if you'll be traveling with children, family, and/or pets. Let your recruiter know if you have any actions against your license in any state. Establishing these things at the outset builds trust.

When it comes to your desires regarding travel assignments, clearly state your priorities whether they be related to pay, location, or any other variable. Your recruiter will appreciate that you've narrowed down the field of possibilities. However, remember that recruiters are sales people and they're treated as such by their employers. As a result, they're going to try to convince you of things you may not want to be convinced of. Don't let them bowl you over. They may still contact you with options that don't entirely meet the criteria, but that's ok. They probably have a good reason for doing so. Simply decline the opportunity if you're not interested. They'll appreciate the fact that you're decisive up front because it will save everyone time and trouble in the long run.

Second, follow through during the entire process. In the beginning of the process be sure to meet timelines that you've communicated. For example, if you let the recruiter know that you will complete the application and skills checklist by a certain time, then follow through or reach out to explain any delays. Failing to do so gives the impression that you're not a serious candidate. Also, always be available for interviews or be sure to return calls for interviews, particularly those interviews that you agreed to be submitted for. Missing interviews weighs heavily on the recruiter. Their supervisors and the hospitals have a tendency to place blame with the recruiter. Besides, you may want to work with the hospital in the future.

Third, be diligent during your assignment. Make sure that you're a prompt, productive, and positive member of the hospital's team. Also, make sure that you comply with the agencies time reporting, compliance, and credentialing policies. Recruiters will fight tooth and nail to keep good employees on board. Additionally, do everything you can to complete the assignment. Recruiters certainly realize that things can sometimes go really bad on an assignment, but terminating an assignment should be the absolute last resort. It too weighs very negatively on the recruiter.

Fourth, send your recruiters referrals. Like all business people, recruiters love referrals. There may be no better way to let recruiters know that you think they're doing a good job than sending referrals. It shows that you're willing to stick your neck out on the line for them. It adds to your value in a way that will make you a recruiter's top priority.

Better yet, most if not all agencies have referral bonus programs. So you'll get paid for sending referrals to your recruiter. I've seen referral bonuses as low as $250 and as high as $1500. Of course, you only get a bonus if the referral signs a contract with the agency. And even then, the bonus is contingent on the referral actually working. Different agencies have different policies for paying out their bonuses. For example, some agencies will only pay the bonus if the referral completes the total number of hours in the contract and others will prorate the bonus by the hour. In any case, you'll want to ask your agency about their referral program because they will most certainly have one.

Finally, give your recruiters the courtesy of full disclosure regarding your search process. Keep them in the loop as to your status and progress with finding assignments. If you've been submitted for an assignment through another agency, let your other recruiters know. It will motivate them to hunker down and find something for you quickly and they'll be gratified not to waste their time on the same assignment that you've already been submitted for. If you've accepted an assignment, let your other recruiters know. They'll be disappointed, but keeping them in the loop is the professional thing to do and will ensure that they contact you for your next assignment.

You may think it might be difficult to manage all of this communication, but recruiters are fine receiving quick email updates. Send updates to all of your recruiters at once using the BCC feature in your email service to minimize your time. Following these suggestions will ensure that you get the most out of the recruiters you've deemed the best.

Chapter 7: Working with Multiple Agencies

I often see travel healthcare professionals and travel healthcare recruiters debate whether or not travel nurses should work with multiple agencies. The simple answer is Yes! You should work with several agencies. In my opinion, you should work with at least 3 agencies, more if you intend to travel the country far and wide.

Of course, travel nursing agencies and their recruiters will tell you not to work with other agencies. It's in the agency's best interest for you to work only with them. They'll offer seemingly convincing arguments in their defense. My favorite is the one about how hospitals "frown upon" travelers being submitted by multiple agencies. It is EXTREMELY rare for this to be of any consequence whatsoever to the candidate. However, it is of consequence to the agency, which is ultimately what this is all about.

Landing a travel nursing assignments can be highly competitive. Assignments are typically released to a multitude of agencies. The important thing to understand is that it's not just competitive for the travel nurse it's also competitive for the travel nursing agency. The travel nursing agency only makes money when their travel nurses work. As a result, nearly every agency makes an attempt to find out what the travel nurse wants in terms of compensation and location, and then submits the travel nurse's profile immediately upon a matching assignment's release, often without first notifying the travel nurse. They are desperate to stay ahead of the competition.

This leads to travel nurses being submitted by multiple agencies. It happens literally all the time. It happens so much that if it were indeed frowned upon as grounds for disqualification, there would be no travelers left to hire. For example, one of the nation's largest hospital corporations sent out a massive list of open travel nursing assignments in January of 2012. The next day, the account manager responsible for handling these openings sent an email to all of the agencies on the mailing list. The email informed the agencies that, among other things, he had received just over 1,200 candidates for the open assignments, nearly 900 of which had been submitted by more than one agency. That's 65%-75% of the candidates being submitted by multiple agencies. My experience leads me to believe that this is the standard.

It happens so much that most facilities and Vendor Management Services have a policy for dealing with it. Some will ask the travel healthcare professional which agency they prefer to work with during an interview. This is the best case scenario for the candidate. However, some have a first come first serve policy. As a result, it's important for you to find out which hospitals an agency works with, and how much they pay so you can compare agency pay packages for the same hospital. Then, inform the agency you choose that they have your permission to submit you for openings, and the others that they do not have your permission. Otherwise, you may risk being required to go with the first agency that submitted your profile, which may not be your top choice.

Additionally, it's not wise to tell agencies that they cannot submit you without speaking to you first about every opening. Time is of the essence. You want to be submitted immediately. Otherwise, you may be out of the running entirely. This is why you should have in depth conversations with your recruiter that lay out specifically what you're looking for in an assignment. Again, get the rates, compare the rates to other agencies at the same facilities, and choose the agency that will represent you for particular facilities. Let these agencies know that they have your permission to submit your profile if an assignment opens that matches your criteria. Also, let them all know that if an assignment pops up that does not match what you are looking for, then they can call you and pitch it. If you agree, only then can they submit your profile. Your chances of landing such an assignment will be diminished as you are not going to be among the first to be submitted, but that's okay. It's not your ideal assignment anyway.

Your goal in all of this is to maximize your potential. By working with multiple agencies you'll realize 2 major potential maximizing benefits. First, you'll maximize your exposure to the market of available assignments. Remember, an agency can only work with the hospitals they have contracts with. It's really rare for an agency to have contracts with every hospital in a given major metropolitan area, let alone every hospital in a given state. By working with multiple agencies you'll gain access to more contracts. Yes, you will get some overlap. It's common for agencies to have contracts with the same hospitals, but that's ok. You just have to manage it to your advantage.

This brings us to our second potential maximizing benefit of working with multiple agencies, competition results in higher compensation. When agencies know that you're working with other agencies, they'll be compelled to offer you a better deal. In fact, it behooves you to find out how much an agency offers for a given hospital and then compare the offer to another agency's offer. For example, let's say you're interested in going to Northern California for a travel assignment. There are 3 major employers in that area, Kaiser, Dignity Health (formerly Catholic Healthcare West), and Sutter. You can ask each agency if they work with these organizations. You then ask the recruiters about the compensation they offer for these particular organizations.

Let's use Kaiser in Northern California as an example. If you'd like, you can select a particular city, Sacramento or San Francisco for example, and ask agencies what the compensation would be for those specific locations. Once the compensation is provided, you can compare the offers you've received and begin negotiating. You can let one company know that another has offered higher compensation in hopes that they may try to outdo one another. Ultimately, you should select one of the companies to represent you for that specific organization. For example, you would tell one agency that they can submit your profile for Kaiser openings, and tell the other agencies that they cannot submit your profile for Kaiser openings because you have selected to go with another agency for openings at Kaiser Hospitals.

The bottom line is that an agency's recommendation that you work exclusively with them is for the agency's benefit, not yours. The vast majority of hospitals and Vendor Management Services have procedures in place for duplicate submissions. Those that don't are the exception, not the rule. Additionally, those that don't, and hold the candidate accountable, are misguided. It's far more reasonable to suspect agencies as the culprit as opposed to candidates. If you take an active role in managing multiple agencies as described above, you will benefit.

Conclusion:

In this section we discussed how agencies find you and how you can find agencies. Letting agencies find you by supplying your contact information to various services will definitely result in a large volume of calls. For some, this is a great option. However, if you prefer to maintain your privacy and ensure that you aren't receiving calls and emails for years to come, then there are many ways for you to target and find agencies. In any case, you'll want to be prepared with your checklist to quickly and efficiently determine which agencies are capable of meeting your needs. Once you have established that an agency can meet your needs, you should evaluate the recruiter you're working with to determine if he/she is experienced, honest, and service oriented. Once you have accomplished this, you're in a position to decide which agencies you're going to work with and move forward with the process.

Section 4: Compensation

In this section, we'll discuss the most complex and least understood aspect of travel healthcare, the compensation package. A solid understanding of how the travel healthcare compensation package works will allow you to confidently compare compensation offers and provide valuable insight to help you make decisions on which compensation components you wish to receive.

I hate to say it, but I have yet to see a blog or book provide a completely accurate explanation of the compensation package. Some of them do a good job of explaining the traveler's side of the compensation package, but nobody comes close to understanding what's happening on the agency's side of the package. Some provide decent information about tax free reimbursements, and others are just plain incorrect. The result is that there is a ton of misinformation out there.

I don't blame the healthcare professionals though. I blame the sales people. The healthcare professionals know what they've been able to piece together from their experience, and what the sales people have told them, which is often a sales pitch. As you'll see, understanding all aspects of the travel compensation package will not only help you negotiate, but it will help you stay out of trouble with the IRS.

Chapter 8: Compensation: The Agency's Perspective

The compensation for every assignment starts with the bill rate. The bill rate is the hourly rate that an agency can charge the facility for the traveler's time at the facility. For example, if the bill rate is $60, then the agency charges the hospital $60 per hour for the traveler's time. There can also be additional rates such as an on-call rate, an overtime rate, a call-back rate, a charge rate, a holiday rate, and others. The bill rate is essentially the base of the compensation package. For the vast majority of agencies, if not every agency, the bill rate is the only source of revenue the agency has. This means that there is no other source of money for an agency. Every single cost that an agency incurs is covered by this rate.

Like all businesses, agencies are fundamentally concerned with their "gross profit" or "gross margin." Gross profit is the difference between revenue and cost before accounting for certain other costs.

Gross margin is the same as gross profit except that it's expressed as a percentage. Also like all business, agencies are fundamentally concerned with their "net profit". Net profit is the difference between gross profit and other costs. Confused? Well, we essentially have three variables to define: 1) Revenue 2) Cost 3) Other Costs.

Revenue is very simple. Revenue is simply the total amount of money that the agency brings in. As mentioned above, in most cases an agency's revenue is the amount of money it receives for its workers' time at the contracted hospitals. Therefore, revenue is the bill rate multiplied by the number of hours worked. Consider a 13 week contract for 36 hours per week with a bill rate of $60 per hour. The agency would receive $2,160 per week ($60*36 hours) and $28,080 for the entire contract (13 weeks*$2160).

Defining Cost and Other Cost is a bit more difficult because agencies can employ different ways of determining these variables. However, these differences will not matter to the traveler because every cost is going to be accounted for and it's ultimately going to have the same effect on the traveler. Therefore, I'll provide you with a general example of how the vast majority of staffing agencies calculate these variables.

Cost is typically defined as the total cost of the product. I hate to say it, but for a contingent staffing company, the contracted workers are the product. Therefore, every penny that is directly attributed to them is the cost. There are two cost classifications: 1) compensation 2) burdens. Compensation is typically defined as any cost or payment that is going to be given directly to the traveler. These items include things like the pay rate, the tax free stipends, travel expenses, medical benefits, rental cars, reimbursements for licenses and certifications, and any other money or benefit provided by the agency and going directly to the traveler. Burdens are typically defined as costs that don't go directly to the traveler, but are none the less attributed to the traveler. These items include things like liability insurance, compliance/credentialing costs, orientation fees charged by the hospital, federal payroll taxes, and workers comp, disability and unemployment insurance.

The cost of capital may also be included in the burdens. Like most companies, agencies must borrow money to meet their payroll obligations. A traveler turns in a weekly timesheet and the agency pays the traveler on either a weekly or bi-weekly basis. But for the agency, the timesheet is more than just a timesheet, it's also a bill. The agency sends the timesheet to the hospital and requests payment. The hospital typically pays within 30, 60, or 90 days. So the agency has to pay the traveler before they actually receive the money. Therefore, they need to borrow to meet their payroll. As a result, the agency is charged interest, and this cost is typically included in the burdens.

Other Cost is typically defined as all of the costs that go into managing and maintaining the business itself. These items include office costs like rent, telephones, computers, copiers, and faxes. They also include marketing costs like web site development, job board costs, advertising costs, and convention attendance fees. Finally, Other Cost also includes the agency's internal staff's payroll.

We have defined Revenue, Cost, and Other Cost. Now let's take a mathematical look at how these variables are calculated.

Revenue = (Bill Rate)*(Contracted Hours)

Gross Profit = (Revenue)-(Cost)

Gross Margin = Gross Profit/Revenue (remember, Gross Margin is expressed as a percentage)

Net Profit = (Gross profit)-(Other Cost)

Net Margin = (Gross profit)-(Other Cost)/Revenue (remember, Net Margin is expressed as a percentage)

Now that we have defined these basic variables, let's turn to discussing how agencies use them. Let's not forget that agencies are businesses. At a bare minimum, businesses need to break even in order to continue doing business. It's true that businesses can take losses, and some businesses can take losses for years on end. However, healthcare staffing agencies aren't in the category of businesses that can take losses for years on end. They need to be break even or be profitable.

Break even means that they don't need to borrow additional money to meet their financial obligations. Profitable means they have some money left over after meeting their financial obligations. Profits can be paid out to shareholders as dividends, or they can be reinvested into the business, for example to purchase additional office equipment. No matter the case, every agency must employ some strategy for forecasting their future profitability to ensure that they don't go bankrupt.

I am sure that there are many methods that travel healthcare agencies use to manage and forecast their financials. However, I'm not aware that there are any specific names used in the industry to define even the most commonly used methods. To keep it simple I'll define and describe two methods that I'm familiar with.

The first method we'll call the "Fixed Gross Profit Method." In this scenario, the agency determines a fixed gross profit figure to target for each contract. No matter what the bill rate is, or the contracted hours, or anything else, in this scenario the agency must always achieve a predetermined gross profit figure. This gross profit figure is typically defined by the agency's "Other Costs." The agency will determine their "Other Costs" down to the penny and set that figure as a gross profit goal. They then know how many contracts they need in order to meet their goal. To achieve even greater detail, the agency may focus on the number of "full time equivalents" they need to meet their profit goal. A "full time equivalent" is basically a full time worker. In healthcare staffing, this could be defined as 36 or 40 hours per week.

For example, let's say an agency determines that its Other Costs will be $200,000 for the fiscal quarter. Now let's say that the agency decides on a fixed gross profit of $5,000 per 13 week, 36 hour contract. This means that the agency needs 40 13 week, 36 hour contracts during the quarter just to break even. Because we don't live in a perfect world, the agency is going to break this figure down to the hour. In this case, the agency needs to make sure that their contingent staff works a total of 18,720 hours (40 workers working 36 hours per week, for 13 weeks = 18,720). The agency is also going to know that their gross profit per hour is going to be $10.69 (13 weeks at 36 hours per week is 468 hours. $5,000 divided by 468 hours is $10.69 per hour). For an agency using this method, it doesn't matter if it's a single PRN shift, a 13 week contract with a $53 bill rate, or a 13 week contract with a $73 bill rate. They are going to target $10.69 per hour no matter what.

The Fixed Gross Profit Method is simple and efficient for the agency to use. The agency knows exactly how many hours they need their contingent staff to work. The agency ensures that all of the staff members who work for them make the same amount of money at a given facility which minimizes compensation complaints. The agency's recruiters are quick and efficient with compensation quotes when they are requested. And the negotiation process is virtually eliminated.

Despite the efficiencies and uniformity of the Fixed Gross Profit Method, I believe that it's used by few agencies. I have spoken to recruiters from agencies that use it, and the agencies have all had one thing in common, besides the use of the model. They all had relatively few contracts. They all derived a major percentage of their revenue from one or two clients. For example, one agency derived over 80% of its revenue from the California Department of Corrections.

I believe they're able to employ this method because they have relatively few bill rates to contend with. You see if an agency has a broad spectrum of facilities and bill rates, then this model becomes less attractive. For example, let's say that the agency was set on achieving $10.69 gross profit per hour, and they had bill rates that were as low as $48, and as high as $82. The agency would have a very difficult time filling the $48 work orders. The gross profit wouldn't leave enough money to make the compensation package competitive with other agencies that were willing to take less than $10.69. Meanwhile, they'd have a very attractive compensation package for the $82 work orders. However, they'd also be leaving money on the table. They may be able to find candidates who would gladly work for a compensation package that would leave the agency $16 to $20 per hour.

For this reason, most agencies utilize the second method that we'll call the "Gross Margin per Contract" method. I believe it's fair to say that the standard gross margin in the healthcare staffing industry is between 15% and 25%. Any lower, and an agency may go out of business because they won't be able to cover their Other Costs. Any higher, and they may get a very bad reputation for paying low rates. Keep in mind, this margin range is a goal.

Remember, this means that when Cost is subtracted from Revenue, the remainder will be 15% to 25% of Revenue. For example, let's say the bill rate on a contract is $60. This means that the agency's gross profit margin will be $9 (15% of $60) per hour to $15 (25% of $60) per hour. While the majority of contracts will fall somewhere in this range, there will certainly be some contracts that have both higher and lower margins.

The Gross Margin per Contract method provides the agency's recruiters with some flexibility. Recruiters can make determinations based on experience, or how well a candidate fits the job description, and pay more or less accordingly. If the recruiter is bidding against another agency, they will be better able to negotiate. Recruiters can reward veteran staff with potential pay increases for extending. They can also engage in retention strategies. For example, they may pay a current staff member a good rate for a hospital with a low bill rate just keep that nurse from going to another agency, hoping that they'll be able to get a better bill rate on the next contract.

The Gross Margin per Contract and the Fixed Gross Profit methods are employed to ensure that agencies are able to forecast, meet their debt obligations, and stay in business. Which method they choose will have an impact on the compensation package they offer. However, it will be virtually impossible for you to tell the difference. Instead, you should focus on comparing rate packages between agencies. In order to successfully do this, you'll need to understand how the compensation packages work, and be armed with effective questions.

Chapter 9: Understanding the Travel Compensation Package

Before we proceed, let's dispel with a couple of travel healthcare compensation package myths. The most prominent myth I've encountered is the "Free Myth." Remember, the only source of revenue for a healthcare staffing company is the bill rate. And because the bill rate is the rate upon which every compensation package is based, every single attributable cost is taken from it. There is no free housing. There are no free medical benefits. There are no free rental cars.

Pitching these items as "free" is a sales gimmick designed to lure you in. When a company says "free", you should interpret that to mean "company provided." There is an important distinction between "free" and "company provided." "Free" implies that there is no cost to you. However, every company that provides "free" housing will offer to pay you a "lodging stipend" if you choose not to take their "free" housing. How is that free? The simple answer is it isn't. If we resolve to accept these items for what they are, company provided, then their true nature becomes apparent. These are nothing more than services that an agency offers for a price.

Some agencies offer every service you can imagine. You can have anything you want for a price. Meanwhile, other agencies don't offer much of anything and I'm often asked why that is. Why would an agency not offer housing, or travel expenses? The answer is risk. If an agency signs a 3 month lease on a nice apartment and the traveler backs out, or gets released, the company is still responsible for the cost of the apartment. Remember, the only source of revenue is the bill rate, and if the hours aren't worked, then there's no money to pay for anything. These losses can be massive and despite what some may think about the contract's ability to shift liability to the traveler, the simple fact of the matter is that in the vast majority of cases there is nothing at all the agency can do to recoup these costs. The important thing to know is that if an agency does not offer something, then it's almost certain that they'll pay more than the agency who does. This is why you must understand how to compare compensation packages to ensure that you're getting the most out of every deal.

The second myth is the "Bill Rate Negotiation Myth." We've touched on this previously. I often spoke with travelers had no doubt been given the impression by some recruiter, either directly or indirectly, that negotiating rates with hospitals on a contract by contract basis is a common practice. This is a sales gimmick. It's like a used car salesman telling you he's going to discuss lowering the price of the car you're buying with his manager and then going back to the break room, munching on some popcorn, exchanging a few jokes with co-workers, and coming back to tell you, "Let me tell you what I'm gonna do."

The fact of the matter is that the vast majority of bill rates are etched in stone. Standardized bill rates are widely embraced. The contract between the hospital and the agency typically determines the bill rate, and these rates are most often negotiated, or at least require the approval of, someone quite high up in a hospital's administration. In the vast majority of cases, it's going to be much easier and more realistic for the hospital to move forward with another candidate than it would be to negotiate a separate rate for your contract.

I'm not saying that negotiating a higher bill rate with the hospital is impossible, it's just extremely rare, and definitely not the norm. As mentioned earlier in the book, there are some VMS systems that offer bidding systems for bill rates. However, these systems typically have a bid ceiling and are designed to bid bill rates down, not up. Additionally, contracts between hospital and agency often times include a standard rate and a higher rate known as a "crisis rate." It is possible that a hospital may extend the crisis rate for what was originally advertised as a standard rate assignment. But again, this is highly unlikely. Finally, we'll sometimes see rates get increased by $2-$5 per hour if a hospital has been unable to fill an opening and they become desperate. Such circumstances are typically only encountered during a very tight labor market.

The third myth involves travel nursing pay rates. There seems to be a commonly held misconception that travel nurses are making tons of money relative to their permanent peers. Unfortunately for travel nurses, this isn't entirely true. In the majority of cases, when you compare the entire compensation package you receive with a permanent job against the entire compensation package you receive on the standard travel nursing assignment, it's going to be about even, give or take a few percentage points in either direction. When making this comparison, it's necessary to account for the benefits packages, the paid time off, the sick leave, and all of the other variables involved. Also, the fact that travel healthcare agencies advertise to hospitals that using contingent staff will save the hospitals up to 10% on their labor costs should be evidence enough that travel healthcare professionals aren't making tons more money than their permanent counterparts.

However, there are certainly situations in which travelers can make very good money. First, when a hospital's permanent workers go on strike the rates for replacement workers tend to be very high. Of course, strikes are typically very short term and certainly can't be relied on for ongoing employment. Second, hospitals sometimes determine that they have an urgent need that necessitates them to institute a "crisis rate" or increase their standard agency bill rate in order to promptly meet their needs. Crisis rates can be $10 to $20 higher per hour than the standard rates. Third, hospitals in certain locations have high rates due to the difficulties they experience in attracting qualified personnel. Bakersfield, California is one example. The rates in Bakersfield are generally much higher than the rates in Los Angeles despite the fact that the cost of living Los Angeles is much higher than Bakersfield. Fourth, contracts that guarantee 48 hours per week can be quite lucrative. Not only are you working more hours, but the agency's fixed costs are reduced because they are spread out over more billable hours. This allows the agency to pay more money than they would on a standard 36 hour contract.

Fifth, travel nurses tend to have higher net pay than their permanent counterparts. This is due to the tax free stipends that travel nurses are paid. We'll discuss this in detail later in the book.

Sixth, travel nurses do indeed make more than their permanent counterparts in certain states. However, this situation never existed in certain states and has begun to level out across the country. For example, permanent nurses in California tend to earn much more than travelers. Meanwhile, travel nurse compensation in places like Texas, where travel nurses used to significantly out-earn their permanent counterparts, have leveled off due largely to increased compensation for permanent employees.

Now, there was a time when it may have been true that travel nurses significantly out-earned their permanent counterparts. However, bill rates for travel nursing assignments have remained flat for many years despite increased inflation and have significantly decreased in many cases. For example, when American Mobile won the contract with Kaiser California in 2010 the bill rates for Registered Nurses decreased between $6 and $12 per hour depending on the specialty. I speculate that there are a couple of reasons for this.

First, the high unemployment rate the country has experienced since the Mortgage Crisis in 2008 has resulted in downward pressure on the travel nursing industry. Healthcare workers who may have otherwise retired or worked fewer hours remained in the workforce to help pick up the slack for losses they or their families may have incurred. Meanwhile, people in America utilized healthcare less because they had lost their healthcare insurance or needed to save money. All of this resulted in a decrease in the total number of travel nursing assignments and an increase in the number of potential candidates.

Second, the proliferation of the Vendor Management Service has resulted in increased competition and downward pressure on bill rates. Cost savings are one of the major selling points that Vendor Management Services offer. In addition, increased competition among the major players in the market has resulted in bidding wars that drive bill rates lower.

The Pie

Now that we have put these myths behind us, let's move on to our discussion of compensation packages and how to compare them. One of the most common questions, and I have to say one of the worst, if not the worst, questions that travelers ask is, "What's the rate?" This question leaves you vulnerable to terrible answers and potential

72

misunderstandings. It also persuades you to focus on only one aspect of the overall compensation package, "the rate", thereby clouding your judgment. For example, let's say you called 3 different agencies about the same exact job and asked, "What's the rate?" The first agency tells you, "$26 per hour." The second agency tells you, "$33 per hour." The third agency tells you, "$40 per hour."

If, "What's the rate?" was the only question you asked, you'd probably go with the third agency. But what if the first agency was also going to provide medical benefits, housing, utilities for that housing, $700 for travel expenses, and $300 per week for Meals and Incidental Expenditures in addition to the rate? If all else stayed the same, then you'd have made a really bad decision because all of those extras are going to add up to much more than the $14 per hour difference between "the rates" offered by agency one and agency three. Meanwhile, you may incorrectly assume that the third agency's pay package also provided housing and the other benefits in addition to the $40 pay rate. You can never assume that such items are included when an agency quotes "the rate" for an assignment.

Along the same lines, I frequently received calls from travel nurses looking for a new agency because they were convinced that they were getting ripped off by their current agency. It was always the same conversation. They had compared "rates" with another traveler who was working with a different agency at the same facility and this other traveler had a much higher "rate." The used car salesman in me always wanted to pounce on this golden opportunity to sell the nurse on my wonderful services, but I could never bring myself to do it. Instead, I'd always ask what else, besides the rate, the traveler I was speaking with was receiving from their agency. Are you getting company provided housing, medical benefits, travel stipends, etc.? I would then ask if they had discussed all of these items with the other traveler who seemed to be getting such a better deal. Every time the answer was, "No." These examples illustrate the importance of treating travel compensation packages like a pie. "The rate" is only one slice of the pie. In order to determine the full value of the compensation package you must know what the rest of the pie is comprised of.

Remember, the compensation package for any given assignment is based on the bill rate. The bill rate determines what the agency is able to compensate for the assignment. Different agencies provide different services. For example, some agencies offer rental cars and others do not. Different agencies also have different methods for splitting up the compensation package. For example, some agencies offer higher lodging stipends and lower hourly pay rates while others offer lower lodging stipends and higher hourly pay rates. Therefore, you could end up with two compensation packages that look entirely different but are exactly the same.

As a result, you should view travel compensation packages as pie charts. In doing so, you'll not only be able to better visualize the compensation packages, but you'll also get into the habit of considering every single thing that an agency offers as a "slice" of your compensation package pie. This is extremely important when comparing packages to ensure that you select packages that have the most to offer.

Your task then becomes to determine the total value of the pie. To accomplish this, you first need to know the number of hours and weeks in the contract. Knowing these variables will provide you with the base for your calculations. In other words, we need a common denominator in order to adequately compare the values that agencies quote. This is because agencies will quote things in different ways. For example, one agency might quote $360 per week for the M&IE stipend and another might quote it at $10 per hour. If both contracts were for 36 hours per week, then these two quotes are the same. Time is your compensation package common denominator.

For example, a 13 week contract for 36 hours per week has 468 total hours (13 * 36) and 3 total months. I've worked with many travelers who have had trouble with determining the months. They always seem to think that there are only 4 weeks in a month. But that would mean there are only 48 weeks in a year when there are actually 52. It would also mean that there are only 28 days in every month, but there is actually only one month that has so few days. These extra days add up. In fact, they add up to 1 full week over a 3 month period, which can throw calculations off by thousands of dollars if not properly accounted for.

Let's stop here and take a quick look at a pie chart for those, like me, who learn better with visualization.

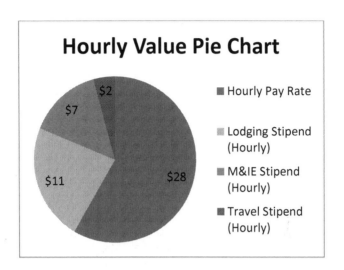

Once you have your time variables locked in, you need to know the dollar values of each piece of the pie being offered. In my opinion, the best way to approach this is for you to take control of the conversation with your checklist. Remember, by the time you're ready to discuss rates with recruiters, you will have already determined what you want as part of your compensation package. You should let every agency know exactly what you need, and then ask them for the values of those items. That way, there are no surprises, everyone is on the same page, there's no room for sales gimmicks, and you'll save a ton of time. We'll start with a simple example. Let's say you decide on the following items:

1) Taxable Base Rate (Always)
2) Taxable Overtime Rate (Always)
3) Lodging Stipend (instead of company provided lodging)
4) Meals and Incidental Expense Stipend
5) Travel Stipend
6) License Reimbursement of $250 for a new state license to practice

Now let's say you follow the previously given advice to determine which agency will represent you at a given facility by asking several agencies to submit a compensation package to you for that given facility. It doesn't matter if there is an opening at that particular facility or not, you're simply making a determination as to who will represent you if and when an opening should arise. For example, let's say you're interested in going to Bakersfield, California because you've heard there are a lot of travel assignments in that city and you want to be sure you're ready with a backup plan if your first choice falls through. Remember to be very specific and ask the same exact questions of all the agencies you speak with. For example:

"Can you please provide me with a written rate quote via email for Bakersfield Memorial? I'm interested in a 13 week contract for 36 hours per week and I'd like the following items as part of my compensation package: Taxable Base Rate, Taxable Overtime Rate, Lodging Stipend (instead of company provided lodging), Meals and Incidental Expense Stipend, Travel Stipend, and License Reimbursement of $250 for a new state license to practice. Also, please include your overtime pay rules for this contract."

The last request in this statement, the one regarding overtime pay rules, is very important. I've found that different agencies have different policies even though state laws on the subject are very clear. Some agencies simply don't abide by state laws, or claim that they have developed some mechanism for circumventing state laws. In addition, because every state has different overtime pay laws, there is not one standard method for payment. You shouldn't have to become an expert on overtime laws in all 50 states. You should however know how the agency will pay the overtime rate because it will make a significant difference in your pay.

Now let's say you speak with three different agencies and you get the following three responses:

Agency 1:

1) Taxable Base Rate: $20/hour
2) Taxable Overtime Rate: $30/hour
3) Lodging Stipend (instead of company provided lodging): $2800/month
4) Meals and Incidental Expense Stipend: $350/week

5) Travel Stipend: $700
6) License Reimbursement of $250 for new state license: $250
7) Overtime is paid after 8 regular hours in a day and 40 regular hours in a week.

Agency 2:

1) Taxable Base Rate: $30/hour
2) Taxable Overtime Rate: $45/hour
3) Lodging Stipend (instead of company provided lodging): $1500/month
4) Meals and Incidental Expense Stipend: $250/week
5) Travel Stipend: $500
6) License Reimbursement of $250 for new state license: $250
7) Overtime is paid after 8 regular hours in a day and 40 regular hours in a week.

Agency 3:

1) Taxable Base Rate: $24/hour
2) Taxable Overtime Rate: $36/hour
3) Lodging Stipend (instead of company provided lodging): $16/hour
4) Meals and Incidental Expense Stipend: $8/hour
5) Travel Stipend: $800
6) License Reimbursement of $250 for new state license: $250
7) Overtime is paid after 8 regular hours in a day and 40 regular hours in a week.

There are several ways to compare these packages. The two I recommend are "hourly", and "total value". To compare them hourly, you're going to break every number down to an hourly figure, and add them all up to arrive at what's commonly referred to as the "blended rate." The term "blended rate" means different things to different people. The basic idea is that variables are going to be added together, or blended, to arrive at a total figure. In this example, we're going to use every variable of the compensation package, as opposed to using just a couple of variables and leaving the rest to the side. I recommend using this approach because it's the best method for making an apples-to-apples comparison between various offers.

To do this, you begin with the total number of hours in the contract. In this case, we are looking at a contract for 13 weeks with 36 hours per week. So the total number of anticipated hours in the contract is 468 (13*36). The next step is a little tricky. You need to determine the average hourly taxable rate. The average hourly rate is the average rate of the regular time hours and overtime hours for the contract. In most cases, you won't really need to worry about this. This is because typically, overtime laws require that employers pay time and a half after 40 hours in a week. And because most contracts are going to be 36 hours per week, you'll never get into the overtime rate. If you land a contract that guarantees 48 hours per week, and the agency pays time and a half after 40, then you'll want to run a calculation to determine the average hourly rate. Basically, if you're going to get any overtime as part of your contract hours, you want to determine the average hourly rate.

In our example, we're looking at a contract in California which requires employers to pay overtime after 8 hours in a day. Additionally, each agency has indicated that they comply with this law. So, to run our "average hourly taxable rate" calculation we use the following formula:

(Regular hours per day)(Regular hour rate) + (Overtime hours per day) (Overtime hour rate)/Total hours for the day

In this example, the contract is for 12 hours per day, and overtime is paid after 8. Therefore, there are 8 regular hours and 4 overtime hours per day. Below is a sample calculation using a taxable base rate of $20 per hour and a taxable overtime rate of $30 per hour.

($20)(8 hours) + ($30)(4 hours)/12 hours = $23.33

With this information at the ready, we're all set to run an hourly comparison for the three quotes we received.

Agency 1:
1) Taxable Base Rate: $20/hour
2) Taxable Overtime Rate: $30/hour
3) Lodging Stipend (instead of company provided lodging): $2800/month
4) Meals and Incidental Expense Stipend: $350/week
5) Travel Stipend: $700
6) License Reimbursement of $250 for new state license: $250
7) Overtime is paid after 8 regular hours in a day and 40 regular hours in a week.

Average hourly rate: ($20)(8 hours)+($30)(4 hours)/12 hours = $23.33
Lodging Stipend per hour: ($2800)(3 months)/468 hours = $17.95
M&IE Stipend per hour: ($350)(13 weeks)/468 = $9.72
Travel Stipend per hour: ($700)/468 = $1.50
License Reimbursement per hour: ($250)/468 = $.53
Blended Rate: $23.33 + $17.95 + $9.72 + $1.50 + $.53 = $53.03

Agency 2:
1) Taxable Base Rate: $30/hour
2) Taxable Overtime Rate: $45/hour
3) Lodging Stipend (instead of company provided lodging): $1500/month
4) Meals and Incidental Expense Stipend: $250/week
5) Travel Stipend: $500
6) License Reimbursement of $250 for new state license: $250
7) Overtime is paid after 8 regular hours in a day and 40 regular hours in a week.

Average hourly rate: ($30)(8 hours)+($45)(4 hours)/12 hours = $35.00
Lodging Stipend per hour: ($1500)(3 months)/468 hours = $9.61
M&IE Stipend per hour: ($250)(13 weeks)/468 = $6.94
Travel Stipend per hour: ($500)/468 = $1.07
License Reimbursement per hour: ($250)/468 = $.53
Blended Rate: $35.00 + $9.61 + $6.94 + $1.07 + $.53 = $53.15

Agency 3:
1) Taxable Base Rate: $24/hour
2) Taxable Overtime Rate: $36/hour
3) Lodging Stipend (instead of company provided lodging): $16/hour
4) Meals and Incidental Expense Stipend: $8/hour
5) Travel Stipend: $800
6) License Reimbursement of $250 for new state license: $250
7) Overtime is paid after 8 regular hours in a day and 40 regular hours in a week.

Average hourly rate: ($24)(8 hours)+($36)(4 hours)/12 hours = $28.00
Lodging Stipend per hour: $16 (they already calculated for us)
M&IE Stipend per hour: $8 (they already calculated for us)
Travel Stipend per hour: ($800)/468 = $1.71
License Reimbursement per hour: ($250)/468 = $.53

Blended Rate: $28.00 + $16 + $8 + $1.71 + $.53 = $54.24

There are a couple of things we can learn from this example. First, these rates are all pretty close to one another despite the fact that all appear to be very different. In fact, they're all within 2% of one another. Second, we can see that the contract with the highest "rate", Agency 2 with $30 per hour, isn't actually the highest paying contract. I hope this drives home the importance of considering every variable of the compensation package. The bottom line is that all of this money is going to make its way to you. All else equal, it shouldn't matter how it's paid to you, it just matters that it is indeed paid to you. Unfortunately, not all else is equal and we'll discuss the inequalities and how they may affect your decisions a little later. For now, we turn to the total value comparison.

The total value comparison is bit more straightforward. Our goal here is determine the total value of the entire contract. To do so, we again begin with the number of weeks and hours per week to determine the total number of hours in the contract.

13 weeks
36 hours per week
3 months (13 weeks = 3 months)

We also need to determine the total number of regular hours and the total number of overtime hours for the contract. Again, for the vast majority of contracts there will not be any contracted overtime hours. However, in our example we do have contracted overtime hours. Each agency is paying overtime after 8 in a day. The contract is for 3 12 hour shifts per week, totaling 36 hours per week. So each week 24 regular hours are worked and 12 overtime hours are worked. Multiply each figure by 13 weeks and we get a total of 312 regular hours, and 156 overtime hours for the entire contract. We are now ready to compute the total value of each contract.

Agency 1:
1) Taxable Base Rate: $20/hour
2) Taxable Overtime Rate: $30/hour
3) Lodging Stipend (instead of company provided lodging): $2800/month
4) Meals and Incidental Expense Stipend: $350/week
5) Travel Stipend: $700
6) License Reimbursement of $250 for new state license: $250

7) Overtime is paid after 8 regular hours in a day and 40 regular hours in a week.

Taxable Base Rate Total: ($20)*(312 regular hours) = $6240
Taxable Overtime Rate Total: ($30)*(156 overtime hours) = $4680
Lodging Stipend Total: ($2800)*(3 months) = $8400
M&IE Stipend Total: ($350)*(13 weeks) = $4550
Travel Stipend Total: $700
License Reimbursement Total: $250
Total Value of the Contract:
$6260+$4680+$8400+$4550+$700+$250 = $24,840

Agency 2:
1) Taxable Base Rate: $30/hour
2) Taxable Overtime Rate: $45/hour
3) Lodging Stipend (instead of company provided lodging): $1500/month
4) Meals and Incidental Expense Stipend: $250/week
5) Travel Stipend: $500
6) License Reimbursement of $250 for new state license: $250
7) Overtime is paid after 8 regular hours in a day and 40 regular hours in a week.

Taxable Base Rate Total: ($30)*(312 regular hours) = $9360
Taxable Overtime Rate Total: ($45)*(156 overtime hours) = $7020
Lodging Stipend Total: ($1500)*(3 months) = $4500
M&IE Stipend Total: ($250)*(13 weeks) = $3250
Travel Stipend Total: $700
License Reimbursement Total: $250
Total Value of the Contract:
$9360+$7020+$4500+$3250+$+$700+$250 = $25,080

Agency 3:
1) Taxable Base Rate: $24/hour
2) Taxable Overtime Rate: $36/hour
3) Lodging Stipend (instead of company provided lodging): $16/hour
4) Meals and Incidental Expense Stipend: $8/hour
5) Travel Stipend: $800
6) License Reimbursement of $250 for new state license: $250
7) Overtime is paid after 8 regular hours in a day and 40 regular hours in a week.

Taxable Base Rate Total: ($24)*(312 regular hours) = $7488
Taxable Overtime Rate Total: ($36)*(156 overtime hours) = $5616
Lodging Stipend Total: ($16)*(468 hours) = $7488
M&IE Stipend Total: ($8)*(468 hours) = $3744
Travel Stipend Total: $700
License Reimbursement Total: $250
Total Value of the Contract:
$7488+$5616+$7488+$3744+$+$700+$250 = $25,286

All of the examples we've looked at thus far include a lodging stipend in lieu of company provided housing. However, many who read this book will opt for company provided housing in lieu of the lodging stipend. You can still use this method. In fact, you can use it no matter what you choose to take from the agency. The method is adaptable. Simply remove the items that aren't a part of your compensation package and/or add the items that are a part of your compensation package. You'll run the same calculation for each variable based on the total number of hours in the contract. We'll discuss company provided housing in detail later in the book.

The Blended Hourly Rate and Total Value methods are the best ways to compare compensation packages for the same hospital, or multiple hospitals within the same region. These methods allow you to make apples to apples comparisons by breaking every aspect of the compensation package down to common denominators. But what if you're comparing compensation packages for offers that are in remotely different regions of the country?

For example, let's say you're currently in Miami, Florida and you're deciding between an option in Tallahassee, Florida and Los Angeles, California. It's going to cost you more to get to California. Housing may be more expensive in California, and the cost of living may be higher depending on your lifestyle choices. Of course, it will be difficult to determine how cost of living differences will affect the value of your compensation. However, there are some useful tools on the internet. For example, you can use the Cost of Living Calculator at payscale.com.

In this situation, many travelers rely simply on the weekly net pay offered by each assignment in an effort to determine which opportunity would be the most lucrative. The idea is that the costs involved are actually costs that you will truly incur. For example, traveling to California is going to be more expensive than traveling to

Tallahassee from Miami. Therefore, who cares what the travel stipend is because it's going to get soaked up by the cost of travel expenses.

Unfortunately, this logic is not sound. It's true that it may work in some circumstances, but it's still not the best way to determine which compensation package is going to net you more money by the end of the contract. I still recommend breaking everything down with the Blended Hourly Rate or Total value method. This is because an agency may provide a larger travel stipend than is required, or they may offer something else that another agency is not offering. If you only look at the net pay that you'll receive for working the contracted hours, you may miss out on some of the additional compensation variables an agency may be offering. In any case, if you stick to your list, and stick to the methods described here, you'll ensure that you're able to make true comparisons that will result in income maximization and increased negotiating leverage.

Conclusion

The travel nursing compensation package can be quite complex. Understanding the agency's side of the equation elucidates the subject and can improve your negotiations. Being aware of some of the compensation myths will help set your expectations and make sure that you don't fall prey to any traps.

Always consider the entirety of the travel nursing compensation package when determining its value. Never focus on the value of just one variable, like the rate. Use the total number of anticipated assignment hours to calculate the hourly value or total value of the compensation packages you're offered in order to compare them. If financial considerations are your primary concern, then be sure to factor in the cost of living and various expenses you stand to incur with the various different assignments you're considering.

Section 5: TAX FREE MONEY

Chapter 10: Tax Free Money: Overview

Now that we have a pretty solid understanding of the travel compensation package basics, let's discuss the "Tax Free" aspect that everyone seems so fascinated with. I mean, what's not to be fascinated about?! You're not going to have to pay any taxes!! Is it possible that Benjamin Franklin was wrong when he said, "in this world nothing can be said to be certain, except death and taxes."? The answer is yes, *possibly*. Please note the emphasis on "possibly." Before I offer any further information it's important to note that I am not a tax advisor, Certified Public Accountant, or Lawyer. I am not in any way providing any tax advice. All information regarding taxes is informational and intended as a jumping off point. You must seek the help of professional tax advisors to gain a clear understanding of your unique circumstances. That said we can move on to a detailed discussion of this issue.

Basic Information

Let's begin by discussing where the concept of tax free money even comes from. In a general sense, the tax code allows for tax write offs or tax free reimbursements for all ordinary and necessary expenses incurred while working away from one's tax home. First let's distinguish between a "tax write off" and a reimbursement. A tax-write-off is when you reduce the amount of your taxable income by a specified amount in the course of compiling your tax return. For example, if you lived in Atlanta and went to Chicago on a business trip and incurred hotel and food charges while in Chicago that were paid out of your own pocket, you would keep the receipts and reduce your taxable income by this amount on your tax returns.

Now let's say you took the same business trip, only this time your employer gave you a fixed amount of money to pay for your expenses before you left; that's a reimbursement or "per diem." Many agencies and recruiters will call a per diem payment, a "stipend" which is a term that is technically used to describe any lump sum of money given for a specific purpose. This is the term that we will use moving forward because in the healthcare staffing world, it helps us differentiate between per diem as meaning PRN shifts worked on an on call basis, and stipends as meaning tax free money. Again, bear in mind that the following terms all mean the same thing: stipends, per diem, tax-free money, and tax-advantage program.

The most common forms of stipends offered by agencies are travel stipends, lodging stipends, and Meals and Incidental Expenditure (M&IE) stipends. Travel stipends are validated by the cost of traveling to and from the assignment. These costs can include airline tickets, or car mileage stipends among other things. The car mileage stipend rates are set and periodically updated by the IRS. For example, the standard mileage rate in January, 2012 was 55.5 cents for business miles driven.

Lodging and M&IE stipend rates are also set by the government on an annual basis. Specifically, these rates are set by the General Services Administration (GSA). The GSA sets these rates for every country in the world and the rates vary depending on the estimated cost of living in a given area. For example, the stipend rates in San Francisco, CA are going to be much higher than the stipend rates in El Paso, TX. When you're looking up rates in the United States, you may see them referred to as the "CONUS Rates". CONUS simply means the Continental United States. **Stipend rates for lodging and M&IE are the maximum rates that an employee can be given without an exchange of receipts while the employee is away from home on the business of the employer.**

I've bolded the definition above to highlight the importance of being familiar with it. It's particularly important to note two aspects of the definition. First, these are the "maximum rates." That means that agencies can pay less if they'd like to, or need to. This is where the idea of "maximized stipends" comes from. One agency might offer a higher percentage of pay in the form of stipends, and another may offer a lower percentage of pay in the form of stipends. Second, these are the maximum rates that can be given "without an exchange of receipts." This means that the employer does not have to collect receipts from the employee for record keeping purposes.

Why Agencies Offer Tax Free Stipends

Every agency you come across will be offering you tax free stipends. In fact, you would have difficulty finding a travel nursing agency willing to pay you an all taxable income with no tax free stipends at all. The very simplified logic for this is that tax free stipends are offered because they can be. But a deeper look at the issue provides insight into how travel nursing agencies benefit from offering tax free stipends and how they are in a sense almost forced to offer tax free stipends.

The first benefit of tax free stipends for the travel nursing agency is that they allow the agency to avoid certain payroll costs. This is because payroll costs are calculated as a percentage of the employee's taxable income. The Federal Insurance Contributions Act (FICA) taxes for Medicare and Social Security are an example. Many employees don't know this, but both the employer and employee pay a tax for these government insurance plans.

In 2012 the FICA Medicare tax was 1.45% and the FICA Social Security tax was 6.2%. This means that both the employer and employee each pay this percentage on the employee's taxable income. For example, if an employee earned $1000 of taxable income for a week's work, then the employee would see a total deduction of $76.50 for these two taxes. In addition, the employer would also pay $76.50 for these two taxes but the employee wouldn't necessarily see this happening. There are similar costs at the state level. Workers Compensation, Disability, and Unemployment Insurance are examples. These costs vary from state to state. Some states have higher costs and other states have lower costs.

When all of these costs are added up on the agency's end, they can be as low as 10% of the taxable wage to as high as 18% of the taxable wage. For example, let's say that the total for a particular state was 15%. If an employee earned $33 per hour as a taxable income, then the agency would have to pay $4.95 for every hour that the employee worked (15% of 33 = 4.95). However, if an agency paid the employee $33 per hour, but split that payment up between a taxable wage of $20 per hour and non-taxable stipend that averaged $13 per hour (total $33 per hour), then they would only have to pay $3 for every hour that the employee worked (15% of 20 = 3). All else equal, they would save $1.95 per hour worked.

The second benefit of tax free stipends for travel nursing agencies is that tax free money is a huge selling point for agencies trying to sell people on travel nursing. Recruiters appeal to candidates with talk of "Weekly Net Pay," which is the amount of money after taxes that will be deposited to the candidate's account for one week's work. This figure is typically much higher than the candidate is used to earning. However, the Gross Pay, or before tax figure, may not be that much different than what the candidate is earning with their current job. The difference comes as the result of lower taxes.

Let's say that a candidate is making $33 per hour at their permanent job at home in Alabama. Their Gross Pay, before taxes, for a 36 hour work week, is $1188. Their Net Pay, after taxes, would be approximately $865 (calculated by Paycheckcity.com based on zero exemptions). Now, a recruiter calls the candidate and says that they have an assignment that is paying $1004 Net Pay per week in California, PLUS the agency will provide free housing and cover the travel expenses. Assuming that the candidate intends to keep paying all their bills back at home (rent, utilities, etc.), then they will receive a NET difference of $149 per week ($1004-$865 = $149).

That's a pay increase of 17%. In the compensation world, that's a huge increase. Imagine getting a 17% pay raise at your job without a promotion. Even with a promotion, that's a significant increase. The trick is that the agency is offering the same Gross Pay per week. The example I just used for California also has a pay rate of $33 per hour. The difference is that only $20 of the $33 is taxable. The other $13 is paid as a tax free stipend. As a result, the taxes are less and the Net Pay is higher.

When selling this benefit, some recruiters will go so far as to quote you what they call the "taxable equivalent." Essentially, they added the tax savings to the total figure and quote the resulting larger figure. Let's say the taxable rate is $20 per hour and the non-taxable stipend totals $13 per hour for a total of $33 per hour. The recruiter will calculate the taxes that you would pay on the non-taxable $13 per hour and add it to the total. For example, they might say you would get taxed at 25% if that $13 were to be taxed. Therefore, you're saving $2.95 per hour and the "taxable equivalent of the total rate is $35.95. This is a sales gimmick that confuses many to believe that they're going to make more than they actually are.

Ultimately, the sales appeal and cost savings represent competitive advantages for agencies offering them versus agencies that do not offer them. Agencies offering the tax free stipends can use Net Pay as major selling point over agencies that do not use the stipends. Meanwhile, the cost savings realized by offering the tax free stipends can be used to increase the rate that the agency pays the traveler making the agency even more competitive, or spent on advertising and other revenue generating objectives, or passed back to the hospital in the form of a lower bill rate. It's better to understand this concept in reverse. That is to say that if agencies didn't realize this cost saving, they would be forced to pass off the extra cost somewhere.

This is one of the main reasons why it's difficult to find an agency that will offer a fully taxable wage. A fully taxable wage is a tough sell in a market that's dominated by companies offering a seemingly much more attractive compensation package, and explaining away the differences is a difficult task. Furthermore, the additional cost would make the agency less competitive, whether with their hospital clients, their contingent staff, or their own internal employees. That additional cost would have to affect something.

You might ask why an agency wouldn't just offer both options. All they would have to do is tell you what the compensation package would be if they provided tax free money and what it would be if they provided an all taxable wage, right? There are two main reasons they don't want to do this. First, offering to pay both ways can potentially complicate payroll processing and other aspects of an agency's internal procedures. Second, and perhaps more importantly, offering compensation both ways exposes them to the risk of getting tagged by the IRS for what is called a re-characterization of wages.

The IRS doesn't want tax free stipends to be treated as part of a wage. Tax free stipends are just that, payments to cover expenses incurred while traveling away from one's tax home. If an agency claims that they'll pay you $30 per hour taxable plus a $360 stipend for working a 36 hour week, or $40 per hour all taxable, whichever you choose, then they may open themselves to a claim from the IRS that the $360 stipend is actually being offered as a wage rather than a stipend. This is a risk that travel nursing agencies don't want to take. It's also one of the reasons that the biggest agencies in the business maintain very structured and inflexible pay package offerings.

Tax free stipends also have benefits for travel nurses. Simply put, travel nurses get to put more money in their pockets. However, there are also disadvantages for travel nurses taking tax free stipends and, as we'll discuss later, travel nurses must be certain that they even qualify to receive the tax free stipends.

Financial Disadvantages of Tax Free Stipends

At this point, you're probably wondering why anyone would want to avoid tax free money. I mean, who could possibly want to pay taxes, right? Unfortunately, there's a catch. In fact, there are quite a few catches. For example, your taxable income affects the amount of money that goes toward your Social Security retirement benefit. The calculation determining your social security benefit is based on your 35 highest earning years. In the long run, the low taxable wage you receive from staffing agencies may not have much of an impact on your future Social Security benefit, but it's still something that you should consider, especially if you intend to do it for a considerable amount of time.

Workers Compensation and Unemployment Payments are also calculated as a percentage of your taxable wage. Workers Compensation is a mechanism designed to protect those who become injured at work and miss out on employment and wages as a result. The payment calculation varies by state, but the payment is typically 66% of the worker's weekly taxable income. As a result, your workers compensation payments would be very low if you were to get hurt on the job while your taxable wage was low.

The same is true for Unemployment Payments. These too are typically calculated at 66% of your taxable weekly income. If you were able to successfully claim unemployment, your unemployment payments would be very low. However, this may not be that important as it will be quite difficult to file a successful unemployment claim when working with a travel staffing company. While every state is different, collecting unemployment payments typically requires that one be laid off without the offer of any further work. In a typical case, a worker in Atlanta who was laid off, but offered work with the same company in Chicago would most likely be able to file a successful unemployment claim. But when you accept a job with a travel staffing company, it's understood that the nature of the job requires traveling to where the jobs are. So an agency can deny claims based on the fact that they have plenty of work for you, albeit in locations that may not interest you.

Your taxable income also affects your ability to borrow. If you wish to purchase a new home, car, or anything else that may require financing, your taxable income is what will determine your eligibility. While I have been involved in instances where a lender was willing to accept some form of written statement from the agency attesting to the employee's full income including tax free stipends, this is the exception not the rule. Financial institutions consider these payments to be stipends rather than income. Trying to justify it to the financial institution is typically futile.

Finally, there is also the possibility that the tax free income and the lower W2 total that results, could potentially impact your future salary negotiations. While this is highly unlikely, it is possible none the less. Potential employers may wish to obtain copies of your W2s during salary negotiations. They may also contact your former employers to verify prior compensation. You'll want to stay ahead of this as best you can by offering explanations up front.

Chapter 11: Qualifying for Tax Free Stipends and Tax Deductions

Yet another catch with tax fee stipends, and perhaps the most important catch, is that you must qualify to receive them. While many agencies, recruiters, and even traveling healthcare professionals will tell you that there is a lot of "gray area" or "wiggle room" with respect to the qualifications, the simple fact of the matter is that the IRS and applicable court rulings have made the qualifications quite clear. And it's certainly clear who doesn't qualify for tax free stipends.

The tax code allows tax free stipends for all ordinary and necessary expenses incurred while working away from one's tax home. Therefore, whether or not you qualify to receive tax free stipends depends on where you're working versus where your tax home is. Defining your tax home then becomes the key to determining if you qualify to receive tax free stipends. According to the IRS, **"Generally, your tax home is the entire city or general area where your main place of business or work is located, regardless of where you maintain your family home."**

To get an idea of how one qualifies under this definition, think of a salesman who has a permanent job and a home both in Madison, WI. As a salesman, she spends 80% of her time working at the office in Madison, and 20% traveling to meet with clients at various locations where she must sleep or rest to meet the demands of her work while away from home. While she is working away from home, all of the necessary and ordinary expenses are tax deductible, or her company can provide tax free stipends to cover the costs.

This is a good place to stop and gain some perspective because it represents the first test in determining whether or not you qualify to receive tax free stipends. Note that the individual in the example has a permanent job that it is primarily based in one location. In addition, the individual travels a small percentage of the time for business.

Let's consider a real world example for traveling healthcare professionals. The simplest example that I've dealt with is the healthcare professional who has a permanent job but schedules time off to work the occasional short term contract or strike in a location that requires rest before returning home. They may also work something out with the scheduling at their permanent job that allows them the opportunity to travel and pick up some shifts in another location on their off days. For example, they may work 6 days in a row and then have eight days off in a row at their permanent job. During these periods they can occasionally travel to another location to work some guaranteed shifts. The important thing to note is that they are maintaining a "regular and main place of business." Essentially, the tax home is where they work a significant amount of time and where they derive the majority of their income.

It's my experience that the vast majority of traveling healthcare professionals do not fall into this category. Don't fret; the IRS and tax courts recognize that there are other scenarios that may qualify someone to receive tax free stipends. First, the nature of the taxpayer's business may be such that it is literally away from home all the time. For example, the captain of a cruise ship could certainly fall into this category. Second, a taxpayer may work at multiple temporary assignments in various locations. To get an idea, think of an oil rig worker who gets sent to multiple locations throughout a 12 state region for temporary periods of time. The majority of traveling healthcare professionals fall into the second scenario. Again, they work multiple temporary assignments in various locations.

In such scenarios, the IRS makes a determination as to whether or not the tax payer even has a legitimate tax home and ultimately whether or not the taxpayer qualifies to receive tax free stipends. To make this determination, the IRS seeks to determine whether the taxpayer has a "regular place of abode in a real and substantial sense." (Blum and Coppage)

This definition is clearly subjective. However, various court cases and IRS rulings have set some pretty clear guidelines. For example, IRS Revenue Ruling 73-529 established a 3 factor threshold test which is now widely used when determining the existence of a tax home. The three factors are as follows:

1) Whether the taxpayer performs a portion of their business within the vicinity of the declared tax home and uses the

declared tax home for lodging purposes while performing business there.

2) Whether the taxpayer's living expenses are duplicated as a result of their traveling for work.

3) Whether the taxpayer has not abandoned the declared tax home. This is typically determined by how frequently the taxpayer uses the declared tax home for their own personal lodging and personal business, and whether or not the taxpayer has direct family members living in the declared tax home (Blum and Coppage).

If a taxpayer working multiple temporary assignments meets all three of these factors, then they are safe with declaring a tax home, and they qualify to receive the tax free stipends. If a taxpayer meets two of the factors, then tax courts will typically employ a more subjective "facts and circumstances" test to determine if a true tax home even exists (Blum and Coppage). Finally, taxpayers meeting only one, or none, of the three criteria are considered "itinerant workers". Itinerant workers do not have a tax home and are therefore not entitled to tax free stipends (Blum and Coppage).

The three factor threshold test makes it very clear that if you qualify for only one of the three factors, then you are not qualified to receive tax free money. Meeting two or three of the factors is not as clear on the surface. Therefore, we'll provide details to clarify these issues shortly. But first, we have to look at how to maintain your temporary worker status. Remember, in order to qualify for the 3 Factor Threshold test, you must be classified as a temporary worker. Let's start with a look at what it takes to maintain temporary worker status.

Defining Temporary

Starting at the beginning, let's recall that, "your tax home is the entire city or general area where your main place of business or work is located, regardless of where you maintain your family home." Take note of the distinction between "your tax home" and "your family home." This is important because it's possible to have both!

For example, I have a friend who had a permanent job in San Jose, CA. He married his college sweetheart who was from Fresno, CA and they purchased a home in Fresno which is a 3 hour drive from San Jose. He kept his job and apartment in San Jose for nearly 3 years before he was able to find a comparable job in Fresno and move there permanently. For that 3 year period, he was not entitled to tax write offs or stipends. Purchasing the home in Fresno was a personal matter, not a business matter. His tax home was in San Jose where he worked, and his family home was in Fresno.

The important distinction between my friend's example and a traveling healthcare professional is that my friend's job was a permanent job and traveling healthcare professionals work temporary assignments. However, I offer this example and stress the difference between tax home and family home for a reason. While the IRS employs a different set of principles when dealing with temporary assignments, namely the 3 factor threshold test or the more subjective facts and circumstances test, the spirit of the original definition is certainly at play. As mentioned previously, authorities have ruled that declared tax homes were "personal in nature" rather than business related when deciding cases involving taxpayers engaged in temporary assignments.

With that in mind let's discuss the difference between temporary assignments and permanent jobs, or "indefinite employment" as it is commonly referred to by the IRS. This is a very important distinction to make because if your employment away from your declared tax home is considered indefinite, then you no longer qualify for tax free stipends.

In defining temporary work, IRS Publication 463 states, "If you expect an assignment or job to last for 1 year or less, it is temporary unless there are facts and circumstances that indicate otherwise. An assignment or job that is initially temporary may become indefinite due to changed circumstances. A series of assignments to the same location, all for short periods but that together cover a long period, may be considered an indefinite assignment."

In this regard, one of the great things about travel healthcare assignments is that you receive a contract which designates a start date and an end date. This provides proof that your employment is temporary without question. You must keep copies of your contracts! I cannot stress this enough. However, if you sign multiple contracts in one location for a total consecutive timeframe of 1 year or more, then you'll most likely run afoul of the rule. This is why you will consistently hear about the "1 year rule."

You'll want to be careful with this rule in order to maintain your temporary status. There are two scenarios under which I believe travelers get into trouble. First, they sometimes take multiple assignments in the same metropolitan region. For example, I've worked with travelers who worked in Los Angeles, California for 9 months, and then worked 30 miles away in West Hills, California for 6 months consecutively. The IRS may claim that this traveler is exceeding the 1 year limit because they are essentially in the same general area. Obviously, the same would be true if a traveler continued to work in the same city repeatedly.

The key to avoiding this is to ensure that you maintain what the IRS refers to as "breaks in service." Unfortunately, the IRS does not provide an exact timeframe defining a break in service. However, there are some very clear guidelines. It's important to note that the IRS considers employment history in 24 month increments when determining breaks in service. Various IRS cases indicate that a 3 week break is not considered significant, a 7 month break may be significant, and a 12 month break is definitely significant. A safe rule of thumb is to never work in one location for more than 12 months in a 24 month period (traveltax.com).

However, it's very important to remember that your approach to this rule should be dependent on which two of the three factors in the 3 factor threshold test that you're aiming to satisfy. If you are incurring duplicative expenses, and therefore satisfying factor 2, then the advice in the preceding paragraph is sound. However, if you are seeking to avoid paying duplicative expenses and instead satisfy factors 1 and 3, then you may need to move around much more. My experience indicates that most travelers fall into this scenario. We'll discuss this in detail shortly.

The second way that travelers can jeopardize their status as a temporary worker is to sign on for PRN with either a local agency or directly with a hospital in the same area as their travel assignment. They see this as an opportunity to supplement their hours and earn extra money. It can certainly be a very attractive option. For example, some hospitals in California will pay their direct PRN nurses over $70 per hour, and making $60 per hour or more is quite common. However, the IRS may view these positions as "indefinite" and reject your claim for tax free stipends. Sure, you may have a travel assignment in the area, but you just accepted a job that has an indefinite end date.

You can try to avoid this pitfall by requesting a contract to work the PRN shifts with clearly defined starting and ending dates. However, you'll likely find that only agencies would be willing to do this. Hospitals on the other hand are looking for people who want to keep the PRN positions long term. They'll have no problem finding them because these positions pay so well and are typically highly coveted. In any case, I strongly advise that you seek the advice of a tax advisor who has experience specifically with traveling and temporary workers on these or similar issues.

Just the Facts...And Circumstances

Now that we have made the distinction between indefinite work and temporary work, and we have discussed the basics of maintaining temporary status, we can move on to ensuring a legitimate tax home. Again, the three factor threshold is fairly straightforward. If you're going to be working temporary assignments, in order to guarantee your ability to qualify for tax free stipends you must meet all three criteria. If you meet one, or none, then you are an itinerant worker and do not qualify to receive tax free stipends. If you meet two of the criteria, then you move into the more subjective facts and circumstances test. This basically means that the IRS and/or courts will make a judgment call as to whether or not the facts of your specific circumstances qualify for receiving tax free stipends.

It's very important to understand how the IRS makes this determination because the vast majority of travelers fall into this category. Among the three factors, there are only three combinations of 2 that are possible, 1 and 2, 2 and 3, and 1 and 3. We are first going to discuss what it takes to meet factors 2 and 3. This is because the methods for meeting factors 2 and 3 have been made very clear. Meeting factor 1 is a bit more subjective so we'll tackle it last.

Factor 2: Duplicative Expenses

The second criteria in the 3 factor threshold test to determine a tax home is that the taxpayer must incur duplicated living expenses. This criterion is relatively straightforward, but it does not involve a specific dollar amount. However, IRS and Revenue Court rulings indicate that the amount is substantial and real. For example, in the case of rent, the amount must be fair market value to qualify. This value is easily discerned from local advertisements for housing and apartment rentals. I have had many conversations with travelers, and read many blog posts or chat room posts in which a creative plan was set forth to somehow circumvent the substantial expense requirement, yet still meet the overall requirement. I strongly recommend against this and urge you to consider the following examples.

There once was a taxpayer who spent most of his time in 1990 traveling about the country while working for Walt Disney's World of Ice. The taxpayer used his parent's home in Boise, Idaho as his tax home. He stayed there between shows, contributed time and labor to the maintenance of the home, maintained his driver's license with the home's address, kept his possessions there, and paid Idaho state taxes. The court ruled that he could not use his parent's home as his tax home. In doing so, the court ruled that the taxpayer's reason for staying there was personal rather than business related and that while his expenses on the road were more expensive, they were not duplicative (Blum and Coppage).

In another court case, two brothers worked for a pipeline company that sent them to complete short term projects at various locations throughout the country. The brothers owned an ancestral home in Vallejo, California and returned there from time to time between projects. They also had a disabled sister who lived in the home on a permanent basis. One of the brothers paid for his living expenses while residing in the home and the other pitched in for bills and even paid the property taxes on occasion. The court ruled that the expenses were financial support for the sister rather than maintenance costs for the home. As a result, they were unable to declare the home as a tax home and therefore did not qualify to receive tax free stipends.

I strongly advise that you seek the advice of a tax advisor who has experience specifically with traveling and temporary workers if you wish to do anything other than pay your own mortgage or rent a property for which you hold the lease. I have had conversations, and read blog posts, in which people claim that a traveler can pay rent for a room in a family member's or friend's home and declare it as their tax home. This may be true, but it's more complicated than simply paying the person rent. The rental payments may have to be declared on the person's taxes as income. Some travelers also choose to rent out their declared tax home while they're on travel assignments. Again, this may cause complications that prevent the traveler from satisfying factor 2. A tax advisor experienced with these issues can help you work out the details.

Factor 3: Maintaining Personal and Personal Business Ties

The third factor in the 3 factor threshold test to determine a tax home is that the taxpayer must not have abandoned the declared tax home which is typically determined by how frequently the taxpayer uses the declared tax home for their own personal lodging and personal business, and whether or not the taxpayer has direct family members living in the declared tax home. The thrust of this test is to determine the strength of the ties that the taxpayer has to the declared tax home.

Family ties and your use of the property are certainly important, but there are many other variables that are considered. In fact, this is the factor for which your personal business ties come into play. There is no magic number or combination of personal variables that will ensure your qualification for factor 3. You should really seek to ensure that all variables are met. Below is a list of personal business variables and pertinent insights for your consideration.

Maintaining Personal Ties and Personal Business in Your Declared Tax Home:

1) Use it for lodging: You can return home between assignments, on holidays, and any other time you're able.

2) Maintain one permanent address at your tax home: You should use one address for all official documents and all mailing purposes. Get a P.O. Box that offers mail forwarding services and use it for everything. As far as I'm concerned, don't use your assignment addresses for anything.

3) One Bank Account: Be sure that your one bank account was opened at a branch in your tax home. Use it for everything. It's best to use a national bank with branches throughout the nation, or at least in the locations you'll be traveling. Trust me nobody likes local credit unions more than me, but they're rarely suited to meet the demands of a constant traveler.

4) File your taxes as a nonresident in **assignment states**: Do not file as a resident, or part time resident, because you're neither one.

5) Keep your driver's license registered at your tax home: Do not get a new driver's license.

6) Register to vote at your tax home: No matter what the

circumstances, do not register to vote anywhere else other than your tax home. And if you're not registered to vote, you should be.

7) Make sure that all financial services you utilize have your tax home address: This goes for automobile insurance, health insurance, 401K, and any other type of financial service you utilize.

8) Maintain a primary doctor and dentist at your tax home: I understand you may need to get healthcare on the road, but you should always see your primary care providers for routine services and as much as possible otherwise.

9) Volunteer and civic activities: If you currently participate in such activities, continue to do so or try to maintain the connection. If you don't participate in these activities, it may be a good time to look into it.

10) Register all vehicles in your tax home state: Despite that fact that you're traveling, you should register all vehicles you own in your tax home state and keep them registered there.

If you're going to satisfy factor 2, then it makes perfectly good sense to also satisfy factor 3, and you can see the discussion above for details on how to accomplish this. Now, it's been my experience that most travelers would like to avoid satisfying factor 2. That is, they'd prefer not to have duplicative expenses. This has become more and more common as the economic circumstances and proliferation of Vendor Management Services have put downward pressure on bill rates making traveling healthcare assignments less lucrative. The only combination of factors that would allow this to happen is 1 and 3, conducting business at the declared tax home and not abandoning it.

Factor 1: Performing Business in the Vicinity of the Declared Tax Home

I chose to tackle factor 1 last because of its subjective nature. Unlike factors 2 and 3 which are straightforward and clear no matter the scenario, the method for satisfying factor 1 may vary depending on whether or not you're aiming to meet 2 or 3 of factors in the 3 Factor Threshold Test.

Qualifying under the 2 factor scenario will require that a significant portion of your income be derived at your tax home. Working some periodic PRN shifts will most likely not suffice. Joseph Smith, a tax consultant specializing traveler tax issues, offers two examples to qualify for tax free stipends using factors 1 and 3 on his web site traveltax.com. In the first example, a young nurse working a permanent job and living at her parent's home for free decides to take up travel nursing. She works out a deal with her current hospital employer to return and work there for three months each year during their busy winter season. She also maintains her personal ties to the tax home, returns there between assignments, and conducts her personal business there. When she's traveling, she makes sure to take temporary assignments in new locations and does not stay in any one location for more than one assignment.

In the second example, a traveling healthcare professional continually returns to Phoenix, Arizona for travel assignments on an annual basis for several years. He then establishes Phoenix as his tax home by first paying taxes on all of the tax free stipends he receives during an assignment there, and by second establishing personal and personal business ties in the Phoenix area. He then purchases an RV and takes travel assignments throughout the country making sure to not return to the same metropolitan areas too often. He returns to Phoenix on an at least an annual basis to complete an assignment and pays full taxes on the income he earns there.

There is a very important principle at play in both of these examples. These travelers are earning a significant percentage of their income at their tax home both as a percentage of their total annual income and relative to any one place that they travel to take an assignment. They also pay income taxes when they work at their tax home. By working 3 months out of the year at their tax home, they are earning approximately 25% of their annual income there. In addition, by never working more than one assignment in any given location they ensure that the income they earn at their tax home is very significant relative to any other location they work. If all of the assignments they take are 3 months or less, they ensure that the ratio between what they earn at home versus what they earn in any other single location is approximately 50/50.

This is important to ensure that the IRS does not rule that your tax home has shifted to another location because you perform a majority of your work at that location. Remember, in the scenario we're discussing, you are not incurring duplicative expenses. Therefore, if you do not ensure that a sizeable portion of your income comes from your declared tax home, the IRS may determine that you're maintaining your tax home for personal rather than business reasons.

Now, I have seen many travelers make the claim that "performing part of your business in the area" could be satisfied by activities other than work. For example, in their book "Travel Nurse Insights" Barry and Donna Padgett state, "Keep in mind that your 'business' activity is not just your work as a traveler. It is all aspects of your business life, such as banking, mortgage payments, doctor's appointments, purchasing a car, paying insurance premiums, repairs of all kinds, etc." They go on to recommend that you keep such activities in the area of your declared tax home as a means to meeting the business requirement.

I have seen similar claims made on message boards and have spoken to travelers who claimed the same. I have been unable to determine where this information comes from as I have never seen a citation. Let me be clear, this information is not correct. These and other such activities do not constitute business activities as the IRS views them. Therefore, they will not count towards meeting the first factor of the three factor threshold test. Such activities would however be considered personal business and could be used to satisfy the third factor determining whether or not the taxpayer has abandoned the declared tax home.

The IRS is very clear that they intend "your business" to mean work, or something from which you derive income. Consider the following example taken straight from IRS Publication 463:

> You are single and live in Boston in an apartment you rent. You have worked for your employer in Boston for a number of years. Your employer enrolls you in a 12-month executive training program. You do not expect to return to work in Boston after you complete your training.

> During your training, you do not do any work in Boston. Instead, you receive classroom and on-the-job training throughout the United States. You keep your apartment in Boston and return to it frequently. You use your apartment to conduct your personal business. You also keep up your community contacts in Boston. When you complete your training, you are transferred to Los Angeles.

You do not satisfy factor (1) because you did not work in Boston. You satisfy factor (2) because you had duplicate living expenses. You also satisfy factor (3) because you did not abandon your apartment in Boston as your main home, you kept your community contacts, and you frequently returned to live in your apartment. Therefore, you have a tax home in Boston.

You can see here that the IRS clearly states, "You do not satisfy factor (1) because you did not work in Boston." Work is the key to satisfying factor 1. There have also been many court cases that have treated "business activity" as income deriving activity. For example, the Markey and Fisher cases both defined it as such (Blum and Coppage). In addition, note the IRS states that, "You use your apartment to conduct your personal business." They are clearly differentiating between business and personal business.

One might argue that this is splitting hairs and taking it a bit too far. However, this is a very important distinction to make. You must meet at least two of the criteria to qualify. If you are confused into thinking that activities such as where you locate your bank account are going to satisfy factor 1, then you could be in for big trouble. You may erroneously believe that you are satisfying both factors 1 and 3 when you are really only satisfying factor 3.

As you can see, avoiding the duplicative expenses factor can be very tricky. However, if you do maintain legitimate duplicative expenses, then maintaining your tax home is much easier. Furthermore, if you are able to maintain duplicative expenses, then you should also maintain strong personal ties to your tax home. In other words, satisfy factors 2 and 3, and use factor 1 as a safeguard if you are able to do so. At the same time, make sure that you move around enough to ensure that your employment cannot be classified as indeterminate. This strategy is best for ensuring that you're able to continue accepting tax free money without penalty.

If you choose to qualify for factors 2 and 3 and want to use factor 1 to provide further credence to your case, then it is highly recommended that you maintain employment, whether permanent or PRN, in the vicinity of your declared tax home. This would allow you to occasionally return home and work in an effort to ensure that the requirement is met. Note that I said "effort". These tests are subjective and in such cases the IRS is going to consider all the "facts and circumstances."

That said, in my opinion, the best option is for you to sign on as a PRN worker directly with the employer you're leaving in order to take travel assignments, or some other employer in the area. They'll typically have requirements for maintaining PRN status which usually involves working a specified number of shifts during a specified period of time. For example, they may require that you work at least 2 shifts every 6 weeks to maintain your PRN status.

The upside with signing on directly with a hospital (or other healthcare provider) to work PRN is that you'll be assured that you get the work you need to meet the requirement. In a sense, the shifts are a sure thing. You're on the schedule to work and the shifts are rarely cancelled. In addition, you'll also be on that employer's books as an employee. The downside is that you'll have limited flexibility. You'll need to meet the scheduling requirements in order to maintain your PRN status. This may require trips home in the middle of your travel assignments.

Another more flexible option would be to sign on with a local PRN staffing agency in the area of your designated tax home. In this scenario, you'll give the agency advanced notice of the days that you'll be available to work, and they'll attempt to get you scheduled for shifts accordingly. You should give them ample notice to ensure the best results. You'll also want to be sure to maintain your credentials with the agency so that you're always in compliance. This will ensure that you're able to quickly make yourself available to pick up shifts when you're home. If you do not maintain your credentials, you may miss your chance to pick up shifts during your windows between travel assignments.

The upside to working with a PRN agency is that you'll have increased flexibility. Most agencies don't have any scheduling requirements, and they're happy to try to schedule you around your availability. The downside is that the shifts aren't guaranteed, so you may not get any work at all. However, this may not be a deal breaker. Your concerted effort to obtain work in the area may be enough to qualify, and you should also be on the agency's books as an employee as long as you keep your credentials current with them.

Chapter 12: Tax Free Myths and Special Circumstances

The 50 Mile Myth

A common fallacy that you will most certainly hear with regard to qualifying for tax free stipends is "The 50 Mile Rule." This too is prominent among both travelers and recruiters. This "rule" is often said to allow taxpayers to accept tax free stipends as long as the assignment they're taking is 50 miles or more from their tax home. This is not correct. The IRS makes no such determination. There is no such rule. Refer to the discussion above for a clear understanding as to how you can qualify to accept tax free stipends.

Remember, IRS Publication 463 states that you can accept tax free stipends if "you need to sleep or rest to meet the demands of your work while away from home. " It does not set a specific distance for what would constitute your need to sleep or rest. So where does this myth come from? Joseph Smith, a tax consultant specializing in traveler tax issues, offers 3 possible origins (traveltax.com). First, there is a 50 mile rule for state legislators to determine if they are away from home and able to accept their per diem payments. Second, in order to write off moving deductions, the IRS requires that a taxpayer's new commute to work be more than 50 miles farther than their old commute. Third, many companies and agencies have utilized the 50 mile rule as an internal policy for so long that it has come to be viewed as an IRS regulation. Elaborating on this third possible origin provides some useful insights on the industry.

The 50 mile rule is not just imposed by agencies; it's also imposed by some hospitals. There are several reasons for the policy. First, it serves as a potential safeguard for agencies in case they are audited. While the 50 mile rule may not be a rule established and recognized by the IRS, consistently enforcing such a rule does, none the less, give the impression that an agency is attempting to ensure compliance with the spirit of IRS regulations. Whether or not the IRS views it favorably in an audit is another story.

Second, agencies may want to demarcate between PRN, local contracts, and travel contracts. There are often times different bill rates for PRN, local contracts, and travel contracts at the same facility. If an agency has one rule for all facilities it can make their internal processes and procedures more efficient than if they were to require their recruiters to check each contract to determine the rules.

In addition, hospitals regularly include a distance rule for travel contracts in their contracts with agencies. I've seen the distance requirements set at 50, 75, and 100 miles. I have heard two reasons given for these requirements, and I'm sure there may be others. First, this is a cost issue for hospitals. PRN bill rates are typically 2%-3% less than travel contract bill rates, and I've seen them be up to 7% less. In addition, PRN shifts aren't guaranteed while travel contracts offer guaranteed shifts. Therefore, PRN shifts give the hospital flexibility to cancel shifts which can also save them money. A hospital will typically try and fill its staffing needs at the lowest possible cost and would prefer anyone within a 50, 75, or 100 mile radius to sign up for PRN shifts.

Second, the hospital's staff also has a stake in ensuring that travelers come from outside a specified distance and, despite popular opinions to the contrary, the hospital has a vested interest in keeping its staff happy. The issue is that travelers often have guaranteed hours. As a result, staff members may get called off in lieu of calling off a traveler if census drops. This doesn't happen very often, but it can and does happen. If the traveler is called off and the staff member is allowed to come in, then the hospital runs the risk of paying for both. As a result, it's in the best interest of the staff to have local health care professionals signed up for more flexible PRN shifts.

No matter the reason that the 50 mile myth exists, or the explanation given to justify it, it's important that you not put any faith into it. Again, at its worst the myth is claimed to allow people to accept tax free stipends as long as their tax address is more than 50 miles from the facility. This claim can get people into a lot of trouble.

Making $10 per Hour: Maximizing Your Tax Free Stipends

When it comes to taxes, there is no doubt a myriad of unique circumstances and issue that can exist. Trying to deal with them all here would be futile. However, there are three unique circumstances that are quite common, low hourly wages (maximized tax free stipends), traveling couples, and independent contractors.

As we discussed in the section on compensation packages, agencies can split up the compensation pie in many different ways. As a result, some agencies will offer a base rate of as low as $10 per hour. You're probably thinking that there is no possible way that you'd work for $10 per hour. But remember, you need to be less concerned with the hourly rate and more concerned with overall value of the entire compensation package. For example, one agency might be offering a $30 per hour base rate plus the equivalent of $12 per hour for stipends for a total value of $42 per hour, while another agency might be offering a $10 per hour base rate plus the equivalent of $35 per hour in stipend money for a total value of $45 per hour. The issue we'll address here is whether or not it's okay for you to take a rate as low as $10 per hour.

Let's look at this from the perspective of the two parties involved, the agency and the traveler. According to the National Organization of Travel Healthcare Organizations (NATHO), a nonprofit association of travel healthcare organizations, agencies should indeed be offering a minimum base rate wage that is higher than $10 per hour for most workers. NATHO states that the agencies should pay an hourly rate that is in line with fair market value for someone in the respective profession. That means that the professional could reasonably expect to make the taxable hourly rate, not including the value of the stipends offered by the agency. From this perspective, paying a nurse or physical therapist a $10 per hour base rate isn't going to cut it.

Despite this advice from NATHO to its members, tax advisor Joseph Smith states that it's okay for travelers to accept low wages (traveltax.com). He does point out that you'd have a higher likelihood of being audited, but as long you had a solid tax home and had properly accounted for your taxes, you should be fine. Remember, if you're making a base rate of $10 per hour, you may be getting the equivalent of $40-$50 per hour in tax free stipends. You'd want to be certain that you had all your records in order to justify those expenses, an issue we'll cover shortly in the chapter on record keeping.

Now we're left reconciling these two divergent viewpoints. One side says it's okay, the other recommends against it. However, Joseph Smith also asserts that he'd rather travelers "work with companies that show better business consciences." His reasons for saying this are the same reasons that reconcile the differences here. You see, providing such a low hourly rate along with huge stipends is a form of wage recharacterization, which is against IRS rules. In this case, the only way that someone in this profession would accept the job would be because of the stipends and there would be no way that a nurse, for example, would accept the straight rate of $10 per hour. As a result, the IRS may claim that the agency is recharacterizing the wage as a stipend and the agency would be violating a rule. However, given the standpoint of Joseph Smith, it appears safe to say that the agency may be at risk, and a little unethical for that matter, while the traveler just needs to cover their bases with documentation proving the tax free money went to cover legitimate costs.

Why would agencies put themselves at risk this way? For the same reasons that any other tax violator does it, either they're unaware of the rules, or they're seeking a financial advantage. Anyone can start agency and one doesn't have to be an expert in all of these issues to do so. Meanwhile, those that are aware are doing so for a competitive edge. As mentioned previously, the lower the taxable hourly rate for the traveler, the lower the payroll costs to the agency. They can pocket this money or offer it to the traveler as an incentive to get the traveler to sign on with them. They can also highlight the higher net pay that a traveler will receive from them due to the lower taxes that the traveler will incur.

You'll find that smaller agencies are more apt to offer these low hourly wages. The biggest businesses in the industry are publicly traded, and/or have investors, and boards of directors. As a result, there are touchy legal issues for the biggest companies. The smaller companies don't have these responsibilities. They also may not be as closely scrutinized as the larger companies. Most large companies are going to have auditors, while the smaller ones may not. In any case, there is no denying that offering these low wages crosses the line into unethical business behavior. As a traveler, you just need to decide if that's an issue for you or not.

And remember, your chances of being audited are real, especially if you're receiving a very low hourly wage coupled with high tax-free stipends. In fact, according to Joseph Smith's October 2012 Newsletter, the IRS is currently auditing at least 12 travel nursing agencies (traveltax.com). Wage recharacterization is one focus of the audit. Furthermore, Joseph Smith states that one agency is considering reissuing W-2s going back 6 years for employees who are not willing or able to provide the agency with receipts to justify the high tax-free stipends the agency provided. If the agency reissues the W2s and the difference between the employees' reported income and the newly reported income is greater than 25%, then the employees may be responsible to pay the IRS additional taxes, penalties, and interest.

This might be confusing for readers who are unfamiliar with these issues, so let's look at an example for clarity's sake. A travel healthcare agency offers a travel contract that pays $10 per hour as the taxable base rate plus the equivalent of $40 per hour in tax-free stipends. The travel healthcare professional accepts the contract and completes it. Of course, both the agency and the travel healthcare professional pay taxes on only the taxable base rate. In addition, the taxable base rate is all that will be reported on the travel healthcare professional's W2. Finally, the healthcare professional reports taxable income from the assignment exactly as stated on the W2 when they complete their taxes at the end of the year.

A couple of years later, the IRS decides to audit the agency and claims that paying the travel healthcare professional $10 per hour appears to be a recharacterization of wages. As a result, the agency will be subject to penalties and additional taxes. The agency contacts the travel healthcare professional and requests receipts and other pertinent documentation in an effort to justify the tax-free payments and avoid the costs. The travel healthcare professional is unable to comply for one reason or another.

The agency then decides to reissue a W2 that increases the taxable base rate and decreases the tax-free stipends by equal amounts in an effort to settle the matter. Of course, this increases the reported income to the IRS. As a result, the agency will be responsible to pay their portion of the payroll taxes and any penalties. Moreover, the travel healthcare professional will also be responsible for additional taxes and penalties as long as the difference between what was originally reported and the newly reported taxable income is greater than 25%.

What does all this mean for you? First, you open yourself to increased risk of audit if you accept really low hourly wages and really high stipends. Second, this may be okay as long as you maintain an ironclad tax-home, maintain your status as a temporary employee, and keep excellent records to justify the tax-free payments. Another possibility is that you accept the tax-free money but declare a portion of it, or all of it, as income on your annual tax return. This would result in your paying the taxes at tax time as opposed to paying them out of your paychecks.

Taxes and Traveling Couples

For traveling couples, most everything is normal with taxes until you get to the housing issue. Joseph Smith offers three scenarios pertaining to married couples on his web site. The first involves a couple who accept contracts through the same staffing agency with one accepting the company provided housing and the other taking the lodging stipend. This is a sales pitch that recruiters often make to traveling couples. They highlight the fact that one of them can get the tax free money and therefore keep a higher percentage of their gross pay. Unfortunately, according to Joseph Smith this is not correct. The stipend would indeed have to be taxed.

The second scenario involves a traveling couple who accept assignments through the same agency and both take the housing stipend. In this case, Joseph Smith asserts that the stipends are not taxable. The third scenario involves a traveling couple who accept assignments with different agencies and one of them takes agency provided housing and the other takes the lodging stipend. Joseph Smith asserts that the lodging stipend is not taxable. I would also assume that a couple working through different agencies could also both accept non-taxable lodging stipends.

Smith states that the explanation for these conclusions would be too long to go into on his site, and we'll take his word for it. It's also not clear if conclusions remain the same if the scenarios pertain to an unmarried couple. However, NATHO offers general information to travelers on the topic. They state that if a company has provided housing to one traveler, and knows the other traveler is staying there, the company would be obligated to tax the lodging stipend. They also assert that if the travelers provide their own housing, then the company must tax one of the stipends if the company knows that both travelers are staying there. Again, this is regardless of whether or not the couple is married.

All things considered, I think it's fair to say that there is no gaming the system when it comes to shared housing with the same agency. It would appear as though couples may both be able to receive non-taxable stipends or have one member take company provided housing and the other take the non-taxable stipend if they were working with different agencies. Again, I highly recommend that you rely on the advice of a tax advisor experienced in these matters.

Independent Contractors

The third unique tax circumstance that we'll discuss is that of the independent contractor. Let me first be short and to the point. The vast majority of healthcare workers do not meet the requirements set by the IRS to be considered independent contractors. All nurses and the vast majority allied healthcare professionals do not qualify as independent contractors. In the healthcare field, only doctors and dentists stand a chance at meeting the requirements for consideration as an independent contractor.

You might be asking why we're spending any time on this at all then. Unfortunately, many agencies staff healthcare professionals other than doctors and dentists as independent contractors. Furthermore, many books on the issue of travel nursing, or travel healthcare in general espouse it as a viable option. You may even know someone who has done it themselves. None of this means that it's accepted by the IRS.

According to the IRS, "The general rule is that an individual is an independent contractor if the payer has the right to control or direct only the result of the work and not what will be done and how it will be done." The main focus here should be on the part of this statement that says, "payer has the right to control *only* the result of the work..." Note the emphasis added by me on "only." In the case of nurses and the vast majority of allied health workers much more than just the outcomes of work are controlled by the contracted facility. For example, in the case of nurses, the hospital will determine the hours worked as well as break times. In addition, there are managers and doctors at the hospital who are supervising the nurse's work and nurses must seek the permission of a physician for decisions outside the nurse's scope of practice. There's nothing independent about this.

Despite this, some agencies still place nurses and allied professionals as independent contractors. To me, the funniest thing about them doing so is that it breaks another standard rule regarding independent contractors. You see, the vast majority of healthcare organizations that utilize agencies require the agencies to carry professional liability and workers compensation insurance for all agency staff. Therefore, there is no way that the individual could possibly be considered an independent contractor because covering such items is a violation of the rules regarding independent contractors.

You may also find hospitals and other healthcare providers who are willing to bring people on as independent contractors directly without an agency in the middle. However, the same rules still apply. If the payer controls anything other than the results of the work, then the situation does not meet the requirements for consideration as an independent contractor. Just because a hospital is willing to do this doesn't make it legal. And both parties could be subject to penalties.

So why does the treatment of healthcare professionals as independent contractor persist? In my opinion, the simple answer is that it's easier and cheaper for the payer, i.e. the agency or the hospital. For example, when an agency treats the worker as an independent contractor, they don't have to deal with payroll taxes, worker compensation, disability, unemployment, or liability insurance. They also don't have to deal with the complicated compensation package that travelers receive which splits money up over various categories and provides various services like housing and travel arrangements. Instead, the agency simply pays an hourly rate to the independent contractor, and the contractor is responsible for everything else. For the independent contractor, handling everything else presents a huge burden.

Independent contractors are really operating their own business in the truest sense. They pay the self-employment tax which accounts for the Social Security and Medicare payments typically made by the employer. They are required to file quarterly estimated tax payments on IRS form 1040-ES, as well as annual tax returns. They are required to carry their own liability insurance. They must keep a very detailed account of all income and expenses in order to write off as much as possible for tax purposes. They must invoice the agency or hospital and run the risk of having to act as a bill collector from the agency or hospital who may pay on normal business terms (i.e. Net 60), or neglect to pay their bills at all. Oh, and let's not forget the fact that you will definitely have to register your business at the federal and state level, and quite possibly the county or local level, in order to legitimately function as an independent contractor. Furthermore, agencies don't typically act as advisors for independent contractors, so you're on your own.

Given the circumstances, I fail to see why any healthcare professional, other than a doctor, would even be interested in working as an independent contractor. Many would argue that the independent contractor makes more money. I'd have to disagree. Any difference in gross figures is typically entirely soaked up by the additional costs of being a contractor. If there is any net revenue beyond that, it's not worth the extra time and effort that contactors have to go through to keep on top of the business issues. There's a reason that the Small Business Administration lists "Savings in labor costs" as one of its top advantages of using independent contractors. It's cheaper for the employer.

Money issues aside, we're still left with the fact that the vast majority of healthcare professionals don't qualify under the IRS definition of an independent contractor. Furthermore, there are fewer and fewer opportunities for them in the industry. Most hospitals will not consider them directly and also forbid agencies from treating agency employees as contractors. In addition, the Joint Commission on Accreditation of Healthcare Organizations (JCAHO) is now scrutinizing agency use of independent contractors and will not certify agencies paying W2 workers as independent contractors. So again, I see no reason why anyone would be interested in going this route.

Chapter 13: Record Keeping for Tax Purposes

Now that we have had a detailed discussion about what it takes to qualify for tax free stipends, as well as some of the common unique circumstances, you can see that despite the subjective aspects of the determination process, the requirements to qualify are quite clear. There is no trick that allows one to circumvent the entire system. Travelers need to have a plan and stick to it in order to ensure that they qualify, and continue to qualify, for tax free stipends. Travelers also need to keep accurate records so that they can quickly and efficiently complete their taxes, or transmit the records quickly and efficiently to their tax preparer.

Maintaining adequate records for tax purposes is extremely important to maximizing your potential and minimizing your input as a travel healthcare professional. It will not only ensure that you are prepared for an audit should one occur, but it will also ensure that you are able to quickly and conveniently complete your own taxes or transmit the required records to your tax advisor. You do not want to be stuck scrambling at the last minute to generate adequate documents. This often requires that you call all the agencies that you worked with and repeat conversations and actions that you've already taken. It's very important to remember that you'll want to keep all of your records for at least 6 years. In this Chapter we'll discuss the important documents, tactics, and tools you need to get organized.

The Contract for Tax Purposes

As mentioned previously, it is of the utmost importance that you receive and keep copies of all your contracts. For tax purposes, you should make sure that all contracts clearly state and contain the following:

1) Start Date
2) End Date
3) Name of Facility
4) Complete Address of Facility
5) Taxable Hourly Rate
6) Amounts of ALL Tax Free Stipends to be Paid

Again, the contract provides you with hard proof that your employment is realistically expected to be temporary as opposed to indefinite. The start and end dates make this perfectly clear. It also verifies the work location is in an area that requires you to rest or sleep to meet the demands of your job while traveling. Finally, the contract clearly quantifies the amount that you are to receive in tax free stipends. This is important because this information will not appear on your W2. Your W2 will only show your taxable earnings. So having the contract allows you to easily quantify the totals of the tax free money. There are many important non-tax related aspects of a travel contract, and we'll discuss those later in a section devoted to the topic.

Pay Stubs

While many may disagree, I would argue that keeping your pay stubs is also an important aspect of maintaining accurate records. There are two primary reasons for this. First, the contract provides evidence that there was an agreement, but does not provide proof that the contract was completed. Contracts can go uncompleted for any number of reasons. If a contract ends early, the chances of you receiving written notification to update your records are slim and none. You are most likely going to pick up another contract, perhaps at another hospital in the same location. This may give the illusion that you were working two contracts at the same time in the same location which would also give the illusion that you were collecting double the stipends. Pay stubs provide a backup record.

Second, it's very possible that you receive less or more in stipend money through the course of your contract. Most, if not all, agencies will only pay stipend money for hours worked. In some cases, the stipends are paid daily. In which case, if you miss a shift or get cancelled, the stipend money for that day would be docked. In other cases, the stipends are prorated by the hour and if your time sheet is short of the contracted hours, then the agency will dock the stipend that they pay by the prorated amount. In this case, you may actually earn less in stipend money over the course of your assignment than the contract indicates. However, you will still incur the same costs related to the tax free money. You are still paying for lodging and M&IE. As a result, you may be able to write off these amounts on your taxes to increase your tax savings.

Furthermore, some agencies will also pay you additional stipend money for working additional hours. In this case, you may end up earning more tax free money than is indicated by the contract. While this may be great on the surface, it may result in your receiving tax free stipends that exceed the GSA limits. You'll want to be sure that you're paying taxes on the difference if you wish to remain squeaky clean.

While both prorating by the hour and paying extra stipend money is probably in violation of tax laws, they both happen none the less, and prorating is very common. It could be argued that they both constitute a recharacterization of wages because they essentially treat the tax free stipends as an hourly wage. That doesn't change the fact they're being paid to you that way and maintaining your pay stub records is something I believe is worth your while.

The best case scenario is to ensure that your agency is mailing the pay stubs to your tax home address. You can easily save them if this is the case. However, many agencies rely on electronic reporting of pay stubs. They provide you with a user name and password to log on to their payroll system and access your pay stubs. The advantage is that you have immediate access from anywhere you have an internet connection. The disadvantage is that you won't be able to conveniently send them to a tax advisor. Also, you will undoubtedly work with multiple agencies over the course of the year, so having your pay stubs in multiple locations will be disorganized. To address this, you can print your pay stubs to PDF and save them in a folder on your computer. We'll discuss this and provide a detailed step by step process for accomplishing this in the section on managing your credentials and documentation.

Travel/Transportation Records

The vast majority of travel contracts are going to include a travel stipend. Different agencies pay these out in different ways. No matter how they are paid, you must justify receiving them with a transportation log and/or receipts. This is very different than the lodging and M&IE stipends. Again, lodging and M&IE stipends are typically based off of the GSA guidelines which represent the maximum amount of tax free money that an employer can provide to an employee without requiring receipts. Travel stipends do require some form of justification. Additionally, the travel stipends provided by agencies often don't cover the total cost of travel that travelers incur. Keeping an accurate record of all travel expenses can possibly give the traveler the ability to write off the excess travel expenses on their taxes. On the flip side, without a transportation record you will have to declare the tax free stipend as income and pay taxes on it when you complete your taxes.

There is no one way to keep a record of your travel expenses. However, there is certain information that must be recorded. For example, a mileage log requires a date, a starting location, an ending location, an explanation, and the number of miles driven. It also requires that you record your starting and ending odometer reading for the year (1/1-12/31).

There are many tools available on line to assist you with maintaining your travel and transportation records. Many of them focus on one aspect of traveling or another. For example, many focus only on mileage. I strongly recommend that you keep a comprehensive Travel Expense Record for each assignment. A comprehensive record gives you one location to record all travel associated expenses. And you will undoubtedly require tracking more than just mileage. For example, let's say you drive from North Carolina to Nevada for a travel assignment. You will certainly do more than just drive. You may stop at a hotel or two along the way, tip the bellman, and have a few meals. A comprehensive Travel Expense Record allows you to record all of these costs in one location. IRS Publication 463 provides a detailed sample Traveling Expense and Entertainment Record that is very useful.

Receipts

I have found that there is some confusion on the issue of keeping your receipts. I believe the confusion originates with the fact that you are not required by the IRS to keep receipts for the lodging and Meals and Incidental stipends that you receive. Remember, the rates set by the IRS for these stipends are the maximum amounts that can be provided without receipts for justification. Additionally, you're not required to keep receipts for gas when driving your own vehicle for business. Remember, the IRS annually publishes the amount that can be declared for using your own vehicle for business purposes on a per-mile basis. As a result, you'll find many people who correctly assert that you are not required to keep receipts for these items.

However, I believe receipts are important for two reasons. First, they are required to justify additional travel nursing expenses as well as miscellaneous expenses such as hotels while traveling to and from an assignment. For example, if you're driving from North Carolina to Nevada, then you're most likely going to have a few meals and stay in a couple of hotels. It's very rare for agencies to cover such costs. Therefore, they can be written off if you keep the receipts.

Second, if an agency pays a stipend that is lower than the maximum amount allowed by the GSA, then you may be able to claim a write off for the difference between what the agency provides and what you actually spend. For example, it's fairly common for larger agencies to pay $250 per week for M&IE. However, the maximum M&IE rate for the year 2012 in Los Angeles, CA is $71 per day. That's $497 per week. If you spent more than the $250 that the agency provided, then you would need to have receipts to justify the write off.

Keeping receipts can be a daunting task. However, I personally believe that it's well worth it. Remember, receipts are required for travel expenses (except mileage which is covered by the mileage log) and miscellaneous expenses. If you get in the habit of saving all your receipts, it will become an afterthought. You'll want to keep the travel receipts, miscellaneous receipts, and M&IE receipts separate to stay organized so that you can remain quick and efficient come tax time.

How you do this is up to you. I worked with one traveler who kept each classification of receipt in a separate Ziploc bag; the kind that have the film on the outside that you can write on. She kept a set of bags for each assignment and wrote the dates of the assignment and the classification of receipts on each bag. Come tax time, she was prepared to send everything to her tax advisor with minimal effort.

We have provided a helpful list of receipts to keep in Appendix C of this book.

Tax Tools and Advisors

One of our main goals in this book is to ensure minimal effort on your part. Keeping your records organized in real time is a huge step toward that goal. You do not want to scramble around at tax time trying to compile a year's worth of travel tax records. You will inevitably run into road blocks that you would not have encountered had you kept your records in real time. This will cost you time and trouble. Another way to cut down on your effort in this area is to get a tax advisor.

If we've learned one thing from this section on taxes, it's that taxes for a traveler are very complex. In addition to what we've discussed, you will most likely have to contend with filing in multiple states. Each state has its own rules and regulations. Making sense of them here would be futile both because they are so extensive and because they are constantly changing. For all of these reasons, finding a tax advisor experienced with these issues will definitely be worth the cost.

You should be very selective with your choice. Make sure that the person you select has extensive experience with these issues. Ask them if they have gone through the audit process and what the results were. Ask them if they guarantee their work and find out how many years of experience they have with these issues. My personal recommendation is the team at TravelTax. They know travel inside and out and are very good at what they do.

Conclusion:

Maintaining your tax home is important when travel nursing. Given the reduction in bill rates over the last 5 years, you need the benefit of tax free money to increase the financial viability of travel nursing. Furthermore, you'll be hard pressed to find agencies that are willing to pay you any other way.

Remember, the primary concern is to ensure that you maintain your temporary worker status so that your tax home doesn't shift to your travel assignment location. As long as your tax home doesn't shift you will remain eligible for the 3 Factor Threshold Test. You'll need to determine the best strategy for meeting the requirements of the 3 Factor Threshold Test given your unique circumstances.

Section 6: Compensation: Determining What You Want

The Compensation Options

Now that you have a fairly solid understanding of the travel compensation package and related tax issues, we can move on to discussing the various compensation options. We'll look at each variable in detail so you can approach the compensation package with complete confidence. You should understand these variables and know what you're looking for before you start contacting agencies so that you can minimize the time spent in accordance with your overall plan of attack. Again, you'll want to be ready to take the lead when speaking with the agencies so that you can easily weed out the ones that don't offer what you're looking for and stick with the ones that do.

Chapter 14: Lodging: Financial Considerations

In every survey that I've seen, housing is cited by the largest percentage of respondents as being the single most important component of the travel nursing pay package. For those who take company provided housing it's understandable why this is the case. I have heard some housing horror stories. From housing located in unsafe neighborhoods, to housing with bed bugs and mold, I've heard it all. There's nothing worse than traveling 1500 miles to find lodging accommodations akin to those in the slums of Kabul, Afghanistan. At the same time, you could get set up in some of the finest digs in town. However, before you even get to that point, you have to make a decision as to whether you're going to take company-provided-housing or take the lodging stipend and secure your own housing.

You must first make sure that your own personal finances are adequate for securing your own housing should you choose to do so. If you're very flexible and you're willing to rent a room in someone's home or if you have family or friends that you can stay with in the area, then you need to determine whether or not you can meet the financial obligations for these unique circumstances.

If you're willing to utilize Extended Stay or Extended Stay type accommodations and/or motels, then you just need to make sure that you have the cash or credit available to pay for the accommodations for the first couple of weeks of your travel nursing assignment until your first paycheck comes in. These housing options tend to charge your debit or credit card on a weekly basis. Your first paycheck will typically be deposited on the second or third Friday of your contract depending on whether or not your travel nursing agency pays weekly or bi-weekly.

If you're only willing to stay in an apartment, then you'd have to be able to pass the credit check and come up with the first month's rent and the security deposit at a minimum. In addition, you'll need to furnish the apartment which will lead to additional costs. If your finances are not adequate to handle any of these options, then it's best to focus only on travel contracts and agencies that provide housing. There's no need to waste your time on anything else.

If you do have the financial capability to secure your own housing, then your next step is to determine what type of housing accommodations you're willing to consider. I've worked with many travel nurses who were very flexible when it came to housing. Some were willing to stay in Extended Stay Hotels, apartments in lower-income areas, and even rent a room in someone's house or apartment. I worked with some travel nurses who didn't even bother to look into housing until they had arrived at their travel assignment destination. They just found an Extended Stay hotel for the short-term, and then found someplace cheap for the duration. If this is you, you're better off finding your own housing. You'll almost definitely find something for cheaper than the travel nursing agency's housing and less than the stipend being offered. In addition, you will probably spend minimal time finding it.

Most people have more stringent housing requirements. Flying by the seat of their pants and a guest apartment above someone's garage just isn't going to cut it. If this is you, then chances are that more time is going to be required for you to lock down lodging accommodations on your own, and in my view time is money. When it's all said and done, you may be able to get a better deal if you take company provided housing.

Financial Considerations of Lodging

Once you've determined the housing options you're willing to consider, you need to consider the housing and lodging stipend options that are available with the various agencies you're speaking with to determine if there will be a financial advantage to securing your own lodging. Different agencies handle lodging in different ways. Some don't offer lodging and therefore only offer the lodging stipend.

Some agencies are flexible and offer many lodging options. They may let you select the housing option that best suits your needs and then adjust your pay rate in accord with the cost, or you can take a lodging stipend instead. Some agencies offer lodging but don't offer any choices; you take what they give you, or you take the stipend.

Furthermore, some agencies offer the maximum allowable stipend for a given area, while others offer less than the maximum allowable stipend for a given area. Small and mid-sized companies tend to offer higher stipends and either flexibility or no housing at all, while larger companies tend to offer lower stipends with limited or no choices for the housing they offer. Your financial considerations are going to be impacted by how the travel nursing agency you're working with handles these issues.

First, let's take a look at the financial considerations as they pertain to the amount of the stipend being offered. Remember, the lodging stipend is the maximum amount that can be provided in a given area without requiring receipts for justification. So agencies can offer the maximum amount or less. Larger agencies tend to offer less than the maximum along with a higher taxable hourly rate. Smaller agencies tend to offer the highest stipend they can, given the constraints of the bill rate, along with a lower taxable hourly rate.

For example, the maximum lodging stipend in San Diego, CA as of July 16, 2012 is $133 per day. That's $4034 per month, $931 per week, and $25.86 per hour assuming a 36 hour work week. Theoretically, this is what an agency could pay for a lodging stipend. However, they most likely wouldn't be able to offer such a high stipend given today's low bill rates. If the agency were to pay the maximum stipend in this case, then they wouldn't have enough money left over to cover the rest of the compensation package and various other costs. Remember, the amount that an agency can pay for any given assignment is contingent on the bill rate, the rate they're able to charge the hospital for the travel nurse's time.

Now let's start off with a simplified example to get an idea of how the size of the stipend being offered impacts the financial considerations. Let's say a travel nursing agency is offering you a lodging stipend of $20 per hour for a 36 hour per week contract. This is the equivalent of $720 per week and $3096 per month (4.3 weeks in a month!). However, if you choose to take their company provided housing, then it will cost $2000 per month and the remaining $1096 that's left over from the lodging stipend they were offering will be added to your hourly wage.

Let's assume that you are able to find your own housing for $2000. If you instead choose to take the company provided housing, then you would end up paying taxes on an additional $1096 that you wouldn't have been paying taxes on if you chose to take the stipend and secure your own housing. At a modest 25% tax, that's $274 per month ($1096*.25) that you would save if you secured your own housing. The way I view it, $274 per month then becomes the cost of having the agency secure your housing. In addition, you may save even more money if you're able to find housing accommodations for less than $2000 per month.

Now let's look at an even simpler example in which the agency is offering a $2000 monthly lodging stipend, or company provided housing. That's it, there is no flexibility. This is the type of scenario you can typically expect from a larger agency. Your financial consideration is simple here. If you can find housing on your own for less than $2000 per month, then you'll save money. Otherwise, it's worth your while to take the company's lodging.

Before we continue, it's important to point out the importance of maintaining proper tax records here again. While it is true that the GSA rates for lodging and M&IE are the maximum rates that employers can provide without requiring receipts for justification, I still recommend keeping proper receipts to justify all tax free money. For some reason, I just think you're safer if you do. Again, the choice is yours.

As mentioned previously, smaller and mid-sized agencies tend to offer larger lodging stipends while larger agencies offer smaller lodging stipends. Remember, if a larger stipend is offered, then a smaller hourly rate is to be expected and vice-versa. In addition, smaller and mid-sized agencies tend to offer several housing options while larger agencies give you what they give you. For these reasons, I believe weighing your options with smaller travel nursing agencies is the way to go, while taking company provided lodging from larger travel nursing agencies is the way to go. Let's look at a couple of scenarios to see how this plays out.

Scenario 1: This is the typical small to mid-sized travel nursing agency scenario. The agency is offering a set of housing options for you to choose from. First, they're offering a housing stipend of $3000.

Second, if you choose to take company provided housing, then they'll offer a range of housing options. If the housing they provide costs less than the housing stipend they're offering, they'll add the difference to your taxable hourly rate.

The first housing option the agency offers is a very nice 1 bedroom apartment for $2400 per month. It includes everything you need. That leaves $600 per month to be added to your hourly rate. Therefore, you're going to get taxed on $600 that you wouldn't have otherwise been taxed on if you were to secure housing on your own at the same cost. At a conservative 27% tax rate, that's $162 per month, or $486 for the total 13 week contract, that you lose to taxes. $486 then becomes the cost to have the agency provide the housing, again assuming that you can locate housing for the same cost as the agency.

The second housing option the agency offers is an Extended Stay Hotel for $1800 per month. It includes everything you need. That leaves $1200 per month to be added to your hourly rate. Therefore, you're going to get taxed on $1200 that you wouldn't have otherwise been taxed on if you were able to secure housing on your own at the same cost. At a conservative 27% tax rate, that's $324 per month, or $972 for the total 13 week contract, that you lose to taxes. $972 then becomes the cost to have the agency provide the housing, again assuming that you can locate housing for the same cost as the agency.

It behooves you to consider your options in such scenarios. As a result of the large lodging stipend being offered, you stand to save a lot of money if you're able to secure your own housing.

Given our previous discussions on the subject, you may notice that the travel nursing agency in Scenario 1 may be guilty of wage recharacterization. They shifted money from the stipend to your wage. Many agencies do this. Again, this is not a risk to you but it is a risk to the agency. This is why you'll typically tend to find rates quoted in this manner at smaller and mid-sized agencies. Smaller and mid-sized travel nursing agencies typically don't have as much oversight in terms of investors, stock holders and auditors. The larger agencies on the other hand do have to contend with this oversight. Therefore, they tend to offer the lodging stipend and the housing for the same value as we'll demonstrate in Scenario 2.

Scenario 2: This is the typical scenario for a large travel nursing agency. In this scenario, the agency offers a very basic choice between a $2000 per month lodging stipend, or a 1 bedroom fully furnished apartment. The financial considerations in this scenario are very basic. You simply need to determine if you're able and willing to secure your own lodging accommodations for less than $2000 per month. If you can find something for $1400 per month, then you pocket an additional $600 per month that you wouldn't have otherwise received if you took the company provided housing.

Again, the larger agencies are less flexible with their lodging offerings for two reasons. First and foremost, they can't risk getting tagged by the IRS for recharacterizing wages. If they tell you that they'll transfer money from your stipend to your wage if they find housing for cheaper than the stipend, then they're guilty. If they pay taxable wages that are unreasonably low for a normal employee in the field and make up for it with a high stipend, then they're guilty. The second reason for their inflexible lodging offering is that it's just plain easier for them to deal with.

My experience tells me that you should always take company provided housing from larger agencies unless you're going to be very flexible with housing and you're willing to live in cheaper accommodations. Larger agencies always seem to offer excellent value for the housing they provide. They typically offer fully furnished , 1 bedroom apartments with all utilities covered in very nice locations for much less than you'd be able to secure on your own, and for much less than their smaller and mid-sized competitors.

I speculate that there are two possible reasons for this. First, larger agencies are able to sign agreements with national property management companies that mange properties throughout the country. The larger agencies are putting several hundred travelers into housing at any given time. As a result, they end up getting volume discounts. For example, larger agencies my get a 5% discount on the standard rental cost of a 1 bedroom apartment.

This may not sound like much, but it represents a huge difference when compared to what the smaller agency is most likely paying. Apartment complexes typically charge more than the standard rental cost for short-term leases. Short-term leases are typically considered to be anything less than 6 months. As a result, the smaller agency may be paying 5%-10% above the standard price. Therefore, we're talking about differences of hundreds of dollars per month between the 5% discount that larger agencies may be receiving and the 10% premium that smaller agencies may be charged.

The same goes for almost every variable involved in housing. Larger agencies are getting volume discounts on furniture rentals. They're getting discounts on cable TV fees. They may be getting deposits and similar additional costs waived. Larger agencies may even sign long-term leases on apartments in major metropolitan areas where they know that they'll always have a travel nurse in need of housing. This will give them yet another price break.

The second possible explanation for the great housing value offered by large agencies has to do with wage recharacterization issues. As mentioned previously, larger agencies are more cognizant of wage recharacterization risk. Therefore, they tend to be confined with respect to their rate offerings. Remember, according to NATHO agencies are at risk of wage recharacterization if they pay wages that are less than would be accepted by a normal worker in the given field. Additionally, an agency is at risk of wage recharacterization if they lower the stated pay rate to make up for other costs. So what does all this have to do with getting a great deal on housing?

First, bill rates at some hospitals have gone down so low that offering housing, M&IE, travel stipends, and an hourly rate that would be accepted by a normal worker in the given field would not be possible unless the agency was taking very low margins. For example, I was seeing bill rates for hospitals in the Los Angeles area as low as $52 per hour for Registered Nurses in 2011. If an agency offered to provide a fully furnished 1 bedroom apartment in the area, then there wouldn't be enough money left over to pay an hourly wage that would be accepted by a normal Registered Nurse while maintaining standard margin rates for the agency. However, I had travelers telling me that larger agencies were providing the housing and paying a normal hourly rate for those assignments.

Second, let's say that the large agency has offered to pay $26 per hour, plus $250 per week for M&IE, and a monthly housing stipend of $1900 or free company provided housing for an assignment in Los Angeles, CA. If you take the company provided housing, then you'll receive a fully furnished 1 bedroom apartment with utilities and cable included for free. In my experience, this is a very realistic scenario. However, I challenge anyone to locate a decent, furnished, 1 bedroom apartment, with utilities included anywhere in Los Angeles for less than $2400 per month. Meanwhile, if the agency is unable to locate housing for the cost of the lodging stipend ($1900 in this example) or less, it will not be able to adjust the offered pay rate or the M&IE rate because of the wage recharacterization rules.

The agency is most likely able to offer the great housing they're offering because they're receiving $500 per month in volume discounts on the cost of the apartment. However, there are many scenarios that could prevent the agency from securing housing at the rates they've planned for. For example, agencies aren't always able to use their preferred vendors. In other words, the apartment management companies they typically work with may not have any available apartments at the time the agency needs one. Or, the agency may have been planning on one of their travel nurses moving out of an apartment with a long-term lease so that the next travel nurse could move in. Then, at the last-minute, the travel nurse scheduled to move out gets a contract extension and ends up keeping the apartment which leaves the travel nursing agency in a bind to find lodging for the new travel nurse.

All of these factors lead me to speculate that large agencies sometimes take it in the shorts when they provide housing. I don't think that the loss they incur on housing is large enough to result in negative revenue, but it can certainly be large enough to result in significantly decreased gross profit margins. For example, they may typically operate at 20%-25% gross profit margins and the extra housing costs might take them down to 10%-15% on that particular contract. For you, this means that you're getting a great deal.

You may think I'm crazy to say that large companies would take losses like this, and I just may be crazy!! However, remember that the agency is constrained by their inability to renegotiate the base rate offered to the traveler because they run the risk of wage recharacterization. They also can't just go to the hospital and ask for more money because the rates are standardized. Furthermore, large agencies are volume operations that operate with a standard script that maximizes efficiency. For them, taking time to research every last detail before submitting the traveler for consideration results in decreased productivity. And besides, their standard script is designed to be profitable by making more money in some circumstances and less money in others. In other words, they'll make up for this loss elsewhere.

There are several ways they can make up for these losses. First, they can place some travelers in crisis rate contracts where the traveler will accept a compensation package that results in 30% gross

126

profit or higher. Second, the agency may set their lodging stipends at levels which result in a 25%-30% profit margin when someone chooses to take the lodging stipend instead of housing. Third, the agency may earn profit margins as high as 40% or more when their travelers work extra hours on top of their regularly contracted hours. So you can see there are ways that agencies can make up for losses they may incur as a result of providing housing at a discount.

Chapter 15: Company Provided Housing

Advantages to Company Provided Housing

Taking company provided housing has several advantages. I believe that the biggest advantage is also one of the more unknown advantages; it shields you from risk, especially when it comes to apartments. Securing an apartment will typically require the signing of a lease and the payment of a deposit. Even if a lease isn't involved, the apartment will most likely require a 30 day notice for moving out. If the contract gets cancelled at any time, whoever signed the lease is responsible for any remaining costs. This means that if you secure your own lodging and the contract is cancelled for any reason, then you're on the hook for all of the apartment costs. On the flip-side, if the lodging is in the travel nursing agency's name, then they're responsible for the lodging costs in the event that the contract is cancelled.

Many travel nurses have heard that agencies may come after them for such costs. However, if the contract was cancelled at no fault of the travel nurse, census dropped for example, then there is no way the travel nursing agency would be able to come after the travel nurse for incurred costs. If the contract cancellation was the travel nurse's fault, poor attendance for example, then the travel nursing agency may come after the travel nurse for costs incurred, but it's highly unlikely. The cost of legal fees and the time it would take the travel nursing agency to settle the matter would most likely outweigh the benefit to collecting the money.

Another advantage when it comes to taking company provided housing is that you're able to rely on the travel nursing agency's expertise in this area. They will most likely have lodging options that they've worked with in the past and they'll know which options are good and which options are bad. They're more likely to know the terrain and which parts of town are better than others. In addition, they'll probably have a furniture provider they use for apartments. In all of these cases, the travel nursing agency may be getting discounts that you might not be receiving and they'll certainly be quick and efficient at securing everything. This could save you a lot of time and trouble.

Tips on Company Provided Housing - Motels, Hotels, and Extended Stays

On the surface, taking company provided housing has the clear advantage of being simple and hassle free for the travel nurse. However, it can end up being a nightmare if you don't establish expectations at the outset. No matter what type of housing you're provided with, from Extended Stays to apartments, there are a host of variables that you must consider.

Many agencies offer lodging options at Motels, Hotels, and Extended Stay type properties. Motels are the lowest budget accommodation of the three options. Motels have room access directly from the parking lot. In other words, the door to your room will be on the exterior of the building and it will typically be facing the parking lot. Additionally, motels typically offer no additional services, and when they do offer additional services, they are very limited. Hotels are typically the most expensive option of the three. Hotels have interior access to the room and are therefore more secure. They also tend to be equipped additional amenities like gyms, pools, Jacuzzis, housekeeping, room service, breakfast service, and restaurants.

Extended Stay properties are perhaps the most commonly utilized of the three and they typically have a price point between motels and hotels. Extended Stay properties are designed for just that, extended stays. They come equipped with a kitchenette that typically includes a mid-sized refrigerator/freezer, a dishwasher, sink, and a 2 burner stove. These properties can be studios, suites, or full on 1 bedroom apartments. They may also have additional amenities akin to hotels and while room access is usually interior, it can also be exterior.

If you are offered or select to go with one of these options, you should determine the following depending on whether or not they are important to you:

1)   Is it a Motel, Hotel, or Extended Stay?

2)   Is room access interior or exterior?

3)   What's the parking situation?

4)   What amenities are included (gym facilities, free breakfast, cafe or restaurant, daily housekeeping, room service, etc.)?

5)   Is free Wi-Fi available for your internet connection?

6)   Is there a kitchenette, and what's included?

7)   Is there a microwave?

8)   Is there an oven?

9)   Is there a coffeepot?

10)   Is there a laundry room?

11)   Is it a studio, suite, or 1 bedroom?

12)   Is there adequate storage for your belongings?

13)   Is there a real bed in addition to a sofa pull out, or is there just a sofa pull out?

14)   What size is the bed?

15)   Will you be responsible for any hidden fees?

16)   If you have pets, will the property accept pets and if so will the company pay the pet deposit or do you have to pay the pet deposit?

It may appear as though some of these variables should be a given and don't deserve to be inquired about. However, I assure you that if it's on this list and it's important to you, then you should ask. This is basically a list of problems that I've had to deal with as a recruiter working with these lodging options over the years.

Tips for Company Provided Apartments

My experience indicates that many first time travel nurses tend to believe that taking a company provided apartment is a matter of simply agreeing to take a 1 bedroom apartment, no questions asked. However, the apartment can be more complicated than the Motel/Hotel/Extended Stay. Apartments come in all grades, shapes and sizes. Both agencies and apartment properties offer varying amenities. Below is a list of items for consideration:

1)   Is the company providing an apartment in an apartment complex, or a condo, or a vacation home? You'll want to know in order to set your expectations. Different places come equipped with different things and you need to be prepared. For example, if it's a vacation home or condo, is there a yard and if so is yard maintenance included in the cost?

2)   Is the lodging furnished? What furnishings are included? What size is the bed?

3)   Are house wares included? House wares typically include pots, pans, linens, towels, silverware, a coffee maker, and a toaster. However, it's best to determine what specifically is included.

4)   Is there a microwave? You'd be surprised. Many apartments have not yet been fitted with a microwave and I've had many occasions where we had to add one after the fact.

5)   Is a cleaning package included? Cleaning packages typically include a broom, dust pan, and mop. They may or may not include a vacuum cleaner.

6)   Is a TV included? If you care about TV, you'll want to find out what size the TV will be. Most standard furnishing packages include a 26 inch TV. If you want to hook electronics to the TV such as a computer to watch Netfilx, or a game console, then you should make sure that the TV has applicable hook ups.

7)   How are the utilities, cable, and other bills handled? Some agencies put everything in their name and the travel nurse doesn't have to do anything. Some agencies require that travel nurses put the utilities in the travel nurses name and then provide a fixed amount per month as a utility reimbursement. They do this to protect against risks such as the purchase of $500 worth of Pay Per View movies, or leaving the Air Conditioner running on 65 for 30 days straight in the middle of summer.

8)   What's the parking situation? Parking costs extra in many urban areas. Some places have parking garages. Some have open parking lots. Some have assigned parking spaces. Some have covered parking. Some have no parking and you need to find street parking nearby. If this is important to you, then you'll want to know.

9)   Do they accept pets? If they do accept pets, what's the deposit and who's responsible for it, or any additional "pet rent" costs?

10)   Are a washer and dryer in unit, or is there a laundry facility on site? Sometimes there are hookups for the washer and dryer in the unit, but the facility charges extra to supply them, or expects you to bring or rent your own.

The main point in all of this is that you should cover all of these issues with your recruiter prior to accepting an assignment if you're going to take a company provided apartment. Ideally, you should let your recruiter know everything you need before agreeing to be submitted for an assignment. Things can move very fast once you're submitted. You may sometimes have an interview and offer in the same day you're submitted.

If you haven't discussed the housing details beforehand, they can become deal-breakers for you. I've had several occasions where these issues became last-minute deal-breakers and that's not a good situation for anyone, including the travel nurse. You'd be stuck at that point without an assignment. Depending on your financial situation, you may get forced into accepting the assignment with lodging that does not meet your standards.

Now, it's always possible that an agency provides something after the fact, but they're not obligated to. For example, you may arrive to find that there is no cleaning package at the apartment and then call the agency to request one. They may or may not provide it. Chances are good that they'd provide an item or two, but beyond that, you can expect them to deny further requests. At some point it becomes an issue of costs that the agency won't be able to afford because they haven't budgeted for them. This means that you would have to purchase items out-of-pocket, or go without for the duration of the assignment.

Hospital Provided Lodging

There is another type of company provided lodging that you should be aware of, hospital provided lodging. I know this sounds funny, but it exists, albeit rarely. In this scenario, the hospital has secured lodging for use by travel nurses. This situation is most common in very remote locations, or in other locations where housing is very difficult to come by. For example, I've often seen hospital provided lodging in some of the more remote parts of Alaska. I've also seen it in expensive resort areas like Aspen, Colorado.

In my experience I have found that hospital provided lodging is typically not glamorous. It can often be more like a barracks than an apartment complex. These accommodations sometimes have communal bathrooms and kitchen areas. They rarely accommodate pets and lack the amenities that typically come with apartments or hotels.

Despite all these potential negatives, hospital provided housing can have its advantages. First, it's not always as described above and can be quite nice and accommodating. It can allow you to travel to some really great places. As mentioned previously, hospital provided housing typically exists in locations where housing would be extremely difficult or even impossible to find otherwise. Hospital provided housing can also result in some really good pay rates. Hospitals will typically adjust the bill rate down to factor in the cost of housing, but the resulting bill rate is typically still enough to offer a very attractive pay rate. In any case, you'll want to approach hospital provided housing the same way you would approach company provided apartments, find out everything you can before proceeding.

Chapter 16: Securing Your Own Lodging

Many travel nurses, especially first time travel nurses, shy away from securing their own housing and opt for company provided housing instead. However, there are many advantages to securing your own lodging. As we previously discussed, in many cases you'll pocket some extra cash. You're also guaranteed to be involved in the decision making process and get to see your potential accommodations in advance, albeit in pictures most likely. Perhaps the most important advantage is increased flexibility. Agencies typically provide only the most basic options, apartments and hotels. They don't want to take chances on anything else. If you secure your own housing, then you can elect to go with any option available, and there are so many options available these days.

Motels/Hotels/Extended Stays

Let's first discuss the obvious options. If you're willing to stay in a Motel/Hotel/Extended Stay, then you should most definitely look into securing it on your own. Many travel nurses think that agencies are getting some kind of screaming deal on these accommodations. However, my experience indicates that unless the agency is doing an extremely high volume of business with a particular location, they're probably only getting a 10% discount off the rate.

There's a catch though. The published rate for these places is negotiable. And your bargaining power increases with the number of nights you intend to stay. If you're staying for 2 nights, then you're going to get the published rate. However, if you're staying for 90 nights, then you need to call and speak to the manager, not the front desk, the manager, to negotiate a better deal. This is what agencies do, and you can do it too. It'll take you 10 minutes.

Extended Stay Hotels are a perfect example. They almost always have a separate unpublished rate for long term stays. Long term stays are considered to be 30 days or more. And in many states and municipalities you won't be charged taxes after the 30th day, and you'll be rebated the taxes that you've paid to date. You'll definitely want to speak to the manager or the owner if it's a franchised property. You may get the same results as speaking with the front desk, but every once in a while managers will give you a better deal. Tell them there's a strong chance that you'll be returning under similar circumstances in the future and your bargaining power will increase.

In my opinion, Extended Stay Hotels and others like them are excellent options. They'll have everything you need. They're typically secure and often times in excellent areas. However, be careful as some of them can be in shady locations. The price is all inclusive which means you don't have to worry about utility costs. They can bill you weekly so you don't need to worry about huge up-front costs. Stay at them enough, and you may get better discounts and even discounts on short term stays. Also, you can inquire to see if they have any rewards programs.

Apartment Complexes

On the other side of the coin is the apartment complex. I believe it's best to let the agency handle matters if you must have a fully furnished apartment. In most cases, it's simply too much of a hassle for the travel nurse to deal with. You'd need to do some research to locate properties that allow month to month or short term leases. Most properties don't allow this option and those that do charge a premium.

If you secure an apartment, you'll also need to get it furnished. This is most often accomplished by contacting a furniture rental company like Brook Furniture Rental or Aaron Rents. However, I've worked with travel nurses who secured all their furnishings on the cheap from the likes of Ikea and craigslist.org. You'll also need to secure all the utilities and any other amenities you'd like to have.

Despite all this, there are circumstances which I believe warrant the consideration of providing your own apartment. The first circumstance is that of the traveling couple. As mentioned previously, if both members of a couple take contracts from the same company, neither of them can technically accept the lodging stipend if one of them accepts company housing and they're living together. So there's a financial consideration. In addition, there's also a division of labor and cost consideration to be made. All of the labor and cost of securing the apartment could be dispersed evenly between the couple and decrease the hassle and cost for each of the members.

The second circumstance occurs when you're able to find the perfect apartment complex for your needs. What exactly does this mean? Well, it means that the complex offers month to month lease terms, can provide furnishings for you at an additional cost of course, and can do it all at a reasonable price. This is a rare circumstance, but one such example is The Springs Apartments in Fresno, California (springsapts.com). Granted, it's not the swankiest place in town, but it's nice enough and I've had many travel nurses stay there without complaint. What's more, it's reasonably priced at $1250 for a 1 bedroom and $1450 for a two bedroom, fully furnished. Of course, prices may change, but at the present time, this is a good deal. Beyond this one location though, you'll need to search for others on your own.

Alternative Lodging Options

With the basic options out of the way, we can move on to some of the more creative options you can explore when securing your own lodging. First, I highly recommend utilizing craigslist.org. Obviously you can search the ads for "roommate wanted" or "Apartments for Rent". However, I suggest placing an ad on craigslist regardless of whether you're taking company housing or finding your own.

Simply create a craigslist account and post an ad for housing wanted in the area you're traveling to. For example, "Registered Nurse seeking accommodations for 13 weeks during a travel nursing assignment in Palo Alto, CA. Please respond via email with any options you may have." You're going to get a lot of people looking to rent out a room in their apartment or home. However, every once in a while you'll find a true gem. I had a travel nurse secure a 1200 square foot fully equipped guest house at a 5500 square foot estate near West Hills, CA for $900 per month all inclusive. I had another sublet a posh condo in Sunnyvale, CA while the owner was traveling for 6 months in South America. It's rare, but it's possible.

Another great option is airbnb.com. If you're not familiar, airbnb bills itself as a community marketplace for booking accommodations. You may be able to find a cheaper price on craigslist, but airbnb offers you reviews, photos, and nicer options. Don't be fooled by the higher nightly rates. You have to open the ads to see the monthly rates which are typically quite reasonable. The properties being offered tend to be quite nice. There are many other options in this niche including iStopOver, Wimdu, 9Flats, Homeaway, Localo, Roomorama, and Housetrip. However, airbnb is the biggest and most utilized option in the US.

In my opinion, the best way to approach all of these alternative options is to schedule visits with a couple of options before leaving for your assignment. Book an inexpensive hotel for the first few days of your assignment while you check out the housing options you scheduled to visit. In the meantime, you can continue to schedule more visits as backups. Chances are good that you'll find a great option for a very reasonable price if you have any flexibility at all. Many travel nurses seem to worry that they're somehow going to be homeless. I assure you that this will not happen. There are tons of great options out there and they're not difficult to secure.

Chapter 17: Medical Benefits

Medical benefits may seem quite simple on the surface, but the issues at play are extremely complex. Ultimately, you'll need to decide whether or not you want to secure your own medical benefits or take agency provided benefits. Each option has advantages and disadvantages. When making this decision, it helps to know a little something about how healthcare coverage works in the United States, and to be familiar with some applicable laws. I say this because unlike virtually every job that provides medical benefits, your travel assignment is temporary. It's pretty rare for temporary jobs to offer medical coverage. And while you may be convinced that you've found the agency that you're going to work with forever, chances are very strong that you'll be bouncing around from agency to agency over the course of your time as a traveler.

The first thing to understand is that if and when you switch agencies, your health insurance provider will most likely change which may interfere with your continuity of care. In other words, you may have to change doctors because no insurance company works with every doctor and vice versa. Additionally, there is no one insurance plan that covers every medication on the market, so you may also have to change prescription drugs. This is especially true if you're using a name brand drug. You can request the plan's formulary, which is a list of covered medications, from the agency or directly from the insurer's web site to find out if the prescriptions you're taking are covered. Furthermore, insurance plans have deductibles that don't get carried over from one plan to the next. So you may get stuck paying a deductible several times over if you change insurance plans several times in a year.

In my opinion, these issues, along with preexisting conditions which we'll discuss shortly, are the biggest concerns that you should be worried about when it comes to deciding whether to take agency provided medical benefits or secure your own. However, most travelers and first time travelers are most concerned about being without coverage for even a single day when they are leaving or changing jobs. In my opinion, this is the least of your concerns as there are options available. For example, in the vast majority of cases, you are guaranteed the option of purchasing health insurance when

136

you leave a job or are terminated from a job that provided you with health insurance. This is the result of what is commonly referred to as COBRA.

COBRA is a federal law that offers former employees and their dependents the right to temporary continuation of health coverage at group rates (the rate the company was paying). In the vast majority of cases, when you voluntarily or involuntarily leave a job and your benefits are terminated, you are eligible for COBRA coverage. Essentially, you are being offered the opportunity to purchase the same exact health plan you had at your old job at the group rate. You can continue the coverage for 18 months and may qualify for extensions under certain circumstances.

When a qualifying event occurs (you quit or are terminated from your job), you'll have ample time to secure COBRA coverage and you are assured uninterrupted coverage once it is secured. First, the employer must notify the plan administrator within 30 days of the qualifying event. Then, the administrator has 14 days to send you an election notice. You then have 60 days to make your decision and get the paperwork back to the administrator. You then have 45 days after electing coverage to pay the initial premium. For all intents and purposes, you're covered during this whole time. As long as you elect coverage and make the premium payments on time you're covered for the whole timeframe.

The number one complaint I hear about COBRA is that it's expensive. Yes, it's expensive, but all health insurance is expensive and you'll most likely be getting a far better deal with COBRA than you would if you went out and tried to secure the same exact coverage on your own. This is because there is a very good chance that your employer received a price cut for purchasing a large volume of insurance for all of its employees. And because COBRA mandates that you can't be charged more than 2% above the cost that the employer was paying, you'll receive virtually the same price as the employer. You'll certainly be able to find less expensive coverage if you shop around, but it will almost certainly not be as comprehensive.

However, if you do choose to purchase coverage on your own (not COBRA) and are concerned about denial of coverage due to pre-existing conditions, then you may find assistance in the recently enacted Affordable Care Act. Beginning in 2014, the Affordable Care Act makes it illegal for health insurance companies to deny coverage based on pre-existing conditions. In the mean-time The Pre-Existing

Condition Insurance Plan makes health coverage available to you if you have been denied health insurance due to a pre-existing condition and have been uninsured for at least 6 months. Details vary from state to state, but you can learn more at healthcare.gov.

Despite all of these issues and protections, you may still prefer to take company provided health insurance. If you choose to take company provided benefits, you'll need to find out everything you can about the coverage being offered. You'll also need to determine how the agency handles healthcare coverage costs.

Different agencies offer different types of health coverage. My experience indicates that a few agencies offer high-level coverage that is very comprehensive, a large number offer mid-level coverage, a few offer low-level coverage, and some offer no coverage at all. With the wide range of possibilities, you're going to want to know exactly what you're paying for.

To get information on benefits, you should request the "schedule of Benefits", as it is typically referred to, from your agency. The schedule of benefits will tell you among other things what the co-pays are, what the annual maximums are for hospital stays, what the monthly maximum for prescription drugs is, and how much the insurance will reimburse for ambulance services. I recommend obtaining the same information from your current health insurance plan to compare the plans your agencies are offering with the plan you currently have. This will give you a reference point.

The other main aspect of agency provided health benefits that you want to determine is how the agency handles the cost of the benefits. Again, contrary to agency sales gimmicks, nothing is free. And because the bill rate is most often the single source of revenue for the company, everything, including the cost of benefits, comes out of the rate. Agencies have many ways of handling this. First, some agencies factor the entire cost of benefits into the rate as a burden, much the same way that they add in the cost of FICA taxes. In other words, they see it, but you don't. They can also factor in a portion of the cost in this way, and leave some for the traveler to pay out of their paycheck. For example, you might be charged $13.34 per week while the agency pays the rest of the cost. Finally, some agencies will offer to add more money to your pay if you choose not to take their benefits, and other agencies will not. In any case, you'll want to know exactly how the agencies you're communicating with are handling this.

Securing your own benefits has its own advantages and disadvantages to consider. One clear advantage is that you'll have continuity of care. You won't have to worry about whether or not your doctor and prescriptions are going to be covered when you switch to a new agency. This may make it easier for you to switch agencies when a recruiter calls with a great opportunity which could lead to your taking more desirable assignments.

Another advantage of securing your own medical benefits is that you'll always know exactly what your medical coverage entails. If you go with agency benefits, then when you switch agencies, the new benefits will undoubtedly have a different "Schedule of Benefits." There will be different deductibles, coverage limits, and other variables. If you utilize your health insurance frequently, then you may spend a lot of time researching medical coverage if you switch agencies often.

Yet another advantage of securing your own medical benefits is that you'll get to shop for the coverage that best suits your needs. If you decide that you only need catastrophic coverage, then so be it. If you decide that you need a very high quality plan with extensive coverage, then so be it.

There are also several disadvantages to securing your own medical benefits. First, there's a strong chance that you'll pay more for less coverage. This is because employers tend to receive discounts for purchasing in volume. However, this may soon change with the purchasing pools created by the new Affordable Care Act which aim to give the power of volume discounts to individual insurance purchasers.

Another disadvantage is that you risk earning less in total compensation if you secure your own benefits. As mentioned previously, some travel nursing agencies will increase your pay if you do not take their medical benefits and some do not. If you sign on with an agency that offers benefits but doesn't increase your pay if you choose not to take them, then you're essentially leaving some money on the table. Not only are you paying for your own benefits, but you're essentially paying for benefits that you're not receiving from the company because, as we've stated several times before, everything that a travel nursing agency provides comes out of the bill rate.

Now, this next issue regarding medical benefits is a little complex because it pertains to both company-provided and personally-secured medical benefits. Typically, medical benefits are intended for use within an individual's home state. The reasons for this are legal in nature and we don't need to go into them here, we just need to understand the ramifications.

Health insurance packages offer medical coverage within a network of healthcare providers established by the health insurance company. For all intents and purposes, these networks are comprised of healthcare providers within a given state. For example, if you purchase health insurance and list Memphis, Tennessee as your home city, then the network of providers you have access to will be within the state of Tennessee, and the original list you receive will be for healthcare providers within the Memphis metropolitan area. The coverage rules will differ if you want to see a healthcare provider outside your network. As a result, you'll need to find out how the health insurance plans you're considering will deal with the fact that you are traveling from state to state on a continual basis.

Don't be dismayed as this may not be a very big deal. In most cases, you'll see your primary physician when you're back at home so this issue will not be of impact in that regard. This is really only an issue for emergency situations. As a result, you'll want to find an insurance plan that pays all costs regardless of where they're incurred once you've paid off the maximum annual deductible. It's probably also advisable to purchase a plan from a carrier that sells insurance on a national level, meaning that they operate in multiple states. Examples of such companies include but are not limited to Aetna, Cigna, Anthem, HealthNet, and United Healthcare. These plans may be able to offer certain advantages over plans that operate in only one state.

Again, it's important to remember that this issue pertains to both company-provided and personally-secured medical benefits. If you're taking company-provided medical benefits, then you'll want to find out how this is handled on their end and what the ramifications are for you. If you're going with personally-secured medical benefits, then you'll want to factor this issue into your decision making process.

Finally, you'll want to consider the issues surrounding pre-existing conditions. The issues vary depending on whether you have company-provided health coverage or have chosen to secure your own coverage. If you elect to go with company provided coverage, then there are various protections regarding pre-existing conditions already in place. These protections come from the Health Insurance Portability and Accountability Act (HIPPA).

HIPPA limits the ability of a new employer health plan to exclude coverage of pre-existing conditions. Specifically, if it's been less than 63 days since your old medical benefits were terminated, then your new employer's health plan cannot deny coverage of conditions that were covered under your old plan. If it's been more than 63 days since your previous coverage lapsed, then the maximum time that coverage can be denied is 12 months. In addition, your new employer's health plan will only be allowed to consider conditions that have been diagnosed or treated within the previous 6 months. This is Federal law and some states have laws that are more beneficial to the employee.

Under current law, this is an important consideration for travel nurses who have pre-existing conditions. This is because some of the nurses I worked with routinely went more than 63 days without coverage. Again, this is one of the luxuries of travel nursing. You can take extended vacations if you choose. However, if you have a pre-existing condition then you'll want to be cognizant of these rules.

When it comes to securing your own coverage, you'll benefit from provisions in the new Affordable Care Act pertaining to pre-existing conditions. Beginning in 2014, the Affordable Care Act makes it illegal for health insurance companies to deny coverage based on pre-existing conditions. In the mean-time The Pre-Existing Condition Insurance Plan makes health coverage available to you if you have been denied health insurance due to a pre-existing condition and have been uninsured for at least 6 months. Details vary from state to state, but you can find out more at healthcare.gov.

If you decide that the advantages of securing your own medical benefits outweigh the disadvantages and elect to secure your own benefits, then you'll need to locate a benefits package that bests suits your needs. I suggest working with a licensed broker who can answer any questions you have and recommend a plan that best meets your needs. The service that I typically recommended to the travel nurses I worked with was ehealthinsurance.com. They have a great website that allows you to compare the plans from various health insurance providers. They also have free telephone customer service so you can call in, ask questions and get the help you need to make the right decision.

Chapter 18: 401K and Retirement Planning

401Ks are another compensation benefit that many travel nursing agencies offer to their travel nurses. In my recruiting days, I found that many travel nurses addressed 401Ks as important variables in our original conversations and then never utilized them. This is an undesirable approach. You may potentially pass up on good agencies because they don't have a benefit that you aren't going to use. You may also select an otherwise poor performing agency because they offer a benefit that you aren't going to use. Like many other aspects of the travel nursing compensation package, there's a lot you need to be aware of when determining how important this variable is for you.

Before we begin, I must point out that I am not a licensed financial advisor. The details I provide are for informational purposes only. I am not making any recommendations. You should consult with a licensed professional to discuss your specific circumstances. That said, I was formerly a licensed stock broker and brokerage principal, and I do have a firm grasp on these issues.

A 401k is a type of retirement savings account that lets the individual make "tax deferred" contributions. Tax deferred means that the individual is not required to pay Federal Income taxes on money contributed to a 401k. For example, if an individual worker made $50,000 in a year and contributed $7,000 to a 401k, then their taxable income would be $43,000 assuming they had no additional adjustments or deductions. This is the first potential benefit of the 401k; you're able to save the money without having to pay income taxes on it. If you have a large income tax burden, then is a great benefit.

However, if you don't have a large income tax burden, then this is not much of an advantage at all. This is because there may be better options out there if you don't pay a lot in income taxes. You see, "tax deferred" means that you don't have to pay taxes on the money now, but you do have to pay taxes on it later when you withdraw it. The fact that you don't have to pay taxes now may not really matter if you're already paying really low (or no) income taxes because you have a low taxable income and/or a lot of deductions.

Many travel nurses fall into this category. This is because travel nurses typically receive a large percentage of their income from tax free stipends. Therefore, they tend to have lower taxable incomes. Furthermore, travel nurses may qualify for other tax deductions that will drive their taxable incomes even lower. As a result, many travel nurses will have a very low, and sometimes no, federal income tax burden.

If you find yourself in this situation, then you could instead invest your money in a Roth IRA which is another type of retirement savings account that allows you to contribute post tax dollars now, but withdraw them later without paying any taxes. As a result, you may end up paying much less in taxes with the Roth IRA than the 401k. Keep in mind that the annual contribution limit for a Roth IRA is currently $5000. So if you choose to go with a Roth IRA and intend on investing more than $5000, then you'll want to also have access to a 401K. This way, you can make your additional retirement contributions to the 401K.

There is another potential advantage to 401ks that must be considered. 401ks are a type of retirement account known as "defined contribution plans." A defined contribution plan is one in which the employer can make specified annual contributions. For 401ks, this is commonly referred to as "matching." The employer will essentially give the employee some extra money in the form of a retirement contribution. For example, the employer will contribute $.10 for every dollar that the employee contributes. This may not sound like much, but that represents a 10% return on your investment and it's free of risk to boot! Matching is a huge advantage for 401ks.

Unfortunately, while many agencies advertise that they have matching contribution benefits, you'll be hard pressed to find one with realistic requirements to qualify. This is typically the result of "vesting periods" that are unrealistic for travel nurses to meet. A "vesting period" is a period of time before the employer contributions are actually owned by the employee.

For example, the travel nursing agency will say that they have 10% 401k matching vesting after 1 year. This means that you'd have to work with the agency continuously for a full year before the matching contributions were actually released to you. This is just one example and you'll see that different companies have different "vesting schedules." Because travel nurses tend to move from company to company in order to land ideal assignments, they rarely meet the vesting requirements. In any case, you'll want to know everything about the company's matching and vesting schedule before making any judgments.

Again, I'm not providing advice and I recommend that you seek the advice of a qualified licensed financial professional. That said, my experience tells me that the vast majority of travel nurses will not utilize 401Ks by choice despite the fact that they treat them as important. Furthermore, the single biggest advantage of the 401k, the employer match, is hardly ever realized in the industry. Moreover, travel nurses will most likely not realize much benefit from the 401k tax deferment feature. The reason is that the typical travel nurse has very low income tax rates because they're getting paid a relatively lower taxable wage and have tax deductions that reduce their taxable income even more.

Therefore, the 401k becomes important for the travel nurse when they have maximized their Roth IRA contribution. The maximum Roth IRA contribution for 2012 is $5000 for individuals making less than $173,000 per year. As a result, travel nurses concerned with retirement investing would be wise to determine how much they're interested in saving each year and splitting that up accordingly between a Roth IRA and 401k.

Managing Your 401K(s)

At this point, you may be wondering what happens to all that money that's getting contributed to your 401K. Typically, 401Ks are administered by an investment company. This means that the investment company holds and tracks the money for the employer and employee by establishing an individual 401k account in the employee's name. The money is put into the employee's 401k account where the employee can invest the money in any number of available investment vehicles. Typically, the employer and the investment company have agreed on a set of investments that will be available. Typically, these investments will include a very low risk money market fund, and a host of mutual funds with varying investment strategies and levels of risk. The employee then decides where the money will be invested. This may be accomplished over the internet or on the phone with the investment company. Of course, you can also choose not to invest the money and just let it sit in the account.

Due to legal issues, I'm not going to provide any type of investment advice whatsoever. However, I can tell you that when you invest in a 401k, you are typically able to designate your asset allocation among the available investment options and then let it run on auto-pilot until you're interested in making a change. For example, if you decided to put $200 per week into the 401k, you could set up the asset allocation so that various percentages of the $200 went into particular investments. You may decide that you want 25% to go to the money market, 25% to go to the Small-Cap Growth Fund, 25% to the International Fund, and 25% to the Growth Fund. Each week, your $200 will split accordingly among the investments you have selected. You can typically change the asset allocation as you see fit.

Now, if you do decide to make 401K contributions while you are engaged in travel nursing, then you'll want to have a plan in place for when you switch companies. If you don't have a plan in place, you could end up with 401k accounts all over the place. This is fine if you're okay with keeping track of all these accounts, but there's another disadvantage aside from the organizational issues.

As mentioned previously, 401k accounts typically have a very limited set of investment options. When you leave a company, you're able to transfer the 401k to a qualified investment account with unlimited options. And having more options is always better than having fewer options. In addition, chances are very good that you'll be charged less in management fees and be able to find investment options with higher returns and lower risk.

To accomplish this, you can set up a 401k rollover account with a brokerage firm of your choice. You can choose a traditional broker, or an online broker like E*Trade. In any case, you're going to establish the 401k rollover account and complete the required transfer documentation when you leave one company for another. The broker you choose will help you with all of this. It typically takes 6-8 weeks for your 401k investments and/or funds to be transferred from your old 401k to your 401k rollover account.

Once the transfer is complete, you can invest the funds as you see fit and you'll have one central location to manage your funds. The one thing you'll want to watch out for in this process is the fees that get charged. The fees will most often be negligible or non-existent. However, you should always determine whether or not the transfer is worth paying the fees involved.

Chapter 19: Travel Stipends

Most of the first time travelers I spoke with had the impression that travel stipends are intended to cover the entire cost of traveling to and from a travel assignment. Unfortunately, this is not the case. Like all other aspects of the travel nursing pay package, the travel stipend is just one portion of the pie. Again, agencies have a fixed amount of revenue (money) that they expect to bring in for each contract. The revenue is determined by the bill rate for the contract and the number of hours to be worked during the contract. For example, a contract may have a bill rate of $60/hour, and 468 (13 weeks at 36 hours per week) anticipated hours, for a total of $28,080 for the entire 13 week period. The important thing to note here is that this figure is not going to change if the travel nurse is traveling from 200 miles away or 2,000 miles away. Let's look at this from the agency's perspective to get a clear picture of what's going on behind the scenes.

First, every travel nursing agency is going to consider the risk involved with the travel stipends they offer. You see, a travel stipend is an expense incurred ahead of collecting revenue. Remember, the travel nursing agency doesn't collect any money until the travel nurse turns in a timecard. In addition, because fixed costs like the travel stipend are spread over the course of the contract, the travel nursing company doesn't actually recoup the entire cost until all the hours have been worked. Let's look at a couple of examples to clarify.

One common method that travel nursing agencies use to pay for travel is to just pay for all the costs up front. For example, the travel nursing agency may purchase an airline ticket for the travel nurse. In this case, the agency isn't going to recoup the entire cost until all contracted hours are complete. To illustrate this, let's say the travel nursing agency pays $500 for a roundtrip ticket between California and Florida. Assuming that this is the total cost of the travel stipend, the agency is going to calculate the cost at $1.07 per hour when determining how much they have left for the rest of the compensation pie. For example, if the bill rate was $60 per hour, then they'd have $58.93 per hour left to work with. They may also view it as a percentage of the bill rate or total revenue. For example, if the bill rate was $60, then $1.07 per hour would represent 1.7% (1.07/60) of the pie.

Now, if, for example, the travel nurse ends up working only 200 hours of the contract because the contract got cancelled for some reason, then these numbers get thrown out of whack and the travel nursing agency is forced to eat costs that it wasn't anticipating. In this case, the $500 travel cost becomes valued at $2.50 per hour instead of $1.07 and it becomes 4.2% of the pie as opposed to 1.7%. While this may not sound like much, it adds up extremely fast and if it happens enough it can result in some serious losses and potentially combine with other factors to put the travel nursing agency out of business.

Another common method that travel nursing agencies use to pay out travel stipends is to provide half of the travel stipend on the first check and the other half on the last check of the assignment. For example, the travel nursing agency may offer $1000 total, to be paid $500 on the first check and $500 on the last check of the assignment. In this case, the travel nursing agency is calculating the cost of the $1000 travel stipend at $2.14 per hour ($1000/468 hours).

However, the travel nursing agency is going to pay only the first $500 on the very first pay check that the travel nurse receives. If the contract is cancelled for any reason before half the contracted hours have been worked, then the travel nursing company will take a hit. For example, if the contract is cancelled immediately after week 2, then the agency will have to eat $345.92 in travel stipend expenses that they weren't expecting. This is due to the fact that only 72 hours have been worked up to this point. Therefore, the travel nursing company has only recouped $154.08 of the travel stipend money (72 hours at $2.14 per hour). The travel nurse must work half the contracted hours before the first $500 is fully recouped as planned (234 hours at $2.14 per hour is $500).

Understanding this issue from the travel nursing agency's perspective helps us understand one of the reasons why agencies are reluctant to provide large travel stipends up front. They risk losing money. This is why many agencies now cap the amount of the travel stipends they're willing to offer. My experience indicates that the most common cap these days is $700. In other words, most agencies are only willing to provide a maximum of $700 for travel stipends. It's not because they're cheap, or they're sticking it to the travel nurse. It's because they're concerned about the risk of losing large sums of money in a very tight business market. That said, if you have a really good track record with a particular travel agency, then they may be more willing to take a chance on you and give you a higher travel stipend. However, remember that this doesn't necessarily mean that they're going to give you more money overall. They may just reduce the amount that they're giving you somewhere else in the compensation package.

This brings us to the other main reason that many travel nursing agencies cap their travel stipends. Remember that moving money from one place to another can get the agency in trouble with the IRS for recharacterizing wages. For example, if an agency gives you a choice between $1000 for a travel stipend or $500 for a travel stipend and an additional $1.07 per hour, then they may be guilty of recharacterizing the tax free stipend as a wage. The same is true for the reverse scenario. As a result, many agencies, and particularly the large agencies are very inflexible with the travel stipends they offer. By keeping their travel stipends and other tax free reimbursements at set levels, they're able to ensure that they don't run afoul of this rule.

Now that you understand the travel stipend issue from the agencies perspective, we can discuss what it all means for you. First, chances are very strong that you'll need to have enough capital to make it out to your assignment, especially if you're driving. There was a time when travel nursing agencies would send a prepaid gas or credit card to the travel nurse to help them get from one place to another, but you'll have difficulty finding that in today's market. Second, you shouldn't really look at the travel stipend as a major selling point unless you need cash immediately. Again, the travel stipend is just one component of the compensation package. You need to compare entire compensation packages in order to determine which is offering the best deal. Finally, chances are high that you will incur more in travel expenses than the agency's stipend will cover. As a result, you may be able to write off the difference on your taxes if you keep adequate records as previously described.

Chapter 20: Rental Cars

I was often asked about rental cars as a travel nursing recruiter. For various reasons, many travel nursing agencies no longer offer them. In addition, there are financial issues for travel nurses to consider when deciding whether or not they want to utilize a rental car for a travel nursing assignment.

I believe it's much harder to come by travel nursing agencies that offer rental cars these days. They're out there, but there are far fewer of them. There are a couple of reasons for this. First, rental cars are extremely expensive. The lowest price that can typically be secured for even an economy class rental car is going to be over $500 per month with tax included. The agency may also incur additional insurance costs depending on the insurance that they currently hold as a company and whether or not it covers rental cars. Given the overall decline in bill rates for travel nursing assignments in the last 5 years, these high rental car costs really eat into the amount of money that the travel nursing agency has left to pay the travel nurse. As a result, offering rental cars may make it appear as though the travel nursing agency is paying terrible rates.

Second, there are wage recharacterization issues. Again, a travel nursing agency is technically not supposed to say something like, "The pay rate is $30 per hour without the rental car and $26 per hour with the rental car." Doing so would open them to the risk of wage recharacterization.

Third, I'm going to go out on a limb and say that travel nursing agencies hate rental cars. I'll bet that even those that offer rental cars aren't too fond of them and wish they didn't have to offer them. Managing rental cars is quite a hassle. There's a lot of paperwork that needs to be completed and kept up on. Because the agency is responsible for the car, they must ensure that the travel nurse takes the car in for regularly scheduled check-ins and maintenance over the 13 week contract. The agency is also liable for any additional charges such as mileage overage charges. Between the paperwork and risk, rental cars are really something that all companies, travel agencies or otherwise, would prefer to do without if they could.

Despite all this, the issue for the travel nurse is to determine if a rental car is the right way to go or not. The first thing to consider is that you'll be hard pressed to find an agency that offers rental cars which could ultimately limit your options if a rental car is a "Requirement" for you. However, if you're unable to find a travel nursing agency that offers rental cars and also meets the rest of your needs, then you can always secure your own rental car. Remember, even if an agency provides a rental car, it's not going to be free to you. You're going to pay in one way or another with reductions in other areas of the compensation package. That said, there are some great sites out there for finding the best deal on rental cars. One of my favorites is rentalcars.com.

Your second consideration should be the financial implications of utilizing a rental car. As mentioned previously, rental cars are quite expensive. The cheapest you'll most likely find them for is $500 per month. After taxes and other costs, you're looking at $1,600 for a 3 month contract. If you don't have a car of your own and you're going to a location where you must have a car, then a rental may be the only way to go. However, if you're concerned about putting the miles on your car and "wear and tear" issues, then you should consider the cost of shipping your car versus the cost of the rental car. You can perform an internet search for "car shipping." The service that I've used in the past is movemycar.com. With this website, you should receive a list of quotes via email from various shippers in your area.

Now, to make a solid determination on whether or not it'll be cheaper to ship or rent, you'll need to consider the length of time that you'll be staying in the area. For example, if you're planning on staying for 3 months, then you'll compare the shipping costs to 3 months' worth of rental car costs. If you plan on staying 6 months, then you'll compare the shipping costs to 6 months of rental car costs. My experience indicates that it's typically even at three months, and it's almost always better to ship the car if you're staying for 5 months or more.

Chapter 21: License and Certification Reimbursements

License and certification reimbursements are one of the many perceived perks of travel nursing. In fact, some agencies offer them and others don't. The agencies that do offer them have many different methods of handling them. Most importantly, in the end, like every other item in the compensation package, these reimbursements should be viewed as just another component of the compensation package pie. In other words, the simple fact that a reimbursement is offered doesn't necessarily make one compensation package better than another that's not offering a reimbursement.

Let's look at this first from the travel nursing agency's perspective. Agencies that offer license and certification reimbursements use the offerings as a selling point. It gives the impression that something more is being offered. However, in the end, it's typically treated just like any other cost is treated. It's calculated into the total compensation package where the increased cost is offset by equal reductions in another compensation item.

Note that I used the word "typically." Sometimes, these reimbursements really can add value to the total compensation package. Agencies may set aside funds for license and certification reimbursements such that if you don't take advantage of the offer, then you're leaving money on the table. In addition, agencies may find themselves forced to provide a reimbursement after the compensation package has been negotiated. This is one of the main reasons that some travel nursing agencies choose not to offer them.

Let's look at an example to illustrate the kind of bind that these offerings can get the agency into. Suppose an agency advertises that they provide "free" license and certification reimbursements for travel assignments. A new travel nurse sees the advertisement, contacts the travel nursing agency, and ends up signing on for an assignment with them. During the process, the issue of license reimbursement is never discussed between the travel nurse and recruiter because the travel nurse assumes that the advertisement means what it says. Then, three weeks into the assignment the travel nurse calls the agency and asks when the license reimbursement will be paid. The recruiter will undoubtedly respond that the license reimbursement will not be paid because it hadn't been discussed during the contract negotiation process. Essentially, the agency didn't factor the cost into the initial compensation package, so adding it now would reduce the profit margin that the agency was counting on.

Now, no matter whose side of this argument you come down on, it's not good business to have disappointed customers. So the agency has a choice between a disappointed customer and paying the reimbursement. Paying out an unanticipated license or certification reimbursement every once in a while isn't going to kill the agency, but doing so on a regular basis could have a significant impact on the bottom line. Again, avoiding this scenario is one of the reasons that some agencies don't offer license and certification reimbursements.

Another reason that travel nursing agencies give for not offering license and certification reimbursements is that the license or certification belongs to the travel nurse not the agency. This logic has merit in certain circumstances. For example, if the agency pays for a state nursing license up front in order to land the travel nurse an assignment at a particular hospital, there's a risk that the assignment falls through for one reason or another and the travel nurse may then use the license to land an assignment through another agency. I realize that this sounds unlikely, but trust me it happens. In addition, even if the travel nurse takes the assignment, the assignment only lasts for 13 weeks, but the license or certification is typically good for 2 or more years. The travel nurse and/or future employers of the travel nurse will undoubtedly benefit from the cost incurred by the travel nursing agency that provided the reimbursement. All this said, I'm not a big fan of this reasoning. Again, agencies are going to factor this cost into the overall compensation package so they'll be able to account for it as long as they don't pay for it up font.

Now that you have an idea about how reimbursements are viewed by the agency, we can discuss what this all means for you, the travel nurse. I submit to you that license reimbursement should not be a big issue in determining which agencies you work with. Ultimately, it's just another component of the compensation pie and you must consider the entire pie when determining whether or not you're getting a good deal. That said, I do believe that reimbursements present an opportunity in the negotiating process.

Let's say that you're speaking with two agencies about two different assignments. You get each of them to email you a compensation package offer for their respective assignments. You could then contact each of them and express that you're interested (assuming you are interested) but that you would really like to get a license reimbursement in addition to what they've offered. Of course, this only works if you have very recently incurred such an expense or expect to incur the expense during the course of the contract. The cost of the license or certification reimbursement is typically within a range that is small enough to have a somewhat minimal impact on the agency's profit margin, but at the same time be a big help to the travel nurse. This approach may be a little shady, but I'll let you be the judge of that.

There's another important aspect for travel nurses to consider regarding license and certification reimbursement. It's highly recommended to stay organized when it comes to your licenses and certifications if you want to maximize your chances of getting reimbursed. You have to know in advance if you have a license or certification that's going to expire during your next contract in order to benefit in any way from a potential reimbursement.

I doubt you'll be able to find an agency that will reimburse for a license or certification that you already have. Furthermore, you'll be hard pressed to find an agency that will reimburse for these expenses after the contract has been negotiated. In addition, you're going to want to obtain and maintain receipts for all of your license and certification expenses. Travel nursing agencies are most likely going to require a copy of a receipt in order to provide any reimbursements.

Chapter 22: Bonuses

Again, like any other compensation variable, assignment bonuses must be viewed as part of the compensation package pie. However, bonuses are quite unique. To simplify our discussion, we'll break down bonuses into 3 distinct categories.

The first category is the "hospital-provided bonus." These bonuses are offered by the hospital and are in addition to the bill rate. They are sometimes offered as sign on bonuses, but more commonly as completion bonuses. Hospitals typically shy away from sign on bonuses for travelers due to the risk that the assignment won't be completed. When the labor market was tight, hospital-provided bonuses were offered quite often. These days, with the slack labor market, they're rarely offered.

There are several things you must know about hospital-provided bonuses. First, the bonuses are really offered to the agency with the expectation that they'll be passed along to the traveler. However, it's not required that the bonuses be passed on to the traveler in most cases. Despite this, you should anticipate that the agency will pass these bonuses on to the traveler when offered. Agencies don't want to look bad if the traveler finds out that a bonus was offered for the assignment but not to the traveler.

Second, hospital provided bonuses often have strict stipulations for collecting. The stipulations often require that 100% of the contracted hours be worked. And yes, you may get dinged even if the hospital calls you off for a shift, or sends you home early. They may argue that it's your responsibility to make up the hours.

Third, your agency may withhold payment of the bonus until it's actually paid to them. Remember, agencies have to bill hospitals to collect their money. Hospitals tend to pay on normal business terms like Net 30, 60, or 90. This means the hospital may not deliver payment for 30, 60, or 90 days.

The second category of bonus is what we'll call the "agency-added bonus." We call this an "added bonus" because for all intents and purposes it represents an addition that the agency doesn't factor into its original compensation calculation. There's a fine and confusing line here. As mentioned previously, agencies typically have compensation calculating programs that account for all costs related to the traveler. These calculators help recruiters determine the compensation package for any given assignment by accounting for how compensation changes affect the agency's gross profit on the deal. An "added bonus" is one that is not factored into this calculation.

In this regard, the agency is willing to take a hit to their bottom line. Obviously, they have a reason for doing this. For example, they may offer these bonuses for extending a contract or taking a new contract within a certain number of weeks of the previous contract's end. They're doing this because it's cheaper and easier to retain current employees than it is to hire new ones. Again, these bonuses will typically have strict requirements for collecting.

The third category of bonus is the "agency-factored bonus." In this case, the agency factors the cost of the bonus into the compensation calculator, which can potentially reduce the value of some other variable. Agencies may do this to mitigate risk. If they are providing compensation variables that entail risk such as housing or a large travel stipend, then they may use the factored bonus to reduce the compensation paid during the contract, making up for it when the contract is completed. Agencies may also use this as a sales strategy, or what I like to call a sales gimmick. They'll toss out a bonus as bait in hopes that an unsuspecting traveler, one who hasn't read this book, will bite.

As you can see, we're back to square 1. Just because a bonus is offered, don't assume that it's an extra. You must incorporate the bonus into the entire compensation package to determine if the deal being offered is a good one. Finally, remember that all bonuses are going to be taxed at a higher rate than regular pay and you will receive the after tax amount from the agency.

Chapter 23: Extra Hours Pay

One of the most overlooked aspects of the travel nursing pay package is "Extra Hours." Extra hours are hours that are worked above and beyond the contracted hours. In this chapter, we'll look at some examples to determine the difference between an extra hour and an overtime hour. We'll also discuss some of the issues at play with extra hours and what it all means for you.

Let's begin with a simple travel nursing pay package example. Let's say you have a 13 week contract for 36 hours per week with the following compensation components:

Taxable Base Rate: $20/hour
Taxable Overtime Rate: $30/hour
Lodging Stipend: $2500 per month
M&IE Stipend: $300 per week
Travel Stipend: $700 total for the 13 week contract.

Now, on a perfect week, one in which everything goes as anticipated, the travel nurse will turn in a timecard with 3 12 hour shifts. This will enable the travel nursing agency to collect the money they were anticipating from the hospital and pay the travel nurse exactly as anticipated. But what happens during the imperfect weeks? Let's take a look at three different scenarios to get a clear understanding of the issue.

Scenario 1: Hours are short: In this scenario, the travel nurse turns in a timecard with fewer than 36 hours on it. For example, the travel nurse may have been called off, or called in sick, for a shift and turns in a timecard with only 24 hours. In this case, the travel nurse will not be paid the taxable base rate for the un-worked hours; but what about the stipends and fixed costs like company provided housing? The agency isn't able to collect the money they need to pay for these items because the hours weren't worked.

Different travel nursing agencies handle this in different ways. Some agencies have penalty clauses in their contracts which essentially breakdown the value of these costs to an hourly value and state that the travel nurse will be penalized that amount for each un-worked contract hour. Other agencies may just literally spell out in their contracts that the stipends are paid hourly. So if the hours aren't worked, then the stipends are automatically reduced in kind. The point is that the vast majority of agencies will have some mechanism in place which attempts to ensure they don't have to soak up all the costs as a result of un-worked contract hours. These mechanisms are never perfect which is why agencies are so adamant that travel nurses work the contracted hours.

Scenario 2: Hours are met, but imperfect: In this scenario, the travel nurse turns in a timecard with 36 hours on it, but it's not for 3 12 hour shifts. Instead, the travel nurse has worked 14 hours, 12 hours, and 10 hours. Essentially, there are no issues here for either party. The travel nursing agency is going to be able to bill the hospital and collect for the hours. In fact, it may even work out in the agency's favor if their contract with the hospital has an increased bill rate for hours worked after 12 in a day. The only difference for the travel nurse will be that the additional 2 hours worked on the 14 hour day may be paid out as overtime or double-time hours depending on state law.

The important thing to note here is that the overtime or double-time rate will be based on the taxable base rate. In our example this rate is $20 per hour so the overtime rate is $30 per hour and the double time rate is $40 per hour.

Scenario 3: Extra Hours: In this scenario, the travel nurse turns in a timecard with more than the 36 contracted hours on it. This could be 38 hours if a couple of extra hours were worked or 48 hours if an entire extra shift was worked. Let's go with the latter example. Let's say that the travel nurse worked 4 12 hour shifts. The issue here is to determine how that fourth shift will be paid out.

Different agencies handle it in different ways. Some agencies simply pay the taxable hourly rate. So the travel nurse will receive $20 per hour for the regular hours and $30 per hour for the overtime hours. However, the agency is still collecting the same bill rate that enables them to pay that base rate PLUS the stipends and other costs. So the agency is making out like a bandit if they only pay the taxable base rate. This is why there is a difference between "Overtime Hours" and "Extra Hours."

You see, once the contracted hours are met, the agency has paid for the stipends and any other costs that they had calculated in when determining the compensation package for the assignment. So if they don't offer some additional form of compensation for hours worked above and beyond the contracted hours, then they are pocketing a far larger percentage of the bill rate for those particular hours.

Again, some agencies are happy to do this. But others offer incentives to work extra hours. There are a number of ways to provide such an incentive. I've seen some agencies simply offer a set additional amount for working extra hours. For example, they may offer an additional $10 per hour for all extra hours worked. Others may simply continue to pay the stipend money as an hourly rate for any extra hours. Others may pay double time based on the taxable base rate.

It's important to note that we looked at examples based on weekly scenarios. I did this because it made explaining the issues easier. However, it's important to point out that extra hours are really hours that are worked in excess of the total number of hours on the contract as opposed to the total number of hours in any given week. In other words, if the contract is for 13 weeks at 36 hours per week, then there's a total of 468 hours. So, extra hours would be those hours above 468 for the thirteen week period. However, this doesn't change the issues at play.

As mentioned previously, agencies have mechanisms in place to ensure that they don't pay out stipends for time not worked. As a result, you want to make sure of two things. First, what are the mechanisms in place to ensure that you're paid back for the penalties on missed hours if you make those hours up in the future? For example, if you work 24 hours one week and get penalized by having your stipends reduced, then you want to make sure that your stipends are increased if you work 48 hours the next week or any time in the future. Second, you want to find out how they pay for any extra hours. If you don't, you may kick yourself later when you work a bunch of additional shifts and find out that you are only paid the low taxable hourly rate quoted in your contract.

Chapter 24: Guaranteed Hours

"Guaranteed hours" is an often misunderstood concept in travel nursing. Some assume that it means they're going to get paid for the contracted hours no matter what. Some assume that it means they're going to get paid for the contracted hours as long as they don't call in sick or otherwise miss a scheduled day of work. Some assume that guaranteed hours are a benefit provided by the agency. In fact, guaranteed hours are determined by the contract between the hospital and agency and exist to protect both the agency and the travel nurse.

The contract between the hospital and agency should spell out the hospital's guaranteed-hours policy. On one hand, these policies serve to protect the agency. You see, the agency is providing a service to the hospital that relies on hours being worked so that money can be collected to cover all of the costs involved with the entire process. For example, the agency may have paid for the traveler's travel expenses, housing, and rental car. The agency's ability to cover these costs depends on their ability to bill the hospital for the hours that the traveler works. And remember, if the agency isn't able to bill 100% of the hours they're anticipating to bill, then their calculations are going to be thrown off at best, and they'll lose money at worst. If the traveler doesn't work, then there's no money for the agency, plain and simple.

At the same time, guaranteed hours policies serve to protect the travel nurse. The travel nurse traveled for the main purpose of working and getting paid. They undoubtedly have bills to pay, and they may even be paying for their own housing and other costs while on the assignment. If they don't work, then they don't get paid.

To a certain degree, guaranteed hours policies are in place to ensure that hospitals aren't gaming the system. You see, hospitals attempt to optimally staff their facilities at all times. They don't want too many workers, or too few workers, at any time given the workload in the facility. This approach is an effort to keep costs down. However, managing this approach is very difficult. It's difficult to forecast hospital census, employee sick calls, and other variables that might affect staffing levels and/or patient population.

When hospitals are short-staffed, their first lines of defense should be agency PRN and the hospital's own PRN and regular staff. If those resources are exhausted and hospitals are still having trouble finding enough staff, then they may consider bringing in a traveler. But if they bring in a traveler and hospital census suddenly returns to normal, or employee sick calls cease, then the hospital will be tempted to start cancelling the traveler's shifts to save money. This is just one example, and it's important to remember that hospital's need travelers for many other reasons that don't fit this description. However, to a certain degree, guaranteed hours policies are in place to ensure that hospitals don't call for travelers unless there is a real need.

It's very important to understand that these policies vary from hospital to hospital. Some policies guarantee every hour. Some policies allow the hospital to call the traveler off up to 3 times within a 13 week period. I've even seen some that allow the hospital to call off the traveler up to once a week. As a result, you must determine what the policy is for each contract. You can't assume that the policy is going to be the same at different hospitals just because you're working with the same agency.

There are some standard issues that you need to be aware of when evaluating these policies. First, I've never seen a policy that guarantees hours if the travel nurse volunteers to leave. For example, the supervisor may ask the travel nurse if they'd like to leave a shift early because the census is low. I'm fairly confident I can guarantee that any hours missed as the result of volunteering to leave in such a scenario will not qualify as guaranteed hours. Second, sometimes the policies will give the hospital the option of cancelling a scheduled shift and offering a future shift to make up for it. If the travel nurse declines, then the cancelled shift doesn't count against guaranteed hours. Third, guaranteed hours are often times a trade-off between the guarantee and the requirement to float to other units. In other words, the travel nurse must be willing to float to other units within their scope of practice in order to get the guarantee. Fourth, sometimes hospitals require travel nurses to float between various hospitals as needed in order to get their guaranteed hours. For example, there may be four hospitals within one metropolitan area that are all part of the same hospital organization. If they don't need you at one of the hospitals, then they can schedule you at another to make sure you get the guaranteed hours.

As you can see, guaranteed hours policies aren't as cut and dry as many make them out to be. If this issue is important to you, then you'll want to find out as much as possible about the hospital's policy AND the agency's policy. The two policies may differ and the differences may have an impact on you. For example, the hospital may not guarantee any hours at all but despite this the agency still offers guaranteed hours with a clause that says you'll need to float to other hospitals in the area as a PRN nurse.

Ultimately, you must discuss this issue in detail with your recruiter, and attempt to discuss it during your interview with the manager at the hospital in question. Discussing it with the recruiter is easy enough. You just need to ask them for their policy. The hospital manager you speak with may not be familiar with the policy. Instead of pushing them to find out or saying that your acceptance of the assignment is contingent on finding out, you should ask other probing questions to get at the heart of the issue. What's the float policy within and between hospitals? Why are you looking for a traveler? How often do travel nurse shifts get cancelled?

In any case, the final word on guaranteed hours rests with the agency. Remember, you're signing a contract with the agency, not with the hospital. As a result, you'll want to make sure that the travel nursing agency's policy is clearly stated in the contract you sign. Also, never assume that the agency has the same policy for all hospitals. It's important to ask about the guaranteed-hours policy for each new contract you take.

Chapter 25: Shift Differential

Many travelers and potential travelers asked me about shift differentials over the years. They wanted to know if they would get paid extra for working nights and/or weekends. When told that there typically was not a shift differential for travel nursing assignments, the candidates would often scoff at the idea of working nights or weekends. This is not a good approach to travel nursing assignments.

159

Shift differential pay may be common for permanent positions. However, it's not common for travel nursing assignments. The same can be said for vacation time, sick days, and other common components of the permanent employee compensation package.

There are few instances in which a true shift differential is offered for travel nursing assignments. A true shift differential is one that results from a difference in the bill rate. In other words, the agency is able to bill a higher rate for night shifts for example. However, this is extremely rare.

It is more common for agencies to offer a shift differential by simply keeping a larger percentage of the bill rate for certain shifts. For example, if the bill rate was $60 per hour for all shifts at a given hospital, then the agency could offer to pay its day shift employees $38 per hour and its night shift employees $41 per hour. Now, you could look at this as the agency paying more for night shifts. However, I would look at it as the agency taking more for day shifts.

The difference is important. You may be able to find an agency that pays $41 per hour or more for all shifts. You'd be better served to work with that agency because no matter what shift you worked, you'd always get the higher rate. Again, in the end, shift differential is just another part of the compensation pie. It shouldn't be used as a determining factor on its own merit.

Conclusion

In this section, we covered the most common offerings of the travel compensation package in detail. We've weighed the pros and cons and advantages and disadvantages of each offering. You can use this information to help you determine what you want out of a travel compensation package. We've also covered several variables that you need to be aware of when discussing compensation, like extra hours pay and guaranteed hours.

Ideally, you'll use this information to compile a list of "must-have" compensation variables. You can then communicate that list to the agencies you speak with in an effort to quickly find the agencies that provide the services you desire. In any case, knowledge of the information in this section provides you with the ability to ensure that all the bases are covered when it comes to travel compensation.

Section 7: Additional Considerations

Chapter 26: Deciding Where to Travel

Deciding where to travel seems simple on the surface. Maybe you have family in a particular location so you'd like travel there. Maybe you've always wanted to see Alaska or Hawaii so you'd like to travel to those places. You are certainly welcome and able to approach your decision with these ideas at the forefront, but I recommend a more logical approach due to logistical issues.

I'm certain that a travel assignment in Alaska would be amazing. However, the entire state has a population of 710,000 people. There are 15 cities in the United States with more people. That's not a shot at Alaska; I point this out because where there are fewer people, there are fewer hospitals, and fewer travel nursing jobs. At the same time, it's going to cost just as much to get the license for that state as it is for any other. Hawaii would also be amazing. However, every travel nurse I've ever spoken to would jump at the opportunity to take an assignment there. Sure, some travel nurses change their minds once they hear that the compensation relative to the cost of living isn't so attractive, but the competition remains fierce to land an assignment in Hawaii.

None of this is to say that you should give up on these options. In fact, your unique circumstances make a difference in this decision. For example, if you have a permanent job that is very flexible and allows you to leave on short notice for periods long enough to complete a travel assignment, then you can definitely focus on only locations where it's difficult to land a travel nursing assignment. However, if you need to land assignments on a continual basis in order to pay the bills, then, in my opinion, these options should be viewed as just that, options. Counting on one single location to come through with a travel assignment when you need it is tough enough and even tougher if that location is already difficult in the first place. Developing a strategy to get where you want to go is the best way to get where you want to go.

Let's remember that these days hospitals are looking for travel nurses who can start within 2 to 4 weeks, and sometimes within 1 week, of the opening being announced. Therefore, it's pretty difficult to give your current employer an adequate resignation notice only after you've landed a travel assignment. You almost have to plan ahead and give your employer fair notice in advance of landing an assignment. In addition, it's pretty rare these days to even be considered for an assignment without the appropriate state license in hand prior to submission for the assignment. In fact, most hospitals require agencies to provide a copy of the license verification from the state board of nursing with the submission profile in order for their candidate to be considered. Because of this, the best licenses to have are compact state licenses and licenses from populous states that use travel nurses.

Many nurses are unaware of the Nurse Licensure Compact (NLC). The NLC gives nurses the opportunity to practice across state lines as long as they have a "compact license" and are going to work in a state that is a member of the NLC. Typically, Registered Nurses and Licensed Practical Nurses who legally reside in a compact state will have a compact license assuming that they are licensed in the state. If you don't have a compact license, you can obtain one by establishing legal residence within a compact state and then applying for a license. A list of compact states as of this book's publication is below:

Idaho, Utah, Arizona, Colorado, Texas, Nebraska, South Dakota, North Dakota, Iowa, Missouri, Arkansas, Wisconsin, Texas, Delaware, South Carolina, North Carolina, Virginia, Tennessee, Mississippi, Maryland, Delaware, Rhode Island, New Hampshire, Maine, Kentucky.

As you can see, this is a great license to have because it opens up so many options. If you're not fortunate enough to have one of these licenses, then the next best thing is to focus on populous states that have a track record of using travel nurses. Again, the logic here is that the more populous states will have more hospitals and therefore more opportunities. The best states in this regard are:

California, Texas, Florida, Arizona, New York (in my opinion, in that order)

In addition to these states, you could also consider the various "walk through" states. Walk through states are called such because they allow you to obtain a temporary license to practice within a very short period of time, typically 1 to 2 days, by simply visiting the state's board of nursing in person and completing some paperwork. Again, even hospitals in these states may require a license in hand prior to consideration so you don't want to rely on them, but instead keep them as potential options. Keep your eyes and ears open for assignments in these states in case you find yourself in a bind. According to travel nursing agency Fastaff, the current list of walk through states is:

Arizona, Illinois, Indiana, Maryland, Missouri, South Dakota, Vermont, South Carolina (Wednesdays only) Massachusetts (reinstatements only), New York (reinstatements only).

Now let's take a look at how a strategy based on this logic could get you where you want to go. Let's say your most desired location is Alaska. You should start the Alaska licensing process immediately in order to ensure that you receive the license as soon as possible. But you don't want to rely only on Alaska so you decide to get a California license as well. This is a good choice because it's the most populous state in the nation, has tons of travel opportunities, and is closer to Alaska than say Florida. Again, you should start the California licensing process immediately.

When you contact travel nursing agencies you'll let them know that you're interested in Alaska as your top choice and California as your second choice. If you're unable to land an assignment in Alaska on your first go around, that's ok. You'll be able to get an assignment in Los Angeles, San Diego, or the San Francisco Bay Area. Once you have an assignment locked in, you'll know when it ends, and when you'll be able to start your next assignment. You can let the agencies you're working with know when you're able to start and they can start trying to land your next assignment in Alaska. You can then repeat this process as needed.

Chapter 27: Hospital Preferences

I worked with many healthcare professionals over the years who had very specific hospital preferences. I've worked with healthcare professionals who would only work with hospitals that had a designated children's ER and others who would only work with hospitals that performed high risk deliveries. People tend to have very good reasons for such preferences. For example, some have told me that they don't want to lose their skills while they travel because they intend to return to their home hospital in the future. Others told me that they were using travel assignments as a means to landing a permanent job at a particular type of hospital. In any case, there are considerations to bear in mind when harboring such preferences.

First, you should consider if you have the qualifications to work in your preferred hospitals and whether or not you're willing to accommodate their common requirements. Many hospitals require that candidates have experience with similar operations. For example, it's very common for teaching hospitals and trauma hospitals to require experience in similar settings. It's also common for units caring for specific patient populations to require experience with similar patients. For example, L&D units taking high risk patients routinely require experience with these patients.

In addition, similar hospitals tend to have similar requirements. For example, rural hospitals tend to require flexibility when it comes to floating. This is due to the fact that the census for many units is highly unpredictable in rural areas. A hospital may perform 20 births per month and only have 1 L&D nurse on staff because of staff departures or scheduled leaves of absence. As a result, they need a traveler to make sure they have coverage. Clearly there won't be enough work to keep both nurses busy in the L&D on a full time basis. Therefore, the hospital may require that the nurses float to MedSurg or some other unit. Furthermore similar hospitals tend to require similar certifications. For example, trauma and/or busy Emergency Rooms tend to require TNCC certification.

Of course, you may be able to get by without heeding any of these qualification and requirement recommendations. However, you'll be limiting your options, which is the second important consideration when harboring specific hospital preferences. Preferences reduce options. This is true for any set of preferences you may have. For example, there may be 1,500 travel assignments available right now, but only 15 assignments with Level 1 Trauma Hospitals looking for night shift Emergency Room Registered Nurses. However, hospital preferences can narrow the field significantly. It's no big deal if you're looking for only rural hospitals, or only big city hospitals. But if you're looking only for teaching hospitals, then there are far fewer of those options available.

There are several steps you can take to counterbalance the difficulties created by hospital preferences. First, you should definitely utilize the third step in our process for finding the right agencies. That is, you should identify your preferences and take a proactive approach to finding agencies that can meet your needs. The more refined your preferences, the more you should rely on our approach to finding the right agencies. For example, if you're interested only in rural hospitals, then you'll probably be able to find plenty of agencies that can meet your needs. But if you're interested only in teaching hospitals, then you should take a more strategic approach because there are fewer teaching hospitals.

For example, you can find all of the teaching hospitals in the states you're licensed in. Then you could do some research on line, or call agencies directly in an effort to find agencies that work with these particular hospitals. You could also call the hospitals directly and ask to speak with someone in the staffing office in an attempt to determine if they utilize travel nurses and if so, which agencies they utilize. Again, this approach is aggressive and you may get rebuffed, but it can also be very successful.

You'll also want to make sure that you have as many licenses and certifications as possible in order to expand your options. Again, hospital preferences will undoubtedly reduce the number of available options. Having as many certifications and state licenses to practice will only serve to increase the available options. Finally, you'll definitely want to highlight applicable experience on your resume as well as the agency applications that you complete. Remember, often times it's not the best candidate that gets the interview, it's the best profile.

Chapter 28: Shift and Contract Length

Shift and contract length are obviously important travel assignment variables. All shifts are available when it comes to travel assignments. It's important to note that hospitals are the ones driving the shift requirements, not agencies. Some hospitals operate with 12 hour shifts, some with 8 hour shifts, some with a combination of the two, and some with 10 hour shifts. 8 hour shifts are more common in certain regions and states. For example, you'll find a lot of 8 hour shifts in California, but even the vast majority of assignments in California still have 12 hour shifts.

Many people think that 8 hour shifts are more common in California because the labor laws require overtime to be paid after 8 hours in a day. There's some truth to that, but it's a little more complicated. At one point, there was a loophole that exempted Union workers in California from the overtime laws in lieu of the Union's Collective Bargaining agreement. I'm not sure if this is still true. However, even when it was, many hospitals with Union nurses were working 8 hour shifts by choice. Some people prefer it. Others argue it's better for patient safety.

It's not really necessary to consider shifts when vetting agencies. However, if you're adamantly opposed to working a particular shift and you're interested in one particular location, then it may be useful to ask agencies if the hospitals they work with in your location of interest staff the shifts you desire. Otherwise, simply letting the agency know what shifts you desire is enough.

Determining the contract length you desire is a little more complicated. The vast majority of agencies will handle assignments that are 13 weeks or longer. In fact, I'd be surprised to find an agency opposed to handling assignments of 13 weeks or longer, including agencies that specialize in short-term contracts. Let's face it. Agencies would love to have you on contract for the rest of your life working 60 hours a week. That's how they make money! You'll also find that the majority of agencies will handle 8 week contracts if that's what the hospitals they work with want. Again, hospitals will be the primary drivers behind contract lengths.

Short-term contracts are another story. Agencies tend to dislike short term contracts unless there is a crisis rate involved. When a contract is for 4, 6, or even 8 weeks, the contract is obviously going to generate less revenue for the agency. Less hours worked means less billing, means less revenue. At the same time, the cost and amount of work that goes into staffing the position remains the same. As a result, agencies may decide that short term contracts aren't worth their time. But a crisis rate might make up for the deficiency.

Short term contracts create opposing concerns for hospitals. On one hand, a short term contract presents difficulty for the hospital's continuity of care. If the traveler is only going to be there for 4 weeks, then they're going to be on the floor for only 3 weeks. The first week will be spent in orientation. And if an orientation is not provided, then it may be difficult for the traveler to get acclimated to the floor. Despite this, some hospitals choose to deal with this pitfall. Sometimes a hospital has a dire short term need for some reason. Furthermore, some hospitals just don't want to commit to 13 weeks. By committing to fewer weeks they mitigate the risk of overspending in case their census drops and they no longer have a need for the traveler.

Travelers will have their own reasons for wanting short-term contracts. However, it's important to consider the potential pitfalls. The revenue decrease that the agency experiences will result in a lower compensation package for the traveler. Again, fixed costs like travel expenses, credentialing costs, and orientation costs will take up a greater percentage of the revenue leaving less for pay. Additionally, the traveler will have to contend with more frequent moves and more paperwork burdens. Finally, if the hospital does indeed rush the orientation, the traveler may be at greater risk of errors in patient care.

If you determine that you want to work short-term contracts, then there are agencies that specialize in them. I believe FastStaff is the most prominent, but I'm sure there are others. Agencies that specialize in short term contracts may have a higher likelihood of having short term crisis rate contracts as well. This is because hospitals turn to them in such circumstances, and especially for strikes. This is not to say that other agencies don't handle short term contracts. You'll just have to ask around during the vetting process.

Chapter 29: "Hybrid" Travel Contracts

Not all travel contracts are the same. With a traditional travel contract, you are an integral part of the hospital's regular schedule. You'll be scheduled just like everyone else. You are essentially part of the hospital's staff for a temporary period. There are also situations out there that are quite different.

I've heard these contracts referred to as "Travel/Per Diem Contracts", "Float Pool Contracts", and "Hybrid Contracts." "Hybrid" is probably the best term to describe these contracts. Essentially, these contracts are a combination of a travel assignment and per-diem (PRN). They typically ask that the traveler provide 5 days of availability each week. In return, the agency will guarantee that the traveler works 3 shifts.

For example, the traveler might make themselves available Monday through Friday, 7PM-7AM. The agency would then schedule shifts for the traveler and call the traveler 2 hours prior to the shift start time to confirm or cancel the shift. If the traveler is conformed and works Monday, Tuesday, and Wednesday, then they wouldn't be obligated to stay on the schedule for Thursday and Friday. In other words, the traveler is obligated to work only 3 shifts.

If this sounds a lot like PRN, that's because it is. The agency is essentially staffing the traveler PRN. The difference is that the agency is offering a contract with a start date, end date, and guaranteed number of hours per week, hence the term "Hybrid". There are variations among agencies with respect to these scenarios. The guaranteed hours may work differently from agency to agency. Some agencies may be willing to provide travel stipends and/or company provided housing, and others may not. Some agencies may require that the traveler be willing to take shifts at multiple hospitals within a reasonable commute, others may not.

I always think it's best to ensure that the agency has some skin in the game. In other words, make sure the agency is providing something, like travel stipends or lodging. This will ensure that they stand to lose something if they are unable to schedule the shifts. For the record, it's fairly common for agencies to offer Extended Stay Hotels for Hybrid assignments because there's a need for flexibility. In any case, like any other assignment, take nothing for granted and make sure that everything is clearly spelled out in the contract.

I've heard mixed reviews on Hybrid Contracts. On the negative side, I've heard complaints that agencies didn't live up to their end of the bargain, mostly regarding the guaranteed hours. I've also heard complaints about the scheduling in some cases. In the worst case, a traveler would be scheduled at one hospital and then be told to go to another hospital 4 hours into the shift for the remaining 8 hours of the shift. To top it off, the traveler came to find that he was only paid for 11 hours because of the time it took him to drive to the other hospital in the middle of his shift!!

Hybrid Contracts aren't all bad though. They can be a great for someone looking to gain travel experience. Hybrids rarely require travel experience because travel experience is not required by hospitals for PRN shifts. Hybrids can also be used as stop gaps in several circumstances. For example, many travelers don't want to work the holidays. However, if you're looking for a contract to start any time around October, then you'll be hard pressed to find a contract that doesn't require working through the holidays. You can use a Hybrid contract because they're more flexible. Simply tell the agency the number of weeks that you can commit for, and they should be fine with it.

Hybrid contracts can also be handy if you're waiting on a state nursing license to come through before taking an assignment there.

For example, I worked with a pair of travelers who had a Compact license, were ready to travel immediately, but wanted to go to California and hadn't started the licensing process yet. We set them up with a Hybrid Contract in Dallas, TX while they were waiting on the California license. Seven weeks into their stay in Dallas, their California licenses came through and we started submitting them for assignments. They landed an assignment within 2 weeks and were off to California. The important point is that Hybrids are flexible because there is no obligation to the hospital.

These types of contracts are always out there, but they have become more prominent during the economic recession. During this time, healthcare workers who may have otherwise worked less or not at all opted to work more. Furthermore, hospitals realized they could get by with PRN staff in lieu of travelers, which hospitals always prefer to do. In addition, people utilized healthcare less in an effort to save money or because they lost their health benefits. As a result, many agencies turned to hybrid contracts as a way to keep revenue flowing and keep travelers working.

Conclusion

In this section we covered some of the additional issues you'll need to consider when deciding what you want out of your time as a traveler. Understanding the nuances of travel assignment location preferences, hospital preferences, shift preferences, and contract length preferences will help you understand the challenges you may face with respect to each of these issues. Certain decisions may limit your options while others may maximize your options. Knowing the differences can help you develop a strategy to achieve your goals.

If things aren't working out exactly as planned when it's time to lock down your first, or next, assignment, then you may be able to fall back on a Hybrid Contract or PRN until the ideal assignment comes through. Again, many agencies and recruiters may not be familiar with this terminology. You may need to explain the scenario for them. In any case, I'm willing to wager that the vast majority of agencies out there are going to be happy to get you working for them under a Hybrid or PRN type scenario especially if it means they'll have a chance to place you in your ideal assignment in a short time down the road.

Section 8: Securing and Completing Assignments

Now that we have a game plan for determining what we want out of our travel nursing assignments and finding agencies that can meet our needs, we can move on to discussing the process of securing an assignment. As a former travel nursing recruiter, my perspective on this process is quite a bit different than the average travel nurse's. In my view, a travel assignment isn't actually secured until the travel nurse has been welcomed to the hospital on the first day of orientation. And some of my former colleagues would argue that an assignment isn't actually secured until the first week of the assignment has been completed and the travel nurse has been scheduled for week two. Please don't let this scare you!! You'll see exactly what I'm talking about and it will make you more prepared than most to conquer the entire process.

It's important to point out that the steps in this process do not always follow the exact order that we're going to map out here. Different agencies, and even different recruiters within the same agency, will utilize different approaches to this process. However, all of the steps described here will play out in one way or another during the process of landing a travel assignment.

Chapter 30: Your Submission Profile

Once you have determined which travel nursing agencies that you're going to work with, you'll almost certainly be requested to complete each agency's on-line employment application as well as their skills checklists for the specialties that you're qualified for. There's a very good reason for this. The vast majority of hospitals that utilize travel nurses have a minimum set of items that they require travel nursing agencies to submit in order to even consider a candidate for a travel nursing assignment. As the industry has matured, these requirements have become pretty much uniform throughout the country. It is standard for hospitals to require an Application, Skills Checklist, and 2 recent references in order to even consider the candidate for open positions. These items constitute the candidate's "Submission Profile." In this chapter, I'll discuss the importance of each item and offer tips and tricks to deal with them efficiently and successfully.

Before we begin, it's important to point out that you should complete your submission profile prior to there being an assignment that you're interested in. I worked with many travelers who refused to complete an application and skills checklist until an assignment that they wanted was available. It is extremely rare that this will work. Again, hospitals receive profiles immediately upon a travel nursing assignment opening. Even if you were to immediately complete your application and skills checklist upon hearing of an assignment that you were interested in, it would most likely take several days before the profile could be submitted. As you'll see references must be checked and it is really rare for references to be immediately available. Therefore, the best approach is to utilize your checklist to decide which agencies you're going to work with, and complete their paperwork in advance.

The Application

On-line job applications are becoming the norm throughout the employment world in general. They are typically required simply to get candidates entered in a company's "Applicant Tracking System". Applicant tracking systems are software services that make the entire hiring process more efficient. While they certainly service this purpose for travel nursing agencies, they also offer much more.

When you fill out an on-line application with a travel nursing company, you are also most often filling out the resume that will be used to present you to the hospital. You see, on the back-end these systems are designed to render the collected data in a format that is similar to a standard resume so that it can be presented to the hospital. There are also features that provide the travel nursing agency with the potential to capture the data that is commonly required by the hospital managers responsible for hiring travel nurses. For example, certain hospitals may require knowing if the candidate has worked in a teaching facility, or how many beds were in the hospitals that the candidate worked with in the past, or whether or not the jobs the candidate has listed are travel assignments, or if the candidate has experience in trauma hospitals. Unfortunately, it's impossible to count on these details to be provided in every candidate's resume. So the agency can simply add fields designed to capture the necessary details in their on-line applications.

As you complete the on-line applications, you'll notice that many of the fields within the applications may not be required. In other words, the application system will allow you to proceed with the process and submit the application even though all the fields have not been completed. This is because agencies don't want candidates to abandon the process out of frustration. They also know that once the electronic file is created and saved into their system, their recruiters can fill in the blanks if necessary.

I strongly urge you to complete the on-line applications in their entirety. Yes, recruiters can fill in the blanks. However, the recruiter may be working with several candidates who already have completed profiles. They may also have a backlog of unfinished profiles for which they need to fill in the blanks. As a result, recruiters need to make a judgment call as to where to focus their time. Your profile may not come up for a day or several days if it is incomplete. However, it will be immediately taken up if it is fully complete. This can make a big difference in the very fluid travel nursing job market. In addition, given the high turnover rate among travel nursing recruiters, you'd be better served completing the details on your own as opposed to taking your chances with a potential rookie.

Many healthcare professionals have trouble with some of the information being sought on travel nursing agency on-line applications. They often times forget the addresses, telephone numbers, and/or number of beds for all of their previous employers. In this case, I highly recommend utilizing the American Hospital Directory (AHD) to track down the information. AHD is a great website that allows you to track down this information quickly, conveniently, and for free.

Many experienced travelers have difficulty completing the on-line applications because they have so many jobs to enter. For example, if a travel nurse has been at it for 5 years, then they may have over 20 separate assignments to enter. This is cumbersome. In this case, I recommend that you review Appendix E titled "Travel Nursing Resume." If you maintain a detailed travel nursing resume that ensures that hospitals and/or recruiters have easy access typically required data, then some agencies may allow you to substitute your resume for the work history section of the application temporarily. However, you will most likely still be required to complete an application sans detailed work history.

In addition to capturing a candidate's vital work history data, on-line applications also serve another very important purpose for the travel nursing agency. They get the candidate to answer various background questions and agree to various application signing statements. There are several reasons that make having these items very important for the travel nursing agency. First, hospitals have various requirements regarding criminal backgrounds. Some have very strict requirements and the agency needs to know if a candidate has violated any of these prior to submitting the candidate to the facility. Second, agencies often need the signing statements to complete other hospital requirements. For example, some hospitals require that a criminal background check accompany the submission profile. The agency needs to have a signed agreement permitting the criminal background check in order for it to be conducted. In addition, hospitals require agencies to check the candidate's references. This often requires a statement from the candidate that grants the references permission to provide the details being sought.

The travel nursing agency on-line application is a vital part in the process of securing a travel nursing assignment. You'll want to ensure that your application is completed in a timely and professional manner. Use capital letters when applicable. Provide details designed to sell your attributes. And remember, the information you provide is not just for the travel nursing agency, it's for the people who actually make the hiring decisions at the hospitals you'll be seeking to land a travel nursing assignment with.

Finally, I think this next point merits its own separate statement. You should include any requested time off on your application. If the agency's application does not provide an option for this, then you should communicate it to your recruiter to ensure it's added. You can always discuss it during the interview, but it's always best for the hospital to know this beforehand. Additionally, the absence of this information can delay your profile from being accepted.

Skills Checklists

A skills checklist is a self-assessment tool designed to give hiring managers and travel nursing agencies a solid understanding of a candidate's experience within a specific skill set. They can be formatted differently, but they are all quite similar. They typically ask candidates to rate their level of experience with various processes, procedures, and equipment that are commonly utilized within the unit or specialty in question. Some skills checklists also ask the candidate to signify the amount of recent experience they've had with the various processes, procedures, and equipment. For example, they may ask the candidate to rate the amount of exposure they've had within the last 2 years. Skills checklists have become a standard requirement for travel assignment consideration.

Skills checklists can be quite lengthy and they almost always are. It's not uncommon for them to exceed 5 pages and ask for ratings on over 100 different topics. While the length of a skills checklist can be quite cumbersome, it's also an advantage for the travel nurse. As we've mentioned previously, your profile is going to compete with other profiles for the hiring manager's attention. If a hiring manager is looking for experience with a specific skill which she can find on one skills checklist but not another, then she is definitely going to contact the person whose skills checklist has the information being sought. Therefore, you should be concerned if a travel nursing agency has inadequate skills checklists.

It's typical for hospitals to require skills checklists to have been completed and signed within a particular period of time. For example, most hospitals will only accept skills checklists that have been completed within the past year. This is understandable because skills both increase and diminish over time. Unfortunately, it means that travel nurses will be filling these documents out on a routine basis.

There's really no trick when it comes to skills checklists. They're simply a part of the game. However, my experience tells me that many healthcare professionals spend too much time on them. They sit and debate whether or not they should rate themselves as a 3 or a 4 for each item being measured. I've also found that most people have a tendency to underrate themselves. I'm not suggesting that you breeze through the skills checklist and just give yourself a bunch of inappropriate high marks. However, you should spend a limited amount of time on them with the understanding that these documents are simply used to provide a rough idea of your skills.

References

References are the third and final component of the submission profile. Again, it's possible that certain hospitals require more, but the vast majority of hospitals will require an application, skills checklist, and references. As a result, maintaining your references is extremely important when travel nursing. It's also important for seeking permanent nursing jobs so these tips will come in handy during your permanent job searches as well.

Every facility has its own requirements regarding references. The standard requirement is: 2 supervisory clinical references covering 1 year within the previous three years in the specialty applied for. Let's examine exactly what this means beginning with "2 supervisory". Hospitals will typically accept references from anyone who served in a supervisory role with the candidate. For nurses, this means anyone who was a Charge Nurse or higher on the management ladder.

Next, let's take a look at what they mean by "clinical references." A clinical reference is one that will attest to the candidate's clinical skills as opposed to simply verifying the candidate's dates of employment. Finally, let's look at what they mean by "covering 1 year within the previous three years in the specialty applied for." This means that the references must combine to cover at least 1 year of experience within the past 3 years. For example, if you worked with one reference for 3 months and another reference for 6 months, then that's only 9 months total. You'd need another reference covering 3 months or more to bring it up to the 1 year requirement. It's important to point out that the best facilities typically have the most stringent requirements. For example, some facilities will not accept a candidate without a reference from the candidate's most recent Unit Manager.

Let's also examine what typically doesn't qualify as a reference. First, co-workers do not qualify as references unless they were in a supervisory role. The reference checker will ask for the role of the reference and in what capacity the reference and candidate functioned together. Second, agency references are typically not accepted for travel assignments. This includes recruiters. This is because agencies are unable to provide clinical references. They are unable to attest to the candidate's clinical skills because they are unqualified to do so and/or they did not work directly with the candidate. Oddly enough, many hospitals seem perfectly content to accept agency references for permanent jobs. I know this because I've provided references for many of my clients seeking permanent jobs. Again, as a recruiter, I'm unable to provide a clinical assessment, but hospitals don't seem to care as much when it comes to potential permanent employees.

Perhaps they still seek out clinical references and don't value the reference I provide as highly as they do the clinical references.

In any case, solid references can be the differentiating factor in determining which candidate lands the travel nursing assignment, or permanent nursing job for that matter. I've heard many travel nurses convey their belief that references were never really contacted anyway and therefore weren't important. This is incorrect.

Hospitals require that references be contacted in an effort to vet all candidates. In addition, hospitals require a report of the questions asked of the reference and the answers provided by the reference. If a travel nursing agency, or recruiter, decides not to do this then they are abrogating their responsibilities and ultimately lying. I've worked with recruiters on many occasions who took it upon themselves to submit falsified references. In one instance, the healthcare professional made serious medication errors that resulted in termination at which point the hospital contacted the references and found out that the references provided by the recruiter were falsified. On another occasion, the hospital checked references as part of their routine quality assurance measures to find that a candidate's references were falsified by the recruiter. These recruiters were dismissed on both occasions.

Now, the problem with obtaining references is that while facilities require references, they also prohibit their employees from providing them. There are several approaches to solving this dilemma. If you're a permanent employee, you should definitely develop close relationships with several charge nurses, supervisors, and others in supervisory roles. I realize that this sounds duplicitous. However, building such relationships is good for many reasons, and besides, this is your career we're talking about. When the time comes, politely ask these individuals if you can put them down as a reference for future employment opportunities. I know this can be a difficult conversation for many to have, but it's necessary none the less.

Keep in mind that the individual checking the reference is going to ask about your level of expertise in the specialty in question, about your ability to handle stress, your quality and quantity of work, and your attendance record. You'll want your references to be able to positively attest to these aspects of your work. You also want to be sure that they don't decline to provide a reference when called. That's why requesting permission from your references before putting them down on an application is important.

You'll want to try and do the same thing as a travel nurse. However, developing this level of relationship when you're a travel nurse can be very difficult. You're most likely going to be there for only 13 to 26 weeks. If you are unable to develop these close relationships in this timeframe, then you can utilize an Evaluation Form.

Typically, the contract between the travel nursing agency and the hospital will require that the hospital provide the travel nursing agency with evaluations for their travel nurses. You can ask your travel nurse recruiter to provide you with a copy of this evaluation for your records. This will probably work for about half of your assignments. Unfortunately, hospitals don't always comply, and sometimes travel nursing companies will refuse to provide you with a copy. I believe that travel nursing companies that refuse to provide copies of references to their travel nurses do so as a way to keep their travel nurses beholden to them.

In the event that you're not able to get a copy from the travel nursing company, you can take your own evaluation form into the facility and ask a charge nurse or supervisor to complete it. You can ask your travel nurse recruiter for an evaluation form, or you can visit my blog thetruthabouttravelnursing.com where one is available for download.

In any case, you'll want to be sure that you have copies of these for your own records. They will be a huge help in landing assignments, especially the best assignments. They'll also be a huge help when you've decided you want to make the transition back to permanent work. If you travel for a period of one or more years, then you'll most certainly need these evaluations when applying for permanent nursing jobs. It'll be very unlikely that you'll be able to rely on conversational references without the written evaluations. When the reference checker for a permanent employer calls to check your travel nursing assignment references, these evaluation forms will ensure that all goes smoothly and the reference doesn't forget who you are. The forms can be faxed to the evaluator in question for verification.

Putting It All Together

Once you have completed the application and skills checklist and provided your references, your recruiter will get everything ready to go. A good recruiter will go through the entire profile to ensure that all of the vital information is present. They will correct any spelling and grammar errors. They may write a summary of your attributes in order to make the profile more marketable. They will highlight certain experiences and attributes that they know to be highly desired. They will also obtain copies of license verifications from the state Board of Nursing for each state license you have listed. The references will be checked in accordance with the travel nursing agency's policy. Finally, it's possible that they run a criminal background check and/or education verification depending on where they're hoping to submit your profile. All of these items will then be packaged up so that they're ready to go at a moment's notice.

Chapter 31: The Green Light for Submission

Once your profile is complete, it's time to start having it submitted for open travel assignments. There are several ways that both you and agencies can approach this step in the process. Therefore, it's easiest for us to take a look at some common scenarios.

Scenario 1: Recruiter Hard Ball: In this scenario, the recruiter is going to try to get you to agree to a set of parameters. Then, if an assignment meets the parameters, they can submit your profile immediately. This approach is very common among larger agencies. Essentially, the recruiter wants to avoid calling you for *every* assignment in an effort to convince you to take the assignment. Instead, they establish what you're looking for in terms of the start date, shift, unit, contract length, and location. Then they get you to agree to a compensation package. They then tell you that you'll be submitted for assignments that meet these criteria, and match or beat the compensation package agreed upon. Some recruiters are so aggressive with this approach that they'll say things like, "OK, so we have a verbal contract agreement, right?" And some will even send you a contract even though there isn't an assignment yet!

There are four reasons that agencies prefer this approach. First, it's very efficient. If the recruiter can have fewer and shorter conversations with any given candidate, then they can talk to more candidates, which leads to submitting more candidates, which leads to more contracts, which leads to more gross revenue. Second, this approach gives agencies a leg up in compensation negotiations. If they're able to get the candidate to agree to a base compensation package, then they'll be in a position to take a higher profit margin on contracts that have higher bill rates. It doesn't always work out this way, but this is a negotiating advantage none the less. Third, this approach enables the recruiter to submit the profile immediately, which is a benefit to both the agency and the travel nurse. As mentioned previously, travel assignments fill quickly. Being submitted early makes a big difference in landing the assignment. Finally, the most aggressive maneuvers are designed to ensure that you are loyal to this one agency and that you don't decline an offer if one is made.

Scenario 2: Recruiter Soft Ball: In this scenario, the recruiter is going to take a more passive and service oriented approach to gaining your agreement to be submitted to an assignment. The recruiter will determine what you're looking for in an assignment in terms of the start date, shift, unit, contract length, and location. Then, when an assignment pops up that meets your criteria, they'll give you a call and run it by you. At this point, you may or may not discuss the compensation package for this particular assignment. The recruiter may or may not address it, and you may or may not ask about it.

Of course, compensation will have to be discussed at some point. If compensation isn't discussed until after you've been offered the assignment, then you'll be in a better negotiating position. Once the assignment has been offered, the agency really wants to get you to accept the assignment. Their client, the hospital, will be counting on them to deliver. When an agency's candidates decline offers from a hospital it negatively affects the agency's value to the hospital. In addition, agency's hate declining offers because doing so represents a missed opportunity. This is why I call this approach "Recruiter Soft Ball."

You may wonder why any recruiter would want to take this approach. In fact, they would prefer not to take this approach. Recruiters often take this approach because they feel their circumstances necessitate them to do so. You see, this approach is more common among mid and small sized agencies that have far fewer hospital contracts than their larger competitors. These agencies also tend to be sub-vendors on a greater percentage of their contracts. As a result they have access to fewer assignments and a higher percentage of their assignments are highly competitive and/or have lower bill rates. They're concerned that if they have to discuss rates up front, they may lose you early. There's a better chance that you'll accept an assignment after it's offered, especially if there are no other options available at the time you're ready to start. Now I'm not saying that you're going to get horrible rates with these companies. You may in fact get a better rate due to any number of reasons including your enhanced negotiating position.

Scenario 3: You Play Hard Ball: In this scenario, you take an aggressive approach to determining where you can be submitted and which agency has permission to submit your profile. This scenario can result in a little more compensation, but it will also require more work on your part in order to maximize the potential. In order to be successful with this approach, you'll need to be familiar with the landscape of your top choice markets. For example, if you're licensed in Colorado and California, and you want to go to Denver or Los Angeles, then finding all of the hospitals in these areas is the first step to determining which agency is going to represent you at each hospital.

Again, you can use the American Hospital Directory's website (ahd.com) to find all the hospitals in a given area. Remember to search for hospitals located within the entire metropolitan area if you're willing to accept assignments within the entire metropolitan area. For example, Denver's metropolitan area includes Aurora and Broomfield. If you search AHD for Denver only, then you won't see the hospitals in Aurora and Broomfield. Once you have a list of all the hospitals in your desired locations, you can begin to determine which agencies are going to represent you at each of the hospitals.

When you speak with agencies, you'll ask them which of the hospitals on your list they have contracts with. You'll then ask the agencies for compensation quotes that include the standard set of compensation variables you've decided are most important to you. This will ensure that you're making an "apples to apples" comparison between agencies that have contracts at the same facility. Once you have the quotes, you can decide which agencies will have the green light to represent you at the various hospitals. Remember, compensation isn't the only variable to consider when making this choice. You'll also want to consider the relationships that the various agencies have with the hospitals, the level of service that the agencies provide, and your relationships with the recruiters.

Once you've decided on an agency for a particular hospital, then I recommend calling the other agencies first to let them know that you're choosing another agency, and why. Doing so may result in better compensation offers. For example, you may call an agency and let them know that you've decided to go with a competitor because the competitor offered a higher level of compensation overall. The losing agency may up its offer to get you to work with them. It's okay if they don't make a counter offer. The important thing is that you've let them know you're going with another agency so that there's no confusion during the submission process, and you've tried to negotiate a better deal in the process. There's no harm in this. It's business, not personal.

This approach accomplishes two key objectives. First, it ensures that you're getting a solid compensation package for travel assignments at the hospitals in question. By shopping around for rates and playing one agency off of another, you can rest assured that you're receiving a good deal. Second, this approach ensures that you can be immediately submitted for travel assignments as they become available thereby increasing your chances of landing an assignment. There should be no confusion among the agencies as to who can, and cannot, submit your profile to any given hospital.

There is another base you have to cover with this approach. You should let all of the agencies know that they're welcome to contact you with other offers that they believe you may be interested in. It's best to keep your options open when it comes to travel assignments. You never know when or where something great will pop up and you can never be certain if the timing will work out for landing an assignment in your most desired locations.

Scenario 4: You Play Soft Ball: In this scenario, you take a more passive approach to dealing with the agencies. Essentially, you let them do what they want. Of course, the basic information is still going to be exchanged. You'll let agencies know what you're looking for in terms of the start date, shift, unit, contract length, and location. You may even give them a basic idea of the minimum compensation package you'll accept. But other than that, you give all the agencies you're working with the green light to submit your profile as they see fit. This approach is great if you're looking to expend minimum effort. It also ensures that your profile will be submitted immediately as assignments become available. However, this approach also has its share of disadvantages and fallout.

You run the risk of getting submitted for assignments you're not interested in with this approach. You may not be interested in a particular assignment for any number of reasons including its location, its shift, or its compensation to name a few. This is a tragedy for some people. I've worked with many travel-health professionals who felt that they had to be 100% willing to take an assignment before they were willing to be submitted for the assignment. However, there's nothing really wrong with declining an offer. Sure, agencies don't like it, but you're their customer. Perhaps they should do a better job at heeding your stated expectations before submitting your profile willy-nilly.

Hospitals aren't too fond of their offers being declined either, but they're a little more understanding than most people think. Hospitals understand that people apply for more than one job at a time. They understand that something may have come up during the interview that deterred the candidate from accepting the position. Furthermore, if you decline an assignment somewhere, then chances are you had a pretty good reason for doing so and probably wouldn't want to work there in the future anyway.

You also run the risk of being submitted by multiple agencies for the same travel assignment. As mentioned previously, this is rarely "frowned upon" by the hospital as many recruiters claim it is. Most hospitals and VMS's have policies in place to deal with multiple submissions for the same candidate. However, this is also where you can run into some trouble. You may end up getting stuck with an agency that isn't your top choice. For example, the hospital may have a "first come, first served" policy that results in the first agency submitting the candidate becoming the agency the candidate must work with. It's also possible that the hospital contacts you for an interview and asks you which agency you're going to work with, which could potentially put you on the spot to make a decision without knowing the compensation packages being offered by the various agencies.

Scenario 5: Talk to Me: In this scenario, you provide recruiters with the basic parameters for your search and require that they contact you for each new assignment that pops up and they refrain from submitting your profile until they have spoken to you and obtained your permission. Many travelers seem to prefer this approach. It ensures that you are only submitted to assignments that you've agreed to be submitted to. It allows you the opportunity to ask any questions you might have about a particular assignment before being submitted. It prevents against multiple submissions for the same assignment. It allows you to negotiate a compensation package for each assignment as opposed to agreeing to a base package. There are several factors to consider if you choose this approach.

First, travel assignments tend to be filled quickly. You have to remember that these aren't permanent jobs and the need is typically urgent. Therefore, hospitals are much quicker to make a hiring decision than they are with a permanent job. These factors, coupled with the high level of competition between agencies, tend to favor the first qualified candidates submitted.

Therefore, it's best to be highly responsive to your recruiters if you choose to utilize this approach. This means taking your recruiters' calls immediately or calling them back quickly. Failing to do so will greatly diminish your chances at landing assignments, especially the most desirable assignments. In addition, your recruiters may question your level of urgency and start spending less time working for you and more time with other candidates who are more responsive. I know this sounds harsh, but recruiters have to prioritize their time in favor of the most "placeable" candidates in order to meet their job requirements. Finally, keep in mind that managing all of the calls you receive as a result of this approach may be daunting.

Second, your recruiter may not be able to answer all the questions you have about every assignment. As mentioned previously, direct relationships between hospitals and agencies are becoming less and less frequent. As a result, agencies typically have far less information about any given assignment. Meanwhile, obtaining specific information that isn't included in the job requisition can sometimes be time consuming at best and impossible at worst.

Therefore, it's best to have discussions early in the process about any and all specific questions that are important to you. This way, your recruiter can keep an eye out for the information you're seeking prior to calling you with a new opportunity. Furthermore, most of the specific information regarding the hospital is obtained during an interview with the hospital. We'll discuss this in greater detail in the chapter on interviewing.

Finally, this approach is better to use in some circumstances than others. It's better to use this approach in tight labor markets than in slack labor markets. In tight labor markets, assignments are open longer before being filled. This allows both recruiters and candidates to take more time with the process. It's also better for to use this approach if you have a license or specialty in very high demand. For example, assignments for Physicians, Physical Therapists, Occupational Therapists, Labor & Delivery RNs, and OR RNs tend to stay open longer than most. Lastly, it's better not to use this approach for high demand markets. Assignments in San Diego, CA and Hawaii get filled very quickly.

Again, each of the 5 scenarios is offered as a possible example of what could transpire in the process of getting submitted for travel assignments. They may not always play out in the manner described here and I'm sure there are other scenarios. What's important is that you have a basic understanding of the mechanisms at play in this process. What's the agency thinking? How can you improve your negotiating position? How can you get what you want out of the process?

Finally, you should be open to having your profile submitted for multiple assignments at the same time. Counting on one assignment to hit is a bad strategy. Again, it's a competitive market. You have to get submitted to multiple assignments to land 1. The agency knows this very well. In fact, this reality serves as logic supporting part of the metrics by which recruiter job performance is measured. For example, agencies may hold a belief that for every 5 submissions a recruiter completes, they can expect 2 interviews and one offer. Many healthcare professionals believe that if they get multiple offers they'll have to let someone down by declining. Trust me, hospitals are aware that people need to find jobs and that they're not the only game in town. Besides, this is business and you have to look out for yourself.

Chapter 32: What Happens When Your Profile is Submitted?

There are two common methods for submitting a candidate's profile to a hospital for a travel assignment. These methods are driven by the type of relationship that the agency has with the hospital in question. Remember, the two main relationship types are direct relationships and Vendor Management Service relationships. Each method is going to play out in different ways for the travel nurse, but the ultimate goal is to land an interview.

If an agency has a direct relationship with the hospital, then the profile will be submitted directly to the designated point person at the hospital. These days, email is the most common method used to submit a profile in this scenario. Depending on the closeness of the relationship and/or the hospital's policies, the point person could be a staffing office representative or even a Unit Manager.

In the vast majority of cases, the profile will be submitted to a staffing office representative. The staffing office representative will screen all profiles received. The representative may or may not contact the candidate to ask some standard preliminary questions. Either way, the representative will forward those that pass initial screening to the Unit Manager or Supervisor responsible for conducting the interview.

Communication between agency and hospital becomes an issue at this point. If the agency has a really good relationship with the hospital, they may have a better chance at receiving frequent progress updates. However, all parties at the hospital have other responsibilities to attend besides travel nursing. As a result, significant delays in communication can occur. Sometimes the candidate will receive a call for an interview immediately. Other times it can take weeks for the candidate to receive a call. Sometimes the staffing office representative will tell the agency that their candidate didn't pass the initial screening process, and sometimes they won't. Likewise, sometimes the agency will find out that the assignment has been filled by another candidate, and sometimes they won't.

Unfortunately, the process can be just as opaque, if not more so, when the agency has a Vendor Management Service relationship with the hospital. Remember, Vendor Management Service relationships entail a middle man between the agency and the hospital. Sometimes the middle man accepts submission profiles via email. However, sophisticated Vendor Management Software is becoming ever more prevalent in the industry. If the Vendor Management Service is using such software, then the agency must log into the system and follow the software's process for submitting candidates. This process typically entails answering a series of questions about the candidate's experience, licenses, and certifications in addition to uploading the candidate's submission profile. Sometimes the software system uses the answers provided to the questions to rank the candidate against predetermined criteria for the assignment in question. Higher ranking candidates are pushed to the top of the list.

In any case, the profile may go directly to the hospital at which point the candidate may receive a call from the unit manager or a staffing office representative for an interview, or to schedule an interview. Alternatively, the profile may get routed to a representative from the Vendor Management Service who may call the candidate with some pre-screening questions before passing the profile on to the hospital or to one of the VMS's own interviewers. Just as with direct relationships, the communication between the agency and the hospital/ Vendor Management Service can breakdown. The fact that there are more hands in the pot with the Vendor Management Service relationship tends to mean that communication breakdowns occur more often.

I was often asked why lengthy delays existed assuming that hospitals had an immediate need for help. There are many reasons for delays, but perhaps the most common reason involves the fact that there is almost always more than 1 candidate for every job. The hospital may have chosen to interview a candidate right away and extend an offer to the candidate immediately. At that point, the candidate may accept immediately, or it may take a few days. If the candidate declines the offer after a few days, then the hospital is back to square one and the process starts over. If this happens once or twice during the process, then we're looking at 1 to 2 weeks before anything is known for certain. Meanwhile, all the other candidates are in a holding pattern

Chapter 33: The Interview

The most important thing to know about the travel assignment interview is that it's your time to find out everything you possibly can about the hospital, the unit, and the expectations they have for you. Furthermore, the interview is your time to make sure that the hospital can agree to any special stipulations you're seeking. Requested time off, floating preferences, and other special requests should all be addressed in the interview.

Even if your recruiter has given you answers to certain questions you had about these subjects, you must still address all questions during the interview. Given the fluid nature of the travel assignment job market, it's very difficult, and often impossible, for recruiters to get timely and accurate answers to questions you may have about the hospital, the unit, and various policies that may be important to you.

It is extremely rare for a recruiter to be permitted to contact the hospital directly. Imagine how many calls unit managers and hospital staffing offices would be fielding if the hundreds of recruiters engaged in staffing a particular opening were to have the ability to call with any question they didn't have an answer for. Instead, when your recruiter answers your questions about the assignment they are at best relying on information they receive their account management team, and at worst the recruiter may just offer fabricated answers. Recruiters may also draw on their own past experiences or a generic unit description provided by the hospital at some point in the past. Moreover, when a travel assignment opening is made public, the notice often includes little more than the unit, the shift, the desired start date, and the contract length.

You must take the interview as an opportunity to get your questions answered if they're important to your decision making process. Some standard questions that I recommend asking are (also see Appendix C):

What's the shift?

Why is there a need for a traveler?

Is there a possibility for extension?

What's the orientation process for travelers?

How many travelers are currently on staff?

Are travelers well received by the staff?

What's the float policy?

Will I be working the same schedule as your permanent staff?

What's the nurse to patient ratio?

What type of support staff is available?

What types of patients does the unit typically see?

What charting system is used?

What medication system and protocols are in place?

How many beds are in the unit?

Are there any examinations given prior to starting the assignment?

If the examinations are failed, is the traveler sent home, or does the hospital remediate and retest?

How is the schedule determined?

Is overtime available? If so, what's the process for travelers to secure overtime?

Did you see my requested time off? Can it be approved?

What's the parking situation at the hospital?

Ask any questions that are specific to your unit.

If you want anything related to your working conditions to be added to your contract, then you should seek agreement from the interviewer.

It's important to note that there are also subjects that the interviewer will not be able to address. Questions regarding the compensation package and anything related to the services provided by the healthcare staffing agency should be taken up with your recruiter. For all intents and purposes, only questions pertaining to the hospital itself should be taken up with hospital personnel. It's not the end of the world if you ask them other questions; they just won't have the answers.

Getting the answers to your questions can prove difficult in some cases depending on who you actually get to speak with. As mentioned previously, there are several interview scenarios. Let's take a look at what you can expect out of each of the scenarios:

Scenario 1: The Preliminary Interview: Preliminary interviews are typically conducted for initial screening purposes and to schedule a full interview for a later date/time. The initial screening questions are often designed to ensure that the candidate meets some standard level of requirements. They may ask if you have certain certifications required by the unit, if you have ever participated in a code blue, if you're proficient with IVs, or any number of other questions that are deemed important to the unit. If all questions are answered as needed, then the preliminary interviewer will schedule a time for a full interview. As long as you're going to get a full interview, you can reserve any questions you have for the full interview.

Scenario 2: Interviewing with the Unit Manager/Supervisor: This is the best case scenario for you. My experience indicates that this is the scenario under which the majority of interviews are conducted. There are several things worth noting for this scenario. First, you really won't know what to expect in terms of the interview itself. Different managers and supervisors approach interviewing in different ways. There is no uniform set of questions that you can expect to be asked. Second, you shouldn't have a problem getting your questions answered and getting all the details ironed out. Third, you may receive a verbal offer from the interviewer on the spot during the interview. You should not accept the offer immediately unless you already have 100% of the details worked out with your recruiter and you are 100% certain that you're going to accept the assignment. If you do not have the details worked out and/or are unsure if the assignment is right for you, then politely request the interviewer to send the offer to your agency so that you can work out the rest of the details with them.

Scenario 3: Interviewing with the MSP: In this scenario, you will interview with a representative from the Managed Service Provider. Interviewing services are one of the services that MSPs offer to their client hospitals. The interviewer is typically a healthcare professional licensed in the field for which the interview is being conducted. You can expect these interviews to be very structured. Typically, there is a standard template of questions that the hospital and MSP have agreed will be asked. The interviewer will record the answers provided and probe for further information where necessary. You can expect questions about medications specific to your unit. They may even ask for medication measurements. You can also expect situational questions like, "What would you do if the doctor gave an order you knew was incorrect?"

Unfortunately, this scenario almost never affords you the opportunity to get your questions answered. However, you should always ask the interviewer if they are able to answer your questions. They will sometimes have the answers albeit infrequently. In this case, you'll need to convey your questions to your recruiter who will forward them through the chain to a point where they can be answered. The predicament here is that it may take quite some time before answers are received. In the meantime, the offer will be extended and the MSP will put pressure on the agency for an answer. You'll have to decide for yourself how best to proceed in this situation.

Scenario 4: No Interview: Believe it or not, there are some instances in which an offer is extended without an interview ever taking place. There are many reasons this can happen, but the bottom line is that the decision maker is comfortable enough with the profile to simply make an offer on the spot. Many healthcare professionals that I worked with took this as a horrible sign, thinking that perhaps the hospital was unorganized and/or unprofessional. However, this is not the case. I've had this happen at some of the most reputable healthcare organizations in the country. Again, there are many reasons that this can happen and they're not all bad. In any case, your only course of action is to send your questions to your recruiter who will forward them along.

Now that we have an idea of the various interview scenarios, we can take a look at some of the more general issues that we haven't covered yet. First, don't get discouraged if you don't get a call for an interview. I often got the impression from healthcare professionals that they thought they were the only candidate, or one of a few candidates, that was being considered for the assignment. Again, hospitals may receive a large or small number of profiles depending on the job market and the desirability of the particular assignment in question. Second, don't be discouraged if you don't receive a call for a scheduled interview. Things come up in the work place and sometimes interviews need to be rescheduled as a result. Third, do a little research on the hospital you're interviewing with. You may not need to know everything you would for a permanent job interview, but you should know the basics. Finally, be ready to discuss your work history and details about your former employers in particular. I recommend knowing the number of beds in the hospitals and units you've worked in as well as whether or not the hospitals were teaching hospitals and/or trauma hospitals. This is all information that you can use to relate to the hospital your interviewing with.

Chapter 34: The Offer and Confirmation

Once you've completed the interview you'll receive word as to whether or not you're receiving an official offer. In my experience, an offer is official when it is communicated to your agency. I point this out because I have experienced situations in which the healthcare professional received a verbal offer from the interviewer, but the offer failed to come to fruition. This can happen for any number of reasons; the main point is that it does indeed happen.

The time it takes for the official offer to come through can vary depending on several factors. Offers that come through immediately happen most when the agency and hospital have a direct relationship. This is particularly true when you get to interview directly with the Unit Manager. For them, it's simply a matter of sending an email signifying that the offer is extended. However, even with a direct relationship, an offer may need to go through communication channels or approval channels where it can be delayed.

The biggest delays tend to take place when an MSP is involved in the process. When you interview with an MSP representative, your interview report is forwarded on to the hospital. In theory, the unit manager will review the interview report and make a decision.

However, we have no idea what the unit manager's schedule is like, so it's difficult to determine how long it may take for them to get around to this task.

Additionally, circumstances may change between the time the order is released and the time the interview report is received at the hospital. The new circumstances may put the need for the job order in question which may not be communicated to the MSP. I once had an offer come back 3 weeks after the interview as a result of uncertainty at the hospital regarding the need for the job order. We had no idea what the delay was for until the offer finally came through.

Even when you are able to interview directly with the unit manager, there still seems to be a bigger delay in offers when a Vendor Management Service is involved. There are simply more links in the chain between you and the hospital and therefore more chance of communication breakdowns. That said, it's possible for offers to come through immediately when a Vendor Management Service is involved.

Once the offer is received, the hospital wants to hear back from you as soon as possible. They need to know if you'll be accepting the offer or not because if you don't accept, they need to interview other candidates. I understand they may not have afforded you the same courtesy if there was a delay in the offer coming back to you. However, they are holding the cards in a sense. They can retract the offer if they feel there's been too much of delay in hearing back from you. The standard expectation is for the hospital to hear back from you within 48 hours of the offer being extended. Some hospitals want to hear back sooner and others are a little more flexible. In any case, you can count on your recruiter trying to seal the deal quickly.

When an offer is accepted, the healthcare staffing agency is going to send what is commonly referred to as a "confirmation" to the hospital. The confirmation is more than just an email or telephone call simply stating that the offer has been accepted. The confirmation is an official document that includes the basic details of the assignment. Confirmations typically include the start date, end date, hospital name, hospital location, the unit, the shift, the healthcare professional's name, social security number, date of birth, the bill rate, and a space for listing miscellaneous items. The confirmation is signed by a designated representative of the staffing agency and sent to the hospital where it will be signed by a designated representative of the hospital with a copy returned to the agency.

Sometimes recruiters will press to get a signed contract back from you before sending a confirmation. They may use this as leverage to get the signed contract back from you quickly by saying that they are unable to send a confirmation without getting the signed contract back from you first. This is not an underhanded maneuver but rather a sound business practice designed to ensure that recruiters don't jump the gun and send confirmations that haven't actually been agreed to. Other times the recruiter will send a confirmation based on your verbal acceptance of the offer.

All things considered, it is highly recommended that you contact your recruiter immediately after your interview if you are interested in accepting the assignment. There are two variables that you'll want to address as soon as possible. First, you'll want to get all of the compensation details ironed out and agreed to if you haven't already. The compensation details can take time to work out depending on the complexity of the compensation package, so getting on top of this immediately is important.

Second, you'll want to immediately let your recruiter know about any agreements you came to with the unit manager so they can be included in the confirmation. This includes things like approval for requested time off and floating agreements among other things. This is very important because such details may not be included in the offer received by the agency. In fact, in most cases, the offer from the hospital is a simple email that says something like, "Please offer" and that's it. Therefore, you can't assume that your recruiter will know about the agreements. And you'll want any agreements made between you and the unit manager to be included in the confirmation that the agency sends to the hospital. Getting these agreements into the confirmation is the only way to ensure that the agency can hold the hospital accountable for honoring them. We'll discuss this in detail in the chapter on contracts.

What happens if you didn't get to speak with the unit manager, or forgot to address a potential need for agreement with them? There are two options. First, you could simply pass the issues along to your recruiter and await reply. I recommend this option if you're trying to buy time for some reason. However, this tactic may backfire and too much time may pass resulting in the offer being retracted. Second, you could simply have your recruiter send the confirmation with the requests included. I recommend this option if you you're 100% willing to accept the assignment as long as your stipulations are agreed to.

At this point, you're probably wondering about the travel nursing contract that you hear so much about. Where does it come into play? We'll discuss the contract next!

Chapter 35: The Contract

As mentioned previously, you want to ensure that the contract includes a certain set of information for tax purposes. This includes the start date, end date, taxable pay rate, non-taxable stipend rates, and the address of the hospital. In addition, you should make sure that *every* compensation variable you're expecting is stated in the contract. You should also make sure that all the pertinent contractual parameters are present such as the unit, and shift to be worked. Finally, you should make sure that every special agreement you've made with the hospital regarding your working conditions or requested time off is included in the contract.

Beyond these items, different agencies have different contracts. The differences lie largely with the various contract clauses that agencies choose to use. I've seen some contracts that are very brief and simple. I've seen other contracts that are very comprehensive. It's important to carefully review the entire contract no matter how big or small it is. You can never assume that something is in the contract, so make sure everything that's important to you is included. In fact, many contracts may have a clause stipulating that the contract represents the entire agreement between you and the agency thereby. Therefore, if it's not in the contract, then you can hold them to account for it. Furthermore, contract clauses can potentially dictate how disputes and various other issues are to be resolved. It's best to know these things in advance.

There are several contract clauses that merit special attention. Let's address them individually.

Missed-Hours-Penalties and Charge-Backs

We've touched on penalties previously. Missed-hours-penalties are mechanisms for the agency to recoup costs when the full contracted hours are not worked. Remember, the agency can only bill the hospital for the hours you work, and billable hours represent the only source of revenue for an agency. If you don't work, then the agency isn't collecting the money it needs to cover the costs of things like housing, travel expenses, and medical benefits. Therefore, a penalty clause may stipulate that the traveler will be penalized a certain dollar amount for every hour not worked in a given pay period. For example, the clause may state that the traveler's pay check will be deducted $20 for every missed contract hour in a two week period.

The amount of the penalty is typically based on the value of all, or some, compensation variables except the hourly rate. For example, the value of the penalty may or may not include the value of the lodging stipend, the M&IE stipend, the travel stipend, company provided housing, company provided medical benefits, and any other variable that costs the agency money. While this action may violate wage recharacterization rules, it is used none the less in some form or another by almost every agency. Don't let it scare you off. Essentially, if you don't work, you don't get paid just like any other job. However, this is where the guaranteed hours come into play.

Guaranteed Hours

Because you can get penalized for not working, you'll want to make sure that the guaranteed-hours policy is clearly stated in your contract. If you're a true traveling worker incurring duplicative expenses, then you didn't travel away from your home to simply duplicate your expenses. The guaranteed-hours policy ensures that you don't get stuck paying for these expenses due to shift cancellations. It's also important to again point out the importance of extra-hours-pay in this regard. If your paycheck is docked for missing shifts, then you want to make sure that it is supplemented by an equal amount if/when you make up the missed shifts.

Non-Compete Clauses and Exclusivity Clauses

Almost every healthcare staffing agency will have non-compete or exclusivity clauses in their contracts. Some people treat non-compete and exclusivity to mean the same thing. I'm not a lawyer. But from what I can tell by reading about this topic, it appears as though lawyers don't know whether they're the same thing or not. Therefore, I'm going to point out 2 key aspects that I believe you should be aware of regardless of what the clause is called.

First, some clauses intend to prevent you from working at the contracted hospital in any capacity for some specified period of time after your contract is completed, typically 1 year. This means you can't work there through another agency and you can't take a permanent job with the hospital directly. However, when it comes to taking a job directly with the hospital, there may be a buyout clause in the contract between the hospital and the agency that allows the hospital to pay the agency a fee if the hospital wishes to hire you on.

Second, some clauses intend to prevent you from working only with another agency at the contracted hospital for some specified period of time after your contract is completed, typically 1 year. This means that you would not be able to work at the hospital through another agency. However, you could become directly employed with the hospital without penalty. A buyout clause may still exist in the contract between the agency and hospital and it would still come into effect if you were to take a job directly with the hospital. However, that's between the hospital and the agency.

Agencies utilize these clauses to protect against loss. The agency has invested significant time and resources in finding the candidate and they want to ensure that their investment is protected. However, it's important to point out that the laws governing these clauses vary by state. These clauses are nearly impossible to enforce in California. In other states, they're nearly impossible to get out from under. If you're highly concerned about these clauses, then I recommend doing some research on the specific state in question and perhaps seeking legal advice if necessary.

Contract Cancellation Clauses

Like every other clause in the contract, cancellation clauses vary from agency to agency. Essentially, contract cancellation clauses seek to govern the circumstances surrounding contract cancellations as well as discourage employees from canceling contracts. Essentially, there are two vantage points at play when it comes to cancellations, the agency's and the traveler's.

From the agency's vantage point, they want to make sure that the contract is completed as intended. After all, they only make money when they're able to bill for hours worked, and chances are strong that they need the contract to be completed in order to cover the costs associated with it. As a result, contracts will typically include some mention of penalties associated with contract cancellations that originate with the traveler. These scenarios may or may not be specifically enumerated in the contract. They include willful disregard of duties, dismissal for poor performance or attendance, and criminal activity among other things.

In essence, the monetary penalties are mechanisms designed to discourage early cancellation. The value of the penalty is typically designed to mitigate the losses the agency will incur if the contract is cancelled early. These expenses can include but are not limited to various compensation variables like company provided housing or travel expenses as well as the cancellation fee that is charged to the agency by the hospital which can run anywhere from 1 to 2 weeks' worth of billing.

It's important to point out that many contracts seek to collect penalties by docking the traveler's paycheck. This may be against state employment regulations depending on the state you're in. It's very difficult to dock an employee's paycheck in many states. Therefore, if your paycheck is docked, you can check with the state's labor board to see if this action is legal. If it's not, then you can file a claim with the labor board and attempt to have the funds returned. The agency may be charged penalties on top of having to return your funds, so the simple act of filing the claim or even threatening to file the claim may get the agency to return the funds. The agency would then be forced to go after you through proper legal channels which may be too costly to justify action.

Of course, contracts can also be cancelled for reasons outside the traveler's control. For example, the hospital may cancel the contract for reasons unrelated to the traveler's performance. Perhaps the hospital experienced a decrease in census or had a permanent employee return earlier than anticipated. In addition, the agency may lose its contract with the hospital which would in turn result in the traveler's contract being cancelled. In this case, it's possible that the traveler stay on at the hospital through another agency.

In any case, the contract will typically stipulate the means for handling disputes regarding contract cancellations outside the traveler's control, as well as other disputes for that matter. The contract may stipulate that disputes are to be addressed through arbitration as opposed to the court system. Or, it may specify a particular court jurisdiction for handling disputes. This would most likely be the jurisdiction within which the agency is centrally located.

Essentially, cancellation clauses are for the agency's protection. In fact, you'd be hard pressed to find a contract that spelled out the

196

conditions under which it was acceptable for the traveler to cancel the contract. Again, this is why it's really important to ensure that everything that is important to you is spelled out in the contract. Doing so is the only defense you have to hold the agency accountable to deliver on the promises they've made.

The Contract in General

Perhaps the most important general concept to understand about the contract you sign as a travel healthcare professional is that it's a contract between you and the agency, not a contract between you and the hospital. Meanwhile, "the confirmation" is the contract between the agency and hospital as it pertains to you. You see, the agency already has a master contract with the hospital. The master contract establishes the business relationship between the agency and the hospital which includes the working expectations for the agency's contingent workers. The confirmation is intended to establish the parameters of each assignment and any special considerations.

This is an important distinction for you to understand for two reasons. First, it highlights the importance of establishing with your recruiter any special agreements you've made, or desire to make, with the hospital prior to the agency accepting the offer. If these items are not included in the confirmation, then they may not be honored by the hospital. Furthermore, attempting to add such items after the confirmation has been sent can be difficult.

Second, this distinction highlights the importance of addressing issues with your recruiter when you feel that they violate your contract. I've read many reputable travel nursing blogs that seem to advocate addressing "contract violations" with the hospital directly. This is fine and you're welcome to do as you please. However, there's a good possibility that the unit manager and/or supervisor you're working with has no idea what has been agreed to. It's very likely that they've not seen the confirmation. It's also possible that the confirmation was sent without the agreements included. This would be unfortunate, but it does happen. In any case, the best approach is to take these issues up with your recruiter to ensure that they are resolved without damaging your relationship with the hospital.

Chapter 36: Credentialing and Compliance

As soon as you accept an offer, the agency will initiate the credentialing and compliance process if they haven't already. Credentialing and compliance is one of the biggest burdens that travel nursing agencies and their travel nurses have to contend with. When I first started as a healthcare recruiter in 2006, it was standard to provide the hospital with nothing more than copies of the travel nurse's licenses, certifications, basic medical records, and a unit test. Now, every hospital seems to have its own packet of hospital specific documentation, testing, and orientation information that must be completed prior to starting a travel nursing assignment. There are some hospitals that require completion of on-line orientation modules that can take up to 12 hours to complete!! It's almost as if they're having the travel nurse complete the same process that a newly hired permanent employee is required to complete.

Additionally, hospitals have become extremely nit-picky with the documents they're willing to accept. They'll decline documents that aren't properly signed or those that aren't in the exact required format. To compound the problem, the facilities often want travel nurses to start within one to two weeks of receiving the offer, leaving very little time to comply. Furthermore, some hospitals require all documents to be in the hospital's possession well in advance of the start, while others are more lax. However, missing deadlines can result in delays, and often times, assignment cancellations.

Due to the urgency surrounding the compliance process, agencies will take an aggressive approach to ensure completion. It's typical for the agency to immediately email a list of required documents requesting that you send them copies of everything you have. I can't stress enough how important it is to immediately send them copies of everything you have on hand. I can't even count the number of times I witnessed contract delays and cancellations as a result of missing documents. Don't wait to get everything together; it's better to send documents piecemeal if you have to. This is because you won't know for certain if the documents you have are going to meet the hospital's requirements.

If your documents don't meet the hospital's requirements, then you and the agency must work together to ensure that a document meeting the hospital's requirements is obtained in time to meet the hospital's deadline. Many of the required documents take time to be received, and the timeframes are often times out of your and the agency's control. For example, MMR results and drug screen results are contingent on labs and can often be delayed. Knowing this, agencies typically make these items a priority over other items that are under the control of the agency and you. For example, nurse testing is a lower priority than getting the MMR results.

Different agencies have different policies for obtaining all of the required compliance documents. I believe that most agencies offer to pay for anything you need in terms of medical documents like MMRs, PPDs, Physical Exams, and Drug Screens. I believe they almost always pay for facility specific items too, such as Respirator Mask Fit Tests. Most agencies also claim ownership of the items they pay for which means they may not provide copies of these documents to you free of charge. They have several concerns that lead to this policy including the possibility that the documents may be used to land an assignment elsewhere.

All things considered, it behooves you to diligently maintain a compliance file to ensure that you minimize the time you spend on compliance and that you're not caught off guard. My experience indicates that travel nurses who do not maintain a high quality compliance file must duplicate their efforts several times throughout the year. Moreover, they routinely miss out on assignments they wanted because they're missing some document or another and can't obtain it by the hospital's compliance deadline. In order to avoid these pitfalls, you should diligently maintain comprehensive electronic and hard (paper) files of your licenses, certifications, and medical records.

Below is a list of documents you should maintain:

Front and back copies of all employment documents (Driver's License, Passport, Social Security)

Front and back copies of all licenses and certifications (SIGNED where applicable)

MMR Titers

VZ (Varicella Zoster) Titer

Hepatitis B Titer

PPD (keep copies of all tests conducted in the past 2 years)

Chest X-Ray if PPD is positive

Physical Exam

Copies of mask fit tests

Try to obtain copies of drug screens and other tests and documents that agencies have you complete. Many times, agencies will accept another agency's tests and documents and they are typically valid for 1 year.

When it comes to licenses and certifications, I recommend making a copy of all licenses and certifications, FRONT and BACK. Be sure they are all signed in the designated signature space. The best thing to do is to go to a FedEx/Kinkos, or some other copy shop, and make a high quality photocopy of the fronts and backs of the licenses and certifications. Then, scan the photocopies to PDF and save the PDF files somewhere safe. You can ask the service folks at the copy shop for help if you're not sure how to do this. You should include your Driver's License (or Passport), Social Security Card, and ALL of your health care related licenses and certifications, including CEU certificates. You never know when some facility may require something obscure. It's best to have copies of everything ready to go, in order to save yourself time and trouble later.

While we're on the subject of copies, I should point out that it's best to maintain copies of all your documents in PDF format. There are many reasons for this. First, PDF is a format that is widely accepted. Second, it results in a smaller file size than image files like JPG, which is what many people use. Third, PDF is printer friendly. The files are typically formatted by default to print out on one page of standard printer paper. Every commercial printing shop should provide you with the capability to get your documents into PDF format. Most home printers will allow you to scan to PDF. You can also download freeware (free software) that allows you to both print to PDF, and scan to PDF. Simply conduct a web search for "print to PDF freeware" or "scan to PDF freeware."

When it comes to medical records, travel nurses should maintain a file of records that will pass the most stringent standards. Here is a list of examples:

MMR, VZ, and Hep B:

Measles, Mumps, Rubella (MMR), Varicella Zoster (VZ: chicken – pox), Hepatitis B: For these, it's best to have a titer report. In case you're not familiar with this, a clinic will draw blood and determine immunity by measuring the level of antibodies present. A simple statement of "Positive" or "Negative" is not good enough as it will not be accepted by many facilities. Instead, make sure that the report you receive displays the ranges of immunity, and your blood's level of antibodies, commonly referred to as "lab values". Hand written titer reports are rarely accepted, so be sure the report you receive is typed out on the clinic's letterhead.

If you MUST get by with immunization records for your MMR, note that most facilities are going to require records of 2 immunization dates. Many facilities also require the immunizations to have been completed within a certain timeframe prior to your starting the assignment. However, just know that hospitals' willingness to accept immunization records is diminishing. This is especially true of VZ. Simply having your doctor state that you've had previous exposure to the virus is becoming widely unacceptable. However, many hospitals are still willing to accept a Hepatitis B declination in lieu of a titer report. If so, your agency will provide you with a Hep-B Declination.

TB/PPD:

Tuberculosis (TB) is screened with a purified protein derivative (PPD) skin test. It is becoming more and more common for facilities to require copies of 2 PPD tests within the last year of your assignment's start date. Many require a PPD be conducted within 30 days of the assignment start date and some require a 2 step PPD. Always be sure that the report you receive shows the date given, the date read, the reading (positive/negative), and the induration. Even when the reading is negative, the induration should be recorded as 0mm.

If you test positive, you'll need a chest x-ray, AND the report that shows you tested positive. The most stringent facilities will require chest x-rays within the last year. However, the vast majority will accept x-rays within five years of the start date. Facilities are very particular about the wording that is provided on the report. You'll want to be sure that at a minimum the report says, "X-ray reveals no abnormalities in lungs. No sign of communicable disease."

Physical Exam:

Physical exams are typically required within 1 year of your assignment's start date. Some facilities have specific wording they want to see on the physical exam. This is typically not a problem as your agency will often provide you or the clinic with a form that has all of the required verbiage. However, it's important to remember to have the clinic, or doctor, stamp the document with the office stamp. Many facilities will not accept the physical exam without the official office stamp or if it's not on the Doctor's official office document.

There are many other medical records and various documents that are standard requirements for travel nurses. You should try and get copies of everything you can. It's true that your agency will send you in for a drug screen, and when doing so, they can schedule the rest of the required exams and screenings. However, trust me when I say, if you rely on this approach for every assignment, it's inevitable that at some point you will be sent to multiple clinics, multiple times, for the same travel nursing assignment because something got botched, or one clinic didn't provide the type of service needed. This will cost you valuable time at a time when you also have to get all of that facility specific paperwork done too. Even worse, you may fall victim to a lab that delays reporting to the point that your assignment gets cancelled because the facility didn't receive the report in time.

When you are sent to a clinic, ask the clinic's staff for copies of everything. They will often provide it to you. If you can't get it from them, ask your travel nursing company for copies. Despite the fact that many agencies will decline your request for compliance documents, it doesn't hurt to ask. By taking the small, easy steps necessary to maintain a great file of documents, you'll save yourself a ton of time and trouble in the future, and ensure that you're able to get the assignments you want when it's crunch time.

Finally, if you take any medications, prescription or otherwise, then you must inform the lab performing the drug screen in advance. The lab will then calibrate the test and results appropriately. It's also recommended that you inform your recruiter in advance in the off chance that something goes wrong with the lab.

Chapter 37: Reporting to the Facility and Working Your Assignment

Reporting Instructions

You should receive reporting instructions for your assignment at some point during this process. Typically, hospitals don't send the reporting instructions until they've received a fully compliant file of documents. The way the hospital sees it, you're not starting until they have a fully compliant file, so there's no need for them to send the instructions until they have the documents. As a result, don't be surprised if you don't receive reporting instructions until 3 or 4 days before your assignment is scheduled to start.

You should expect to receive fairly limited information in your reporting instructions. Many times, the agency receives nothing more from the hospital than a date, time, and location. Therefore, if something is important to you, then you should request it well in advance. Don't wait for the reporting instructions to arrive before asking your questions. It may be too late at that point to get answers.

You should communicate your questions to your recruiter as soon as possible and I recommend sending an email so there's a verifiable trail. This approach shifts responsibility to the agency. There's really not much that can go wrong with your reporting instructions, but in the off chance that there is something important that doesn't get communicated to you, then it's best to be able to hold the agency accountable.

I've had my own share of encounters with poor reporting instructions. There have been small instances like nurses showing up in business casual attire as opposed to the hospital's desired scrubs. Such instances aren't that big of a deal. They're easy enough to remedy. However, I've also encountered instances that resulted in substantial setbacks. For example, one time I had a Physician Assistant show up for the first day of orientation at the wrong address. The hospital had multiple campuses and he was sent to the wrong one. He was unable to get to the orientation in time to meet the hospital's stringent attendance requirements. As a result, the hospital delayed his start date for two weeks for their next orientation. Luckily, the PA was very flexible and had no problem with this. However, setbacks like this could be a disaster. As a result, I highly recommend that you email the following questions to your recruiter for each new assignment.

What's the exact address I am to report to?

Is there a particular room number or location in the building where I am to report?

Is there a contact person at the hospital?

Is there a contact telephone number at the hospital?

What is the schedule for the first day of orientation?

What is the dress code for the first day of orientation?

Does the hospital require a certain color of scrubs?

What am I required to bring with me to the orientation?

Ask any other questions that you feel are important.

You may not get answers to all of these questions and that's okay. The important thing is that you ask them to ensure there's no pushback from the agency in the event that something goes wrong.

Orientation and Testing

Typically, the first week of orientation is spent completing paperwork, learning hospital policies and procedures, getting acclimated to the hospital and unit, and taking tests. Everything is easy enough with the exception of the tests. The tests can sometimes get you in trouble. This is why it's highly recommended that you ask about the hospital's testing policies during the interview. You see, some hospitals administer tests and offer remediation which allows you retake the tests. Other hospitals cancel the assignment if you fail.

Hospital testing policies have their genesis in the Joint Commission on Accreditation of Health-care Organizations' (JCAHO) guidelines regarding staff qualifications and competencies. For those unfamiliar with JCAHO, it's an independent non-profit organization that accredits and certifies healthcare organizations based on their commitment to meeting certain performance standards. With regard to staff competencies and qualifications, JCAHO's HR.3.10 stipulates, "Competency to perform job responsibilities is assessed, demonstrated, and maintained." JCAHO defines competency as "the knowledge, skills, ability, and behaviors that a person possesses in order to perform tasks correctly and skillfully."

As you can see, JCAHO does not lay out specific guidelines for meeting the requirements. As a result, hospitals establish their own guidelines based on their individual interpretations of JCAHO's requirements. This is why different hospitals will utilize different tests and have different policies regarding remediation or contract cancellation for travelers who fail the tests. The hospitals that cancel contracts most likely believe that in the case of travelers, they will not be able to document proof of adequate training that results in the ability to demonstrate and maintain the skills measured by the tests. Meanwhile, hospitals that remediate clearly believe that their remediation process satisfies the requirements.

In any case you'll definitely want to know everything you can about the hospital's tests and their policies regarding cancellation or remediation prior to accepting an assignment. You may wish to decline assignments that cancel due to test failures. Why risk the time and money involved with getting to the assignment if you may be cancelled at the outset for failing a test? On the other hand, if you know about the tests in advance, you may be able to adequately prepare for them.

For the most part, the tests administered by hospitals are going to be very easy for you to pass. In fact, you may have already taken many of the tests through your agency. I've never encountered a problem with medication tests, unit tests, OSHA tests, HIPPA tests, fire safety tests, or other standard tests administered by hospitals and agencies.

The tests that tend to cause problems are EKG examinations, the Performance-Based Development System (PBDS) examinations, and the Basic Knowledge Assessment Tool (BKAT) exam. Everyone may be familiar with EKG exams, but if the hospital intends to cancel your contract if you fail one, then you should most definitely study up on the topic. EKG exams may measure dysrhythmia interpretation and measurements. They are designed to assess the test taker's ability to interpret the cardiac rhythm as presented on an EKG tracing and/or perform accurate measurements on an EKG tracing.

Many people believe these tests will pose no problem because the material is so common to their jobs. However, the use of advanced bedside monitoring technology results in an environment where nurses can forget some of the basics. The exam is not going to include the familiar beeps and alerts of the ECG monitors in wide use today. I highly recommend studying for these exams in advance. I've had more than a few nurses run into trouble with them.

The PBDS exam is a whole other story. If you decide to accept a contract with a hospital that administers the PBDS, then you most certainly need to study for it. The test is unorthodox in both administration and assessment. The test taker is shown brief videos that simulate clinical situations. The test taker must then determine the primary problem or diagnosis as well as all the steps needed to address the clinical situation. The test taker will record their answers by writing them down, or typing them into a computer. This is not a multiple choice exam. It's a written examination.

The answers are graded in 1 of 2 ways. First, the answers can be graded by the company that created and markets the test, Performance Management Services, Inc. (PMSI). PMSI's raters are clinical educators with a Master's degree in Nursing, and an active RN license. This is a paid service. The hospital is typically charged $100 per graded test. Second, the hospital may have members of its own staff evaluate the examinations. This is typically the case for travelers as hospitals are not interested in spending money on travelers and do not need the detailed rating reports that PMSI's raters provide.

You see, the PBDS is designed to determine an individualized orientation for each newly hired clinician. The general idea is to reduce the costs of standardized orientations by determining the proficiencies and deficiencies of each new hire, and then focusing the orientation on the deficiencies. So when PMSI rates the examination, they offer a detailed report that outlines the deficiencies and recommends a plan of action for the orientation. However, hospitals are using the exam for travelers only as a means to determine if the travelers will be able to perform with limited to no orientation. So hospitals don't need PMSI's detailed reports.

Obviously, this exposes the fundamental problem with using the PBDS as a PASS/FAIL examination. It was never designed to be used in this manner. It's actually designed to determine strengths and weaknesses so that the weaknesses can be focused on in an effort to improve. Using the PBDS as a PASS/FAIL exam is antithetical to its true intentions.

The good news is that there are only 500 hospitals that currently use the PBDS. And a very small percentage of them administer the test as PASS/FAIL to travel nurses. In addition, PMSI claims that travel nurses have a strong tendency to score as well as permanent hires, which is most often good enough to pass. Additionally, pantravelers.org claims that failure rates for travel nurses taking the PBDS are quite low (pantravelers.org).

I have to be completely honest. My personal recommendation is to stay away from any hospital that administers the PBDS in this fashion. There's simply too much risk involved with taking a test that's not even being applied in its intended manner. If you fail, you'll certainly miss out on a few weeks' worth of work. There's the orientation week and the weeks that it will take to get to another assignment. Not to mention the stress and time involved. In addition, there's a chance that the hospital records the result in their database and maybe even shares it with other hospitals within the same hospital organization.

If you do decide to take an assignment at a hospital that administers a PASS/FAIL PBDS, then you should take steps to limit the risk. First, you should study for the exam to the extent possible. I'm not an expert on these issues so I won't overstep my boundaries and offer direct information here. However, there are many great resources available. Simply conduct a web search for "PBDS test" or PBDS test preparation. Second, I recommend discussing the ramifications of failure with your agency. Are they willing to cover the entire cost of travel should your contract be cancelled? Do they have more available assignments in the same area or state that they could quickly transition you to should you fail? Knowing these things in advance and having a back-up plan can help keep you prepared and mitigate the risk of failure.

The BKAT has many differences and similarities to the PBDS as they pertain to travel nursing. In contrast to the PBDS, the BKAT is more of a traditional test. It is unit specific, meaning there are different tests for different units. I've read that the tests are comprised of 85-100 questions depending on the unit. The tests tend to cover the major body systems as well as general areas of medicine common to the respective unit. I've heard that the questions are very similar to the questions found on the NCLEX and cover basic every-day scenarios.

Similar to the PBDS, the BKAT was not designed for "screening, hiring, or firing situations" as the creator points out. However, some hospitals neglect the creator's intentions and use the test for these purposes anyway. There are hospitals that will cancel a contract based what they determine to be a failing score.

As a result, I offer the same advice for the BKAT as the PBDS. However, I do believe that you should be less concerned given the nature of the exam, what it measures, and how it measures. It's simply an easier exam to contend with. Also, the creator's web site claims that you can order copies of the exams. The web address is bkat-toth.org. However, I've also heard that people have had difficulty actually obtaining copies of the exams. Therefore, I recommend getting a head start if you're concerned. Be proactive and order a copy in advance, just so you have it on hand should you need it. This could end up saving you time and trouble in the future.

Managing Your Time Reporting and Pay

Different hospitals have different ways of keeping track of your time. Some hospitals have electronic time keeping systems. Other hospitals require that you keep a paper timecard and turn it into the staffing office at the end of the week where it is supposed to be reviewed and forwarded to your agency. Still others require that you keep a paper timecard and get a manager to sign it so that you can send it to your agency. The bottom line is that all of these systems are flawed and you should take control in order to ensure that you get paid correctly and on time.

First, we have to understand the challenges facing the travel nursing agency with respect to payroll processing. Remember, as a travel nurse you're paid by your travel nursing agency not the hospital. In many cases, the travel nursing agency is processing payroll on a weekly basis. The payroll processing systems that travel nursing agencies use typically require them to have everything entered no later than Wednesday in order for the service to process on Thursday so that the money can be in your account by Friday. The typical work week is Sunday through Saturday. That gives the agency 3 days to collect and review the timecards, fix any problems, and enter all of the data into the payroll processing system. And even when hospitals are keeping time electronically, they still send a report that must be entered manually into the agency's payroll processing system. Furthermore, a travel nursing agency's payroll is much more complex than most. Everyone has a different rate. Some are receiving stipends and some aren't. The complexity requires more time be spent to properly enter the payroll.

This all results in a time crunch for the agency. To compound the problem, there are regularly delays and errors in time card reporting. Delays are most common when paper timecards are utilized, but they can also occur with electronic timekeeping systems. When it comes to timecard errors, amazingly they're always in the hospital's favor. In other words, reporting errors have a strong tendency to be short of hours rather than long of hours.

Remember, the travel nursing agency really has no clue how many hours you've worked because you're not really under their direct supervision. As a result, it is highly recommended that you keep your own timecard and send it into the agency with or without a signature as early as possible. A signature is always necessary when required, but getting something turned in is a must. Doing so will ensure that the agency has a report of the hours that you're expecting to be paid for. You can request a timecard from your agency and/or the hospital. Always be sure to inquire with your agency whether or not they have specific time reporting guidelines they want you to follow.

If the agency is good at what they do, they'll match the time report you send them to the hospital's report and address any discrepancies. In addition, the timecard you send to your agency will signal to them that you didn't somehow take the week off and that they should be expecting a timecard from the hospital. If the agency is good at what they do, they'll use the timecard you send into be proactive in addressing delays from the hospital. All of this will ensure that you're paid accurately and on time.

Even if you take these actions, and certainly if you don't, you may still experience delays and errors. I highly recommend that you check your pay as early as possible to see if an error has occurred. Determining if there is an error is not always cut and dry. Again, travel nursing payroll is typically very complex. The complexity can sometimes result in errors that aren't always obvious. This is why I believe that working with an agency that provides on-line payroll and pay-stub services is a big advantage. You'll need to look at the details in order to confidently determine the veracity of your paycheck. That said, it'll clearly be cut and dry if you receive nothing!

Checking your pay as early as possible will ensure that you can contact your agency early in the business day if you need and choose to. This will give them time to address any issues and hopefully get you paid the same day. The best agencies will make this effort. Bear in mind, it is highly unlikely that the agency will be able to process a direct deposit to get funds into your account in case of an error. This is because direct deposits aren't processed on an individual basis. They are processed in batches. As a result, there are typically two options to quickly address payroll errors.

First, the agency can walk in a deposit to your bank if there is a branch in their vicinity. This is one of the reasons I recommend having a bank account with a national bank that has branches in your agency's physical vicinity. However, if you need immediate access to the funds, then you'll want to be mindful of bank holds in case the agency offers to deposit a check directly to your account. Typically, the bank will place a hold period on checks to wait for them to clear before you can withdraw the funds unless the deposited check is from an account with the same bank. If you need the funds immediately, you can request the agency to deposit cash.

If the agency is unable to walk in a deposit to your account, then the only immediate remedy in case of a payroll error will be a wire transfer. Funds sent via wire transfer typically do not have hold periods. They are guaranteed funds. They can also be available the same day the transfer is made as long as the transfer is conducted before the 4pm EST cutoff. Bear in mind, wire transfers can incur fees on both sides of the transaction, meaning your account can be charged for receiving a wire transfer. In addition, many banks don't process wire transfers on a daily basis, and a few don't even accept wire transfers. You should find out your bank's policies prior to leaving for your assignment. While doing so, it's a good idea to also check on your bank's policies regarding any service costs you may experience while traveling. Getting these issues covered early can save you time and trouble later.

Handling Problems While on Assignment

Unfortunately, things aren't always sunshine and daydreams while on a travel assignment. Like any other time in life, there are a slew of potential pitfalls. In fact, there are too many issues for us to enumerate and address here. However, we can take a look at some of the overarching themes and offer some recommendations for handling them professionally and successfully.

First, you may encounter personal or family issues that necessitate your immediate attention while on assignment. For example, you may become ill, have a family member become ill, or have a death in the family. Such issues may require that you miss a little time at best, or cancel the remainder of the contract at worst. When such issues arise, it's always best to personally inform both your agency and the hospital. This is the most professional approach. You don't want to leave either party without direct personal communication.

Which party you notify first is your choice. I tend to side with letting your agency know first. This is a courtesy to let your agency get ahead of the issue and formulate a plan. They may have a candidate that can take your place, or they may wish to contact the hospital in advance of you speaking with the hospital to see if they can work something out that benefits all parties. Also, agencies have a tendency to believe it makes them look bad to be the last to find these things out.

In any case, you should document the issue as best you can. If it's a personal health issue, try to obtain an official notice from your healthcare provider. If there's a death in the family, try to obtain a copy of the certificate. I understand that this may seem callous, but your goal is to mitigate any potential problems that result from contract cancellation. Hospitals certainly appreciate the effort. Moreover, agencies may be more understanding and overlook any contract cancellation penalties if they receive documented proof.

Second, you may encounter problems with your agency and/or the services they provide. For example, you may encounter payroll errors or problems with inadequate or unsafe housing. My experience is that all agencies desire to provide a high level of service. Retaining business is the easiest way to grow their business. As a result, you'll be able to resolve these issues with your agency in the vast majority of cases.

However, in the off chance that you cannot resolve issues with your agency, you must document these issues as if you're building a case. Maintain copies of official documents such as pay stubs and keep a record of the discussions you have with your agency and other applicable parties. If you have a problem with housing or some other physical item, then take pictures to verify the issues. By adequately documenting the issue, you will ensure that you have proof of the problem and your efforts to deal with it in the off chance that you terminate the contract.

Third, you may encounter problems with the hospital. There are problems that may arise with the hospital that while problematic can none the less be resolved through normal channels. For example, the hospital may not provide the access codes you need to perform your job adequately and efficiently. They may continually schedule you for the wrong shifts or float you despite the fact that you have an agreement not to float.

In all such scenarios, some combination of working directly with the agency, hospital, or both, will generally result in resolution. You'll have to make a judgment call as to how you approach these issues as they're all quite unique. Many people would advise that these issues be addressed with the hospital first. By doing so, you'll be dealing with the problem at the source and ensuring a quicker resolution. However, remember that if it's an issue related to the contract, then there is a possibility that your connections at the hospital are unaware of your contractual agreements. Therefore, alerting your agency first may be the best route.

It's also possible to run into personality conflicts that result in a hostile work environment. Again, you'll need to determine the best approach given the circumstances. One of the best nurses I've ever worked with ran into a hostile co-worker while on assignment in Los Angeles, CA. The permanent employee was upset that the traveler was getting scheduled for extra shifts. She felt the shifts should be going to a permanent staff member. However, the traveler was simply abiding by the hospital's policies when securing the extra shifts.

The traveler attempted to deal with it directly with her unit manager who addressed the issue with the permanent employee. The problem subsided for a while but then flared up even worse a few weeks later. The traveler contacted me and we addressed the issue with my agency's Chief Nursing Officer who wrote a report and sent it to the hospital. The permanent employee was actually released from duty. Things may not always turn out this way, but it gives you an idea of how to resolve these issues professionally and productively.

You may also have difficulty adapting to the hospital's policies and procedures which can negatively impact your ability to provide the patient care you're accustomed to. Remember, hospitals typically have very good reasons for doing things the way they do them. Their processes and procedures have typically been in place for years without incident. Part of travel nursing is being able to adapt to these circumstances.

That said, there are hospitals in need of travelers because they're poorly managed and can't retain staff. If you strongly believe that you're at one of them, then you should immediately take the issue up with your recruiter. It's always good to ask your recruiter if they've had complaints about the unit in the past. This will give you an idea of whether or not there is a history of problems with this particular hospital, but it won't solve the problem. You should be specific with your recruiter regarding the problems you're encountering and provide potential solutions. That way, your agency can report to the hospital in an effort to resolve the issues.

If you're unable to resolve the issue through your recruiter, then you can ask to speak with the agency's Chief Nursing Officer or clinical liaison. Sharing your concerns with an experienced clinician can result in several positive outcomes. First, you will ensure that your concerns are documented appropriately should there be any legal action. Second, the clinician may be able to provide valuable insight to help you overcome the issue. Third, the clinician may validate your concerns and seek to address them with the hospital. Finally, if a resolution still cannot be reached, then the agency may be willing to help you find another assignment and/or let you out of the contract.

Finally, you may run into to the unfortunate circumstance of having your contract cancelled by the hospital for performance related issues. Just like any other job, there are many reasons that this can happen, from attendance issues to vital mistakes that jeopardize patient safety. Unfortunately, there is typically nothing that you or your agency can do in these situations. Typically, the hospital is in the position of power to take this action as they see fit. There may be legal remedies, but they're typically not going to be worth the trouble involved.

When this happens, it's standard procedure for the agency's Chief Nursing Officer or clinical liaison to file a report. They should receive something in writing from the hospital detailing the reasons for termination. This information will be reviewed with the traveler and the traveler's side of the story will be taken into account. The Chief Nursing Officer will then make a recommendation to the agency as to whether or not the agency should continue to work with the traveler. This is all typically based on a system that assigns points for activities that violate the agency's policies. Obviously, more severe circumstances will garner more points and increase the likelihood that the agency will be unable to work with the traveler moving forward. A similar decision will also be made at the hospital.

When an agency or hospital determines that they will no longer work with a traveler, then the traveler is labeled "DNU", "DNS", or "DNR" in the database. These are acronyms for Do Not Use, Do Not Send, and Do Not Return respectively. They all mean the same thing.

These significations can have a major impact when they are levied by entire hospital organizations or by the largest agencies. For example, if you receive this label with the Hospital Corporation of America (HCA), or Kaiser, then this constitutes a significant number of hospitals at which you will no longer be able to work. If you receive this label at one of the large staffing agencies, then it could be even worse. As mentioned previously, the largest staffing agencies are often involved in the MSP business. They will apply this designation to all of their clients. If another agency attempts to submit your profile for an opening through the MSP, then the MSP agency will reject it.

Unfortunately, this can happen to anybody. I've had it happen to some of the best nurses I've ever worked with. Fortunately, it's not the end of the world. There are many hospitals in America that use travelers. However, you want to learn from it and take step steps to ensure it doesn't happen again.

Chapter 38: Considerations for Future Assignments

Extensions and Future Assignments

Assuming that you're still having fun as a travel nurse, you'll need to continue to secure assignments. If you're looking to secure an assignment at a new hospital, then you should take the same approach as you did in securing the first assignment. Of course, you'll have your current agency on the hunt. You'll also want the other agencies you work with to be on the hunt as well. Remember to make sure that the agencies you're working with provide adequate coverage of the markets you're interested in. If not, then find some agencies that do.

Of course, the easiest assignment to secure is the extension assignment. An extension is a contract with the hospital you're currently working with. It's the easiest to secure because you're already there, already established, already compliant, and already oriented. Contract extensions are typically offered if the facility has a need and has been pleased with your performance. Hospitals typically wait until the final 3-5 weeks of the assignment to make an extension offer. However, I recommend that you discuss an extension with your recruiter as soon as possible; don't wait for the hospital to initiate the process.

I recommend the following approach for every assignment. First, contact your recruiter as early as 3 to 4 weeks into your 13 week assignment to discuss the compensation for an extension. Be clear that you're not certain you want to accept an extension just yet, but you want to get the compensation details ironed out so that you're ready to go without surprises or delays should the opportunity present itself. Taking this step early in the contract helps you establish a game plan in advance so that you're not scrambling at the last minute to negotiate the extension compensation and/or find your next assignment.

There are several important variables to keep in mind when you're negotiating an extension contract. First, extensions are easy for both you and the agency. Second, the agency should incur much lower compliance and credentialing costs than they did on the original contract. Third, the agency will not incur any non-billable orientation expenses typically charged by the hospital for orientating the agency's employees. Fourth, the extension will require less man hours for the agency than a new contract. They won't have to submit your profile, find housing, coordinate compliance with the hospital, or engage in a host of other time consuming activities. Finally, be mindful of the fixed costs that the agency incurred on the first contract such as travel stipends and license reimbursements.

All of these variables represent costs that the agency incurred on the first assignment, but stands to avoid on the extension. In addition, it is most likely that the bill rate will be the same for the extension as it was for the original contract. This may not be true if the first contract was offered at a crisis rate and the extension is offered at the lower standard rate, but that is rarely the case. As a result, when you negotiate an extension you should be doing so with the understanding that it's possible to get more money because the agency is incurring lower costs and therefore has more money overall.

Let's single out one of these expenses, the travel stipend, as an example. If an agency provided $700 for a travel stipend on the original contract, then they may not incur this expense on the extension. This is because you may not need to do any traveling. It's possible that you may want to return home between contracts, but not necessary. Regardless, the agency may or may not add the travel stipend to your extension. If they add it in, then there's no problem. If they keep it out, then you should try to make sure that you get an equitable increase somewhere else, like your base rate or lodging stipend. Remember, to calculate the hourly value of the $700 travel stipend, simply divide the $700 by the total number of contracted hours.

Something else to watch out for when it comes to travel stipends and extensions is agencies holding the second half of your original travel stipend until your extension is complete. For example, let's say the agency offered a $700 travel stipend for the first contract to be paid $350 on the first paycheck and $350 on the last paycheck of the assignment. When an extension is offered, they may try to hold the second $350 installment claiming that you'll receive it when you complete the extension. Don't fall for these gimmicks. You should demand that you're paid what you're due on the first contract, and then try to ensure that you receive another $700 travel stipend for the extension or the equivalent in some other compensation component.

All of this said, it's also important to remember that an agency may not be able to pay you additional money for the extension for a couple of reasons. First, they may have offered you a great deal on the original contract to get you to accept in hopes that you'd extend and they could even things out on the extension. Second, the agency may have bonuses and other increases already built into their contracts. If they do, then it's fair to assume that the cost savings we've discussed are being used to provide the bonuses and increases.

Just like any new travel contract, extension contracts are a negotiation. It's very difficult to know if you're getting a good deal. Again, it's my belief that most agencies are giving good deals these days because the competition is so fierce. However, you should still negotiate to get the best deal. If an agency seems to be shorting you on an extension based on the variables we've discussed here, then you can always politely let your recruiter know that you may still want to extend, but you're going to look for contracts elsewhere that have better compensation. This may be all it takes to squeeze juice from the turnip. Your recruiter won't want to lose you to another agency and it'll be more work for them to move you to another hospital. It may be worth it for them to just increase your compensation if it's possible.

Finally, if you're very intent on getting the best deal and want to take a shrewd approach, then you can look into other agencies that might be able to bring you on for the extension. Remember, sometimes your contract will have a non-compete clause. However, these clauses are not enforceable in many states. You can seek out other travel nurses at the hospital who are working through other agencies and ask them for their recruiters' contact information. Then, you can call and speak with these recruiters about the possibility of extending through them. The recruiters should know if it's possible and/or should be able to provide you with a compensation quote at the very least.

No matter what course you decide, if you come to terms with your agency on extension compensation early in the contract, you'll be in a better position to secure your next assignment, whether it be the extension or a new contract somewhere else. If you start this process 3 to 4 weeks into your assignment, then you should have it completed 3 to 6 weeks into your assignment depending on the approach you take. This leaves you plenty of time to secure your next assignment.

You'll find many folks who disagree with my recommended approach. They argue that there's no point in getting started this early. The hospital isn't going to offer an extension until the last month of the contract. In addition, the vast majority of travel assignments don't become available until 1 to 4 weeks out. As a result, you'll be wasting your time if you get started any sooner. They say when you're a travel nurse, you just have to be prepared to go wherever the jobs are available when you're available to go.

While I agree that there's a certain element of truth to this argument, I reject the notion that it must be this way for every assignment you take. If you follow the steps we've discussed previously, you can gain more control of the process. Remember, most travel nurses ask what assignments a travel nursing agency has open before they complete the agency's application and skills checklist. If you always take this approach, then you'll always be behind in the process. But if you do your research, target agencies that can meet your needs, and complete their applications and skills checklists in advance, then you'll be ahead of the game. Furthermore, your opportunity to gain more control over the process is increased when you have a set start date, and this is the situation you're in when you're working a travel assignment. You'll always know when you can start and you can have agencies target that date.

It's also important to point out that assignments regularly become available in advance; you just have to be ready to go when they do. In fact, there is a cyclical pattern that a large percentage of travel assignments follow. A large number of assignments start in January, April, July, and October. This cycle revolves around the holidays. Hospitals need to make sure that they have coverage for the holidays. Therefore, they start many assignments in October which end at the beginning of January. There's a huge turnover when these October contracts are complete and that takes us straight into winter when hospitals in many regions experience spikes in census. The rest of the year flows from there in 13 week intervals. Hospitals routinely release their holiday and winter needs well in advance, and they're more prone to release their April and July needs in advance as well. As a result, staying on top of things as we've discussed can give you the edge in getting the assignments you want.

Taking Time Off Between Assignments

Taking time-off more frequently is one of the potential benefits of travel nursing. You can take as much time-off as you'd like between assignments if you prefer. However, there are several issues you must consider before taking time-off between assignments.

I was often asked how much time-off could be taken between extension contracts. Ultimately, that's up to the hospital. They may not want you to take any time-off if they're in dire need of coverage. However, hospitals are typically pretty flexible. The best course of action is to discuss your requested time-off directly with your Unit Manager. That's typically the quickest and most effective alternative.

I can tell you one thing for sure. Your agency wants you back to work immediately regardless of whether or not it's an extension or a new contract. The agency only makes money when you work. The ideal scenario for them is to have you work 52 weeks a year. However, while you're technically the agency's employee, you're also their customer. So, they'll try to persuade you to take less time-off but they can't force the matter.

However, bear in mind that the agency is unable to provide their services if you aren't working. If you're not working, then the agency can't bill. And if the agency can't bill, then it has no money to pay for things like medical benefits, housing, or any other services they may be providing. Different agencies are going to have different policies for dealing with this issue. The most common services in play in this scenario are medical benefits and company provided housing. A rental car may also be in play. Let's take a look at each of these services.

Obviously, company provided housing is only in play when taking an extension, or maybe in the off chance that you've accepted your next assignment at a different hospital in the same vicinity. In any case, housing represents a significant expenditure. If you have a fully furnished apartment, then costs are going to run between $350 and $600 weekly. Some agencies may be willing to pick up the cost for a week or two, but I'd be surprised if any agency was willing to pick up more. When they're not willing to pick up the cost, they may just opt to find a new housing option. Obviously, if you're in a hotel or Extended Stay, then there would be more flexibility because the agency would most likely be able to check you out and then check you back in.

There's a little more flexibility when it comes to rental cars. Returning the rental car is the easiest thing to do. You could then check out another car when you returned. You may find some agencies that are willing to let you avoid the hassle for a week or two. But remember, the rental car is intended for business purposes and it typically comes with mileage limits. So, driving it cross country for a vacation is not an option.

Medical benefits are a little more complicated. In many cases, medical benefits are paid for on a monthly basis. In fact, I'd be surprised if this wasn't true in all cases. This means that your contract could end at some point before the benefits are set to expire. For example, if the agency paid for the benefits on the first of the month, then they're going to run through the end of the month. If your contract ends in the middle of the month, then you'll still technically be covered until the end of the month.

However, it's also possible for the benefits to be paid for based on your contract's start date. In this case, the benefits would end on your contract's end date. For example, if your contract started on March 15th and ended on June 15th, then it's possible that the agency started paying monthly premiums on March 15th and will therefore end the benefits on June 15th. You may think this is the obvious scenario, but I don't believe it is. It's pretty difficult for agencies to offer "Day 1" health insurance coverage. It's also difficult to find insurers that will provide the service.

So, what does this all mean for you? Well, first it means that you need to ask agencies in advance how they handle this if it's important to you. Again, different agencies will utilize different methods. Many agencies will be happy to pick up the cost for a week or two if that's what they need to do to secure another contract with you. Others may request that you pay for it. In any case, when making your decisions, you should always consider the effects of COBRA and HIPPA's Creditable Coverage rule.

In addition to compensation considerations, you should also consider the ramifications of time off for your career. Time off may not look so great on your resume if it's excessive. I know that many hospitals require explanations of gaps in employment that are greater than one month in order to consider a candidate for a travel assignment. In addition, the modern electronic application process utilized by the vast majority of hospitals for their permanent employment needs may ding your resume for time off. These "Applicant Tracking Systems" are designed to rank candidates electronically. Gaps in employment may hurt your ranking. You may be able to patch over the gaps by citing the agency as your employer and not including the gaps, but the system may possibly ding your resume for not working at a hospital.

I hope this doesn't make time-off seem more complicated than it actually is. Taking time-off between contracts is very common and there's really not much to it. You just need to be mindful of the issues at play.

Treat Every End as an Opportunity

The vast majority of travel assignments are wonderful experiences. You'll enjoy the hospital, they'll enjoy you, and it will end amicably. I recommend treating every contract-end as an opportunity to advance your career for three primary reasons. First, you may wish to return to the hospital in the future either as a traveler or a permanent employee. Second, you'll want to ensure that you have references for future travel assignments and permanent jobs. Third, travel nursing presents a unique opportunity to expand your professional network.

The first two reasons are pretty obvious, but the third reason warrants discussion. As a permanent nurse, your professional network tends to be limited to the people you work with at your one and only job. As a travel nurse, you may become a part of a new team every 3 months. This significantly enhances your networking opportunities. Taking advantage of these opportunities will have a positive impact on your career.

Many people are quick to scoff at the idea of professional networking. In my opinion, this is unwise. The vast majority of job openings are never advertised. In fact, I've seen numbers from recruitment industry surveys indicating that only 20%-35% of job openings are advertised. A majority of jobs are either filled from within or filled based on referrals from colleagues, current staff, and former staff.

Have you heard of the concept known as "6 degrees of separation"? Most people associate this with the movie star Kevin Bacon. However, there's a whole interdisciplinary academic field of science devoted to the study of networks, Network Science. Social networks are one of the main topics of study within this field. Researchers have shown that every human on earth has just 6 degrees of separation between every other human on earth through their social networks. Imagine how closely connected the relatively small world of American healthcare professionals is. Meanwhile, the advent of social and professional networking web sites has made it easier than ever for you to manage your own professional network, and for employers to find talent by leveraging their employees' networks.

There's a reason that LinkedIn is on pace to generate $915 million in revenue in 2012, just 9 years after being founded. It's a highly effective tool for both employers and employees. A professional networking service like LinkedIn allows job seekers to view jobs and then see if they have a connection with someone who currently works with the employer, or worked with the employer in the past. Even if the job seeker doesn't know someone directly, they may have a 2nd or 3rd degree connection. They can then leverage their 1st degree connection to get introduced.

Meanwhile, human resource costs are typically among the largest expenses, if not the single largest expense, for employers. Talent acquisition is a big part of that cost and employers are always looking for ways to reduce their costs. Employers resoundingly believe that interviewing and hiring candidates based on the recommendations of their great employees is a low cost solution in talent acquisition. They figure birds of a feather flock together. Employers are also more welcoming of those who may be 2nd and 3rd degree connections of their great employees. Professional networking services allow employers to take full advantage of this networking solution to talent acquisition.

I have worked with many healthcare professionals who capitalized on this opportunity. In one case, a travel nurse who had traveled for 2 years ended up marrying her high school sweet heart who lived in Kansas City, MO. She moved there and had difficulty landing a job until she sent messages to her LinkedIn connections asking if anyone had any connections to hospitals in Kansas City. She received a response from a nurse she had worked with in San Francisco, CA who was originally from Kansas City, MO. The travel nurse was put in contact with a Unit Manager at one of the hospitals in Kansas City and ended up landing a job.

In another instance, a travel nurse who had previously completed a travel assignment in Houston, Texas decided she wanted to move there when she was done traveling. When the time was right, she contacted her old Unit Manager in Houston via Facebook. The Unit Manager had switched to another hospital and offered to bring the traveler on staff at the new hospital. The traveler accepted and has been working there for 4 years now.

There are many things you can do to take advantage of networking opportunities, garner positive references, and be welcomed back to the facility. Obviously, being a pleasant, productive, team-player always helps. Participating in extra-curricular activities with your coworkers helps too. Beyond that, there are steps you can take at the end of the assignment that will go a long way.

Be sure to let your coworkers know that you're leaving. Let them know you've had a good time and thank them for any assistance they've provided. Bring treats for your co-workers before you leave if you'd like. Pay particular attention to your supervisors and Unit Manager. I recommend requesting some one-on-one time with them to let them know you're leaving and ask them how they think you can improve. This shows both that you care and value their input. Ask everyone if they are on a social network. If they are, then ask them if you can connect with them to stay in touch. If they're not, then ask them if it would be alright to stay in touch via email. Finally, try to leave every assignment with at least 1-2 solid references.

You never know where life is going to take you, especially when you're out there traveling around. Remember, there are only so many hospitals and potential healthcare employers in any given area. Chances are very strong that you're going to want to settle down as a permanent staff member at some point. Having a strong professional network and references can go a long way toward helping you achieve your career goals.

Appendix

Appendix A: Comprehensive Agency Checklist

This is a comprehensive checklist to help you determine what you want out of an agency and your assignments. Use the list to help determine your "Requirements", "Preferences", and things that are "Irrelevant." Use your requirements and preferences to guide your dealings with agencies.

Compensation Package:

Medical Benefits
Day 1 Medical Benefits
Dental Benefits
Vision Benefits
401(k)
Travel Stipend
Rental Car
License Reimbursement
Certification Reimbursement
Lodging Stipend
Meals and Incidental Expenditure Stipend
Do you want to maximize your tax free stipends?
Do you prefer to have no stipend at all and take only taxable wages?
How will you be paid for "extra hours" (hours over and above the contracted hours)?
On Call Rate
Call Back Rate

Service (questions to consider regarding agency services):

How frequently does the agency pay (weekly, bi-weekly)?
Does the agency offer on-line access to your pay stubs?

Do they mail pay stubs?
Is the recruiter going to be your single point of contact for all issues, or will you work with multiple departments?

Are there any circumstances under which you'll need to change recruiters (i.e. recruiters assigned to specific territories)?

Company provided Lodging

Do you want company provided lodging?
Will you accept an Extended Stay Hotel, or do you require an apartment?
Will you be bringing pets? Who will be responsible for pet deposits?
Will you be traveling with other people?
If you take an apartment do you want it fully furnished?
If you take an apartment do you need a house-wares package (pots, pans, linens, towels, and silverware)?
If you take an apartment do you need a cleaning package (vacuum, etc.)?
If you take an apartment do you need a washer and dryer in unit, or on grounds?
If you take an apartment do you want a specific type of parking at the complex?
If you take an apartment do you want utilities to be covered by the agency?
If you take an apartment do you want cable and internet covered by the agency?

Agency/Hospital Relationship:

What hospitals does the agency work with in (city/state)?
Do they have a direct relationship with the hospital, or are they a sub vendor on a VMS contract?
If they're a sub-vendor, is the VMS a staffing agency, or a just a VMS like Medefis?
Who is the VMS?
How many healthcare professionals do they have working at the site?

Location:

Where specifically do you want to go (city/state)?

Hospitals Types:

What type of hospital do you want to work in?
Will you only work in large teaching facilities?
Will you only work in small rural hospitals?

Appendix B: Sample Checklist for Company Provided Housing

Questions to consider for company provided Motels, Hotels, and Extended Stays:

Is it a Motel, Hotel, or Extended Stay?

Is room access interior or exterior?

What's the parking situation?

What amenities are included (gym facilities, free breakfast, cafe or restaurant, daily housekeeping, room service, etc.)?

Is free Wi-Fi available for your internet connection?

Is there a kitchenette, and what's included?

Is there a microwave?

Is there an oven?

Is there a coffeepot?

Is there a laundry room or laundry service?

Is it a studio, suite, or 1 bedroom?

Is there adequate storage for your belongings?

Is there a real bed in addition to a sofa pull out, or is there just a sofa pull out?

What size is the bed?

Will you be responsible for any hidden fees?

If you have pets, will the property accept pets and if so will the company pay the pet deposit or do you have to pay the pet deposit?

Questions to consider for company provided apartments:

Is the company providing an apartment in an apartment complex, or a condo, or a vacation home? You'll want to know in order to set your expectations. Different places come equipped with different things and you need to be prepared. For example, if it's a vacation home or condo, is there a yard and if so is yard maintenance included in the cost?

Is the lodging furnished? What furnishings are included? What size is the bed?

Are house wares included? House wares typically include pots, pans, linens, towels, silverware, a coffee maker, and a toaster. However, it's best to determine what specifically is included.

Is there a microwave? You'd be surprised. Many apartments have not yet been fitted with a microwave and I've had many occasions where we had to add one after the fact.

Is a cleaning package included? Cleaning packages typically include a broom, dust pan, and mop. They may or may not include a vacuum cleaner.

Is a TV included? If you care about TV, you'll want to find out what size the TV will be. Most standard furnishing packages include a 26 inch TV. If you want to hook electronics to the TV such as a computer to watch Netfilx, or a game console, then you should make sure that the TV has applicable hook ups.

How are the utilities, cable, and other bills handled? Some agencies put everything in their name and the travel nurse doesn't have to do anything. Some agencies require that travel nurses put the utilities in the travel nurses name and then provide a fixed amount per month as a utility reimbursement. They do this to protect against risks such as the purchase of $500 worth of Pay Per View movies, or leaving the Air Conditioner running on 65 for 30 days straight in the middle of summer.

What's the parking situation? Parking costs extra in many urban areas. Some places have parking garages. Some have open parking lots. Some have assigned parking spaces. Some have covered parking. Some have no parking and you need to find street parking nearby. If this is important to you, then you'll want to know.

Do they accept pets? If they do accept pets, what's the deposit and who's responsible for it, or any additional "pet rent" costs?

Are a washer and dryer in unit, or is there a laundry facility on site? Sometimes there are hookups for the washer and dryer in the unit, but the facility charges extra to supply them, or expects you to bring or rent your own.

Appendix C: Sample List of Receipts for Records

Below is a list of receipts to keep for your tax records. This is not a comprehensive list. It is a list to give you an idea of what should be kept.

Licenses and Certifications

Physical Exams

Work Related Testing

Fingerprints

Work Related Verifications (i.e. education verifications)

Professional memberships

Professional insurance

Uniforms and work clothing

Work boots and Safety footwear

Safety and Protective equipment

Postage and Fax

Work Related Books, Journals, Magazines

Union Dues

Work Related Supplies

Work Related Equipment

ATM fees

Work Related Legal fees

Work Related Security clearance fees

Computer cost

Impairment/handicap related work expenses

Cell phone bills

Pager bill

Internet

CEUs (include all related expenses including travel expenses)

Laundry costs (Keep a log book if receipts are unavailable)

Hotel stays

Shipping

Plane fares

Tolls

Parking

Taxi

Car rental costs (you still will need to keep a mileage log)

Gas receipts (only if you are using a rental car)

Transit fares (Keep a log book if receipts are unavailable.)

Meal Receipts (Only if your agency pays much less than GSA per diem rates and you wish to declare the difference)

Appendix D: Questions to Ask During Hospital Interview

Below is a list of questions to consider asking during your interview with the hospital. Obviously, you won't have to ask them all, but you should ask those that are most important to you.

Orientation

What's the orientation process for travelers?

Are there any examinations given prior to starting the assignment?

If the examinations are failed, is the traveler sent home, or does the hospital remediate and retest?

Shift and Scheduling

What's the shift?

Will I be working the same schedule as your permanent staff?

How is the schedule determined?

Can your shifts be scheduled back to back?

Is overtime available? If so, what's the process for travelers to secure overtime?

Did you see my requested time off? Can it be approved?

How far in advance is the schedule available?

What type of notice is given for scheduling changes?

Is there mandatory overtime?

Is there On-Call?

Unit Specific

What's the patient ratio?

What type of support staff is available?

What's the float policy?

Do travelers always float first?

Are all nurses rotated to float?

What types of patients does the unit typically see (i.e. age range, acuity, and classification...Renal, Cardiac, Neuro, etc.)?

What charting system is used?

What medication system and protocols are in place?

How many beds are in the unit?

How is shift report conducted?

Is Charge duty required?

Will you attend Unit meetings?

How are unit meetings scheduled?

Traveler Specific Questions

Why is there a need for a traveler?

Is there a possibility for extension?

Does the hospital regularly use travelers?

How many travelers are currently on staff?

Are travelers well received by the staff?

Hospital Specific Questions

What's the parking situation at the hospital?

What's the dress code?

Are there multiple campuses?

If so, will you be required to float between them?

If you want anything related to your working conditions to be added to your contract, then you should seek agreement from the interviewer. This includes floating policies and Requested Time Off!!

Appendix E: Travel Nursing Resume

Below is a checklist for the ultimate travel nursing resume. Again, agencies are going to want you to fill out their applications because they need to get you into their applicant tracking systems, they need you to answer certain questions, and they need you to sign that you agree to their policies. However, if you're in a pinch for time, ensuring that you have a resume with the standard information may allow the agency to at least submit your resume for consideration.

Licenses and Certifications:

List EVERY license and certification you have by their correct significations (i.e. RN...not Nurse).

List the license or certification number if applicable.

List the licensing or certifying body for EVERY license and certification you have.

List the expiration date for EVERY license and certification.

If there is no expiration, then list date obtained.

If it's a compact nursing license, then clearly state it.

Facility Information:

Include the following information for EVERY facility you've worked for:

Facility's full official name.

Job Title

Exact start and end dates (4/4/2008...not 4/2008)

Facility type: Short term acute care? Long term acute care? Teaching Hospital? Children's Hospital? Trauma Hospital? Etc.

Number of beds in the entire facility

Unit worked (i.e. MedSurg...not 4 West)

Number of beds on the unit.

Caseload or Patient Ratio

List some of your specific duties (i.e. started IVs...not patient care), patient types (i.e Neuro, Cardiac, Rehab, ETC.), and patient age range. If you took Charge duty, then clearly list it.

List the types of computer and/or charting systems used.

Supervisor name and contact number if the supervisor can be contacted (Remember this is for a travel nursing assignment not a permanent job).

Reference Names, job titles, and contact information.

State whether it was a permanent job or travel assignment.

If it was a travel assignment, then list the agency's name and contact information.

I highly recommend against lumping all travel assignments under one agency on your travel nurse resume. For example, if you worked for one agency for several assignments, then you should list each assignment separately and highlight the hospitals as opposed to the agency. This is because some hospitals will not accept a profile without a list of the hospitals complete with all the necessary details including unit worked, number of beds, dates of employment, etc.

Education:

For all education pertaining to healthcare:

Institution's full official name.

Full address.

Telephone number.

Exact dates of attendance.

Name of degree achieved.

Miscellaneous:

List all professional affiliations.

List all professional honors and awards.

Appendix F: List of helpful web sites

City/Location Research

homefair.com: offers comprehensive information by zip code.

yelp.com: local business reviews.

meetup.com: find locals with similar interests

Lodging

rent.com: Find apartments for rent.

apartments.com: Find apartments for rent.

forrent.com: Find apartments for rent.

mytravelershaven.com: Provider of corporate and temporary housing solutions.

housingtravelnurses.com: Listings for lodging dedicated to travel nurses.

bfr.com: Furniture rental company.

aarons.com: Furniture rental comany.

ikea.com: You'd be surprised how cheaply you can furnish an apartment!

extendedstayamerica.com: Great hotels for long term stays.

airbnb.com: Book accommodations with local residents.

apartmentratings.com: The site offers peer reviewed apartment ratings.

Paycheck Calculations

paycheckcity.com: This site will help you calculate your potential tax burden to determine your expected net pay for an assignment.

Rental Cars

rentalcars.com: This site aggregates rental car quotes from across the web to help you find the best deals.

movemycar.com: Receive a list of quotes for having your car moved if you'd prefer not to put miles on your car.

Hospital Research

ahd.com: The American Hospital Directory provides free information on every hospital in America.

hospital-data.com: The site offers information on staffing levels and quality measures.

healthgrades.com: Offers detailed hospital ratings.

Travel Nursing Sites:

thetruthabouttravelnursing.com: This is the blog I manage.

travelnursingcentral.com: Agency and hospital reviews, and more

highwayhypodermics.com: Agency reviews and information from an experienced traveler.

thegypsynurse.com: Blog managed by an experienced travel nurse.

Healthcaretravelbook.com: Like Facebook for travel healthcare professionals.

forums.delphiforums.com/travelnurses: Delphi Forums, Travel Nurses and Therapists: Delphi Forums has a forum for travel healthcare professionals.

pantravelers.org: The Professional Association of Nurse Travelers is an Organization dedicated to the interests of travel healthcare professionals.

natho.org: The National Association of Travel Healthcare Organizations. A non-profit association of travel healthcare organizations, founded in 2008 to promote ethical business practices in the travel healthcare industry, setting the gold standard for conduct among member agencies on behalf of travel healthcare candidates and clients.

Tax Information

IRS Publication 463: Travel, Entertainment, Gift, and Car Expenses. You can search for it on the web, or use this link: http://www.irs.gov/pub/irs-pdf/p463.pdf

traveltax.com: Web site run by Joseph Smith who specializes in taxes for traveling professionals

GSA Per Diem Rates: Lodging and M&IE rates set by the General Services Administration.You can search for it on the web, or use this link: http://www.gsa.gov/portal/category/21287

Resources

1) Blum, Lisa and Coppage, Richard. Location of Tax Home Determines Travel Expense Deductibility. http://www.thetaxdude.com/uploads/LOCATION_OF_TAX_HOME_DETERMINES_TRAVEL_EXPENSE_DEDUCTIBILITY.pdf

2) National Association of Travel Healthcare Organizations. Natho.org

3) Smith, Joseph. traveltax.com.

Made in the USA
Las Vegas, NV
11 November 2021